RSES

Compressors, Condensers, and Cooling Towers

ISBN-13: 978-1-61607-001-4
ISBN-10: 1-61607-001-3

© Copyright 1996 by the Refrigeration Service Engineers Society. All rights reserved.
First paperback edition published 2009.

No part of this publication may be reproduced or distributed in any form or by any means,
or stored in a data base or retrieval system, without prior written permission of the publisher.

TABLE OF CONTENTS

Lesson 1
Compressors 1

Lesson 2
Open-Type Compressors 23

Lesson 3
Hermetic and Semi-Hermetic Compressors 39

Lesson 4
Refrigeration System Accessories 59

Lesson 5
Desiccants and Driers 77

Lesson 6
Air-Cooled Condensers 99

Lesson 7
Water-Cooled Condensers 119

Lesson 8
Evaporative Condensers and Cooling Towers 129

Lesson 9
Water Treatment (Part 1) 147

Lesson 10
Water Treatment (Part 2) 179

Lesson 11
Closed-Circuit Water Coolers 197

Lesson 12
Air-Cooled Condensing Unit Room Requirements 213

Lesson 13
Heat Transfer Coils 225

Lesson 14
Multiple Rack Systems 243

Appendix
Student Supplement

INTRODUCTION

Congratulations on your decision to further your education and career by participating in an RSES training course!

This book belongs to you. It is your primary learning tool, and should serve you well as a source of reference in the future. Feel free to write in your book, and make notes as needed in the page margins. Note that the information contained in RSES training courses reflects "standard" trade practices in the U.S. Some information may not be in compliance with regulatory codes in your area. Be aware that *local codes always take precedence*.

RSES comprehensive training courses cover all aspects of the HVACR service industry, beginning with basic theory and extending to complex troubleshooting. Training courses can be conducted by local Chapters, corporate training facilities, or through self-study. RSES training course series include refrigeration and air conditioning, electricity, controls, heating, heat pump, and the RSES Technical Institute Training Manuals.

Continuing education units (CEUs) are issued only to those students who participate in an instructor-led course. Some courses have been recognized by North American Technician Excellence (NATE). Technicians who successfully complete one or more of these instructor-led courses may receive credit toward renewing their NATE certification.

In addition to its renowned training course manuals, RSES offers a selection of CD-ROMs, DVDs, and other materials intended to assist technicians enhance their skills and knowledge of the HVACR industry. Membership in RSES offers a wide variety of benefits. For membership information and to find out more about RSES, please visit the RSES Web site at www.rses.org.

OBJECTIVES

Lesson 1
Compressors
- Distinguish the different types of compressors.
- List the advantages and disadvantages of open-type, semi-hermetic, rotary, screw, and centrifugal compressors.
- Describe the basic functions performed by each type of compressor.
- Define compressor efficiency.
- Explain the effects of high suction and discharge pressure.

Lesson 2
Open-Type Compressors
- Explain the difference between an open-type compressor and a hermetic compressor.
- Explain how the same compressor can be used for different temperature applications.
- Describe the steps necessary to service the electric motor on an open-type compressor in the field.
- Explain the effect of suction pressure on motor load.
- Describe the installation procedure for a direct-drive open-type compressor.
- Determine by calculation the motor pulley diameter when the compressor flywheel diameter, the compressor speed, and the motor speed are given.

Lesson 3
Hermetic and Semi-Hermetic Compressors
- List the five types of compressors used in the mechanical refrigeration system.
- Describe the basic operation of the five types of compressors.
- List the advantages of a hermetically sealed compressor over an open-type compressor.
- Explain the methods used to remove heat from the motors of hermetic and semi-hermetic compressors.
- Describe the procedures involved in replacing a hermetic or semi-hermetic compressor.
- Identify some of the factors that affect compressor capacity.

Lesson 4
Refrigeration System Accessories
Describe the operation, selection, and application of the following accessories:
- condensing water regulators
- check valves
- safety relief devices
- discharge oil separators
- liquid level indicators and moisture indicators
- discharge mufflers
- compressor lubrication protection controls
- strainers and filters
- vibration eliminators
- suction-line accumulators
- heat exchangers
- receivers.

Lesson 5
Desiccants and Driers
- State the purpose of a desiccant.
- Name and explain the ways in which a desiccant works.
- List three common desiccants used today.
- Describe the properties required of a desiccant.
- Define the terms *mixed desiccants* and *solid-core desiccants*.
- Identify the locations in which a drier can be installed, and explain the advantages and disadvantages of each.
- Describe the differences between a drier and a suction-line filter.
- Explain what is meant by the term *hydrophobic behavior of desiccants*.
- State the principle on which all moisture indicators work.

Lesson 6
Air-Cooled Condensers
- Explain the function of an air-cooled condenser.
- Describe the effect of non-condensable gasses.
- Identify various types of air-cooled condensers.
- Determine where the condenser should be located.
- Explain the refrigerant piping arrangement for a remote air-cooled condenser.

Lesson 7
Water-Cooled Condensers
- Describe the function of a shell-and-tube water-cooled condenser.
- Calculate condenser capacity.
- Explain how a tube-in-tube condenser works.
- List the pros and cons of using a water-cooled condenser.
- Describe the operation of a shell-and-coil water-cooled condenser.

Lesson 8
Evaporative Condensers and Cooling Towers
- Determine which condensing method should be used for applications in which plenty of cool water is available.
- Explain how an evaporative condenser works.
- Identify the factors that must be considered when you install an evaporative condenser.
- Describe the operational characteristics of an evaporative condenser water pump.
- Explain how a cooling tower operates.

Lesson 9
Water Treatment (Part 1)
- Determine why water treatment is necessary.
- Identify the basic causes of corrosion.
- Define *pH*.
- Explain galvanic action.
- Discuss the importance of condensing temperature.
- Describe procedures for the field testing of water.
- List safety precautions for using scale removers.
- Describe cleaning procedures.

Lesson 10
Water Treatment (Part2)
- Explain why preventive maintenance is necessary for condensers and cooling towers.
- Add different types of algaecides to water-cooled equipment.
- Discuss the methods of scale prevention.

Lesson 11
Closed-Circuit Water Coolers
- Explain the difference between a closed-circuit water cooler and an evaporative condenser.
- Discuss the factors that should be considered in selecting a closed-circuit water cooler.
- Describe how to regulate the capacity of a closed-circuit water cooler.
- Determine the location of louvers in a cold-climate application.
- Define the terms *cooling range*, *approach*, and *temperature difference*.

Lesson 12
Air-Cooled Condensing Unit Room Requirements
- Explain why the majority of supermarkets use air-cooled condensing units.
- Describe the basis on which wall opening area is calculated for intake air in the condensing unit room.
- Determine factors governing the unit room planning.

Lesson 13
Heat Transfer Coils
- Describe the design characteristics that apply to heating and cooling coils.
- Identify problems that cause improper performance of coils.
- Discuss important features to be considered in the selection of piping coils.

Lesson 14
Multiple Rack Systems
- Explain the operation principles of multiple rack refrigeration systems.
- Describe the various components of one rack refrigeration system in particular (the Hussmann SUPERPLUS®)—and, by extension, of rack refrigeration systems in general.

LESSON 1

Compressors

A MAJOR SYSTEM COMPONENT

The compressor in a refrigeration system can be compared to the human heart. The compressor pumps refrigerant, the "blood" of the refrigeration system. Evaporation of liquid refrigerant into vapor causes the cooling effect in mechanical refrigeration. A refrigerant can be reused over and over again if it is condensed from a vapor back to a liquid. To be condensed, the vapor must be pressurized. The compressor serves a dual purpose. It circulates and pressurizes the refrigerant vapor before the vapor is condensed for re-use.

The refrigeration compressor is similar to the heart in another important way. It performs its function efficiently over long periods of time. Few problems develop if it is properly cared for and given proper maintenance.

COMPRESSOR PRESSURE

The pressure produced by a compressor is measured in pounds per square inch (psi). It is stated as gauge pressure (psig) or absolute pressure (psia). Atmospheric pressure at sea level is about 14.7 psia. Gauge pressure can be converted to absolute pressure by adding 14.7 psi to it. For example, a compressor discharge pressure of 100 psig would be 114.7 psia at sea level. At one mile above sea level, the same 100 psig would be 112.3 psia. That is because atmospheric pressure at that altitude is 12.3 psia. (Note: When a pressure reading is given as psi, it is assumed to mean psig.)

Compressor operation involves two different pressures. One is *discharge pressure*, often referred to as *head pressure* or *high-side pressure*. The other is *suction pressure*, also called *back pressure*, *inlet pressure*, or *low-side pressure*. System pressures produced by a compressor are measured in two ways. Discharge pressure is measured with a gauge that shows only pressure above atmospheric pressure. Suction pressure may be above or below atmospheric pressure, so it is measured with a *compound* gauge. A compound gauge shows pressures above atmospheric pressure as psig and pressures below atmospheric pressure as inches of mercury vacuum.

The first function of a compressor is to remove the refrigerant vapor from the evaporator by way of the suction line. This creates a low pressure in the low side of the system. It allows the liquid refrigerant in the evaporator to boil at a low temperature. In the process of changing state, the refrigerant absorbs heat.

The second function of the compressor is to raise the pressure and temperature of the refrigerant vapor. This allows the refrigerant to condense into a liquid as it circulates through the condenser. The difference in pressure and temperature forms the basis for mechanical refrigeration systems.

COMPRESSOR TYPES

Compressors are commonly classified by the method used to compress the refrigerant vapor. The most common types are:

- reciprocating

- rotary

- screw

- centrifugal

- scroll.

Compressors also may be classified by how the prime mover (often an electric motor) is connected to the refrigeration system. Compressors may be classified as:

- open

- semi-hermetic

- hermetic.

Open-type compressors

Figure 1-1 shows an *open-type* reciprocating compressor. An open compressor has a drive shaft protruding from the compressor. An electric motor or some other form of prime mover is connected to the shaft, either through couplings or a pulley and belt arrangement. A shaft seal is required to prevent the refrigerant and system oil from escaping from the system into the atmosphere. The seal also prevents contamination by air and moisture from outside the unit. A worn seal can allow either of these undesired conditions. This is the major disadvantage of the open-type compressor. An important advantage is that it can use drive sources other than electric motors. The compressor can be powered by gas, gasoline, diesel, steam, or even water. It can be driven at different speeds by changing the pulleys and belts to match the evaporator load.

An open compressor has service advantages over semi-hermetic and hermetic compressors. Since the compressor and the prime mover are separate units, they can be serviced independently. An electric motor used to drive an open compressor can be replaced without removing the compressor from the system. The compressor can be serviced by unbolting the components. Parts may be replaced without replacing the complete compressor.

FIGURE 1-1. *High-speed open drive compressor*

Semi-hermetic compressors

Figure 1-2 shows a typical *semi-hermetic* (sometimes called a *bolted hermetic*) reciprocating compressor. It has no shaft openings. The driving motor is completely enclosed in one section of the assembly. The compressor is in the other section. The motor shaft is an extension of the compressor shaft. The two sections are gasketed and bolted together.

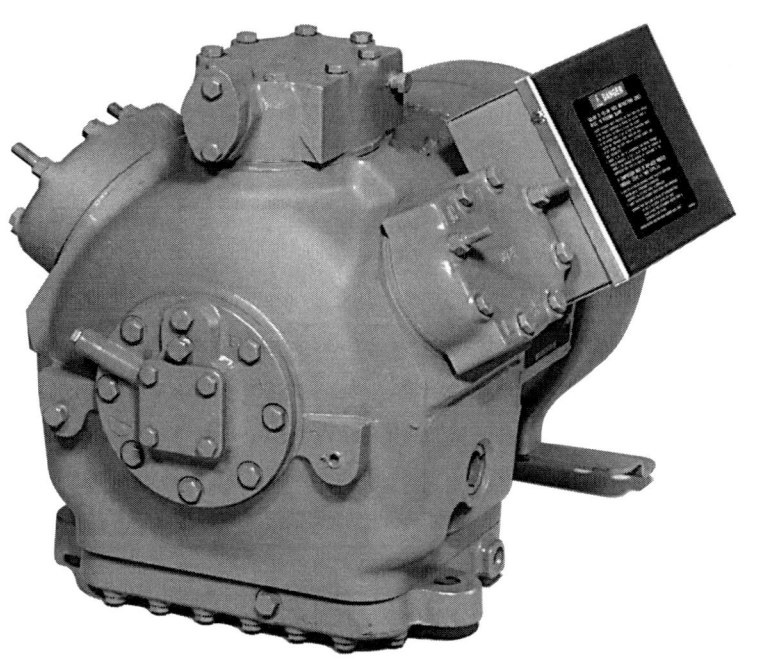

FIGURE 1-2. *Semi-hermetic reciprocating compressor*

Semi-hermetic compressors do not have the disadvantage of open-type compressors—that is, they do not have an exposed shaft prone to leak refrigerant and oil out of the system and air and water into the system. However, semi-hermetic compressors do not have the service and power source advantages of open compressors, either. The compressor speed is fixed by the speed of the motor. Servicing the compressor or motor takes both off line.

Semi-hermetic compressors have an advantage over the welded, or sealed hermetic compressor. Since they are bolted together, they can be disassembled and serviced in the field. The semi-hermetic compressor has a proportionately higher cost than an open-type compressor or sealed hermetic compressor of equal capacity.

Hermetic compressors

Figure 1-3 shows one of the many *hermetic* compressors available. Hermetic compressors also do not require a shaft seal. The drive motor is completely inside the compressor shell. External terminals are air- and moisture-tight. There is a major difference between the *sealed* hermetic and the bolted, or semi-hermetic compressor. The hermetic is in a two-section housing of stamped or formed sheet steel, instead of cast iron. After the motor and compressor are assembled, the housing or shell sections are welded together.

The sealed hermetic compressor has three basic advantages over the open-type compressor. It requires no shaft seal. It is more compact. It costs less than either the open-type compressor or semi-hermetic type compressor. There are some disadvantages, too. If either the motor or compressor malfunctions, the entire unit must be replaced. The motor is actually a part of the refrigerant circulation system. This means that a burnout can contaminate the entire system. In most sealed hermetic compressors, the motor has the advantage of being cooled by refrigerant vapor from the suction line. It flows over the motor windings after entry into the housing.

Hermetic compressors may be installed in hermetically sealed systems. These systems have no access for service to the vapor compression portion of the system. These systems are normally small systems and are sealed at the factory. This allows the system to operate trouble-free for many years without loss of refrigerant or contamination of the system.

FIGURE 1-3. *Hermetic compressor*

Reciprocating compressors

A *reciprocating* compressor is a positive-displacement compressor that can have one or more cylinders in various configurations. Figure 1-4 shows a cutaway view of a reciprocating compressor. All reciprocating compressors have the same basic parts. There is a piston with sealing rings for each piston. A crankshaft has a connecting rod for each piston. Discharge and suction valves (usually reed or ring type) are assembled on valve plates. These are separated by a dividing wall in a removable cylinder head for each cylinder. (While the cylinder head may be removed by removing the bolts, hermetic compressors cannot be serviced without first cutting apart the compressor shell. This is usually considered impractical.)

FIGURE 1-4. *Cutaway view of a reciprocating compressor*

Refer to Figure 1-5 for a brief review of the cycle sequence in a reciprocating refrigeration compressor. In Figure 1-5A, the piston is moving downward in the cylinder. Refrigerant vapor is flowing from the suction line, through the intake (suction) valve, and into the cylinder space. In Figure 1-5B, the piston is moving upward toward top dead center, compressing the refrigerant vapor into a much smaller space between the top of the piston and the valve plate. This is known as *clearance volume*. The clearance volume contains refrigerant vapor at high pressure that will not be discharged to the rest of the system. As the cylinder moves downward again, the pressure in the cylinder decreases. The vapor left in the clearance volume from the previous compression stroke expands to fill the cylinder. It expands until the pressure is lower than the pressure in the suction line, at which point the intake valve opens.

When the piston reaches bottom dead center, the crankshaft starts it upward again. Pressure builds up as

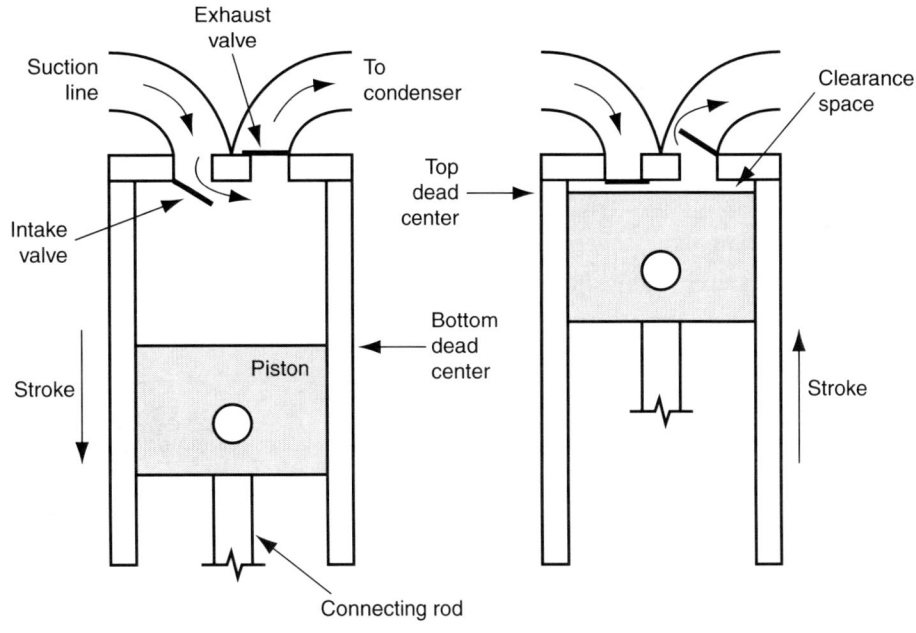

FIGURE 1-5. *How a reciprocating compressor works*

the piston compresses the refrigerant vapor. When the pressure in the cylinder exceeds the pressure in the discharge line, the exhaust (discharge) valve is forced off its seat, allowing the high-pressure refrigerant to move from the cylinder to the discharge line. It then flows into the condenser. When the piston starts downward again, spring tension and discharge vapor pressure close the exhaust valve. This action completes the cycle. The entire sequence is repeated in each cylinder in the reciprocating compressor.

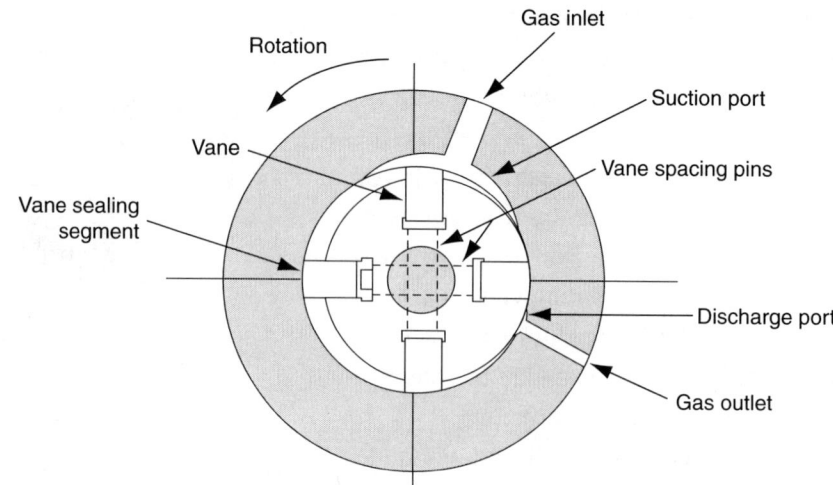

FIGURE 1-6. *Cross section of a vane-type rotary compressor*

The reciprocating compressor is by far the most widely used. It is found in household refrigerators, residential air conditioning, and commercial refrigeration and air conditioning systems. It also is used to some extent in large industrial applications.

Rotary compressors

Figure 1-6 shows a vane-type rotary compressor. The *rotary* compressor, like the reciprocating compressor, is a positive-displacement compressor. Instead of pistons that move up and down, it uses an off-center rotor that rotates inside a compression chamber fitted with suction and discharge ports. A vane is held snugly against the outer ring of the compression chamber by spring tension. Figure 1-6 shows a vane-type rotary compressor. There are also multiple-vane compressors. In these, the vanes mounted in the rotor are held against the chamber wall by spring tension and/or centrifugal force.

Either design pumps and pressurizes by trapping and compressing vapor between the chamber walls and the

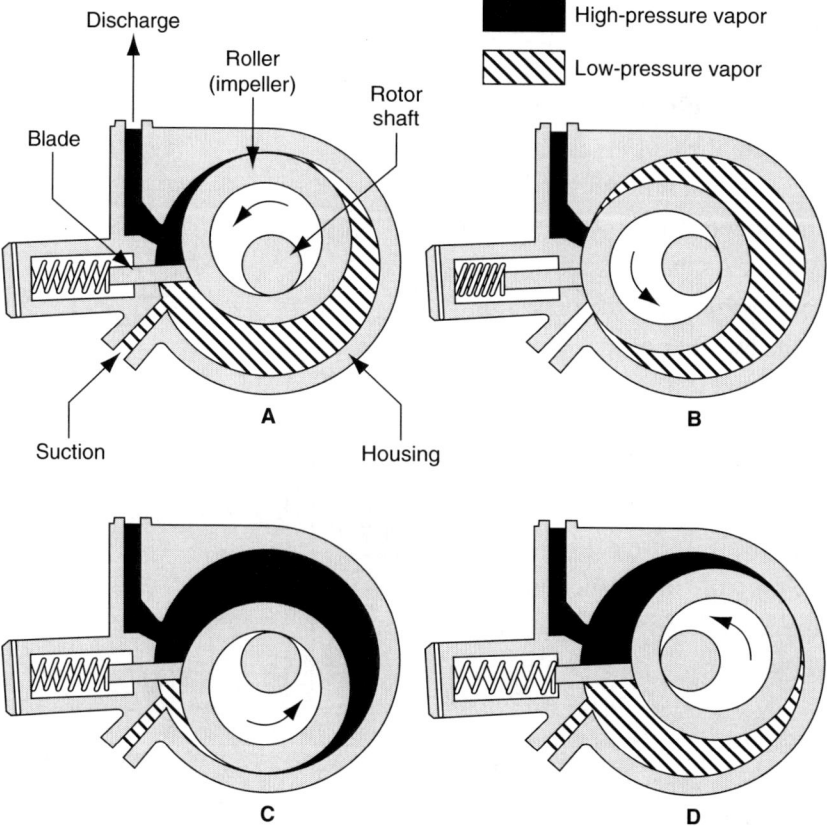

FIGURE 1-7. *Cycle of a blade-type rotary compressor*

turning rotor. Rotary compressors do not have suction valves. Some have a check valve in the suction or discharge line. This keeps discharge vapor from driving the compressor in reverse during the off cycle, which would let refrigerant back into the low side of the system.

Figure 1-7 shows a blade-type rotary compressor. This type has a spring-loaded blade similar to a vane. It protrudes from the outer ring and seals against an eccentric rotor. Rotation of the center lobe squeezes the refrigerant from the low side to the high side of the compressor.

FIGURE 1-8. *Screw compressor*

Rotary compressors may be constructed as open compressors for direct-drive, belt-drive, semi-hermetic, and sealed hermetic types. Full hermetic compressors are most common. They are used mostly in household refrigerators and low-capacity air conditioners (60,000 Btu and under.)

Screw compressors

Figure 1-8 shows a screw compressor. Figure 1-9 illustrates its operation. The *screw* type is also a positive-displacement compressor. It compresses vapor between intermeshing helical rotors. Suction vapor from the evaporator fills the area between the unmeshed lobes of the rotors and the cylindrical housing wall. As the rotors turn, the intermeshing lobes trap the vapor.

The vapor is compressed as the interlobe area (the space between the lobes) is reduced. The rotors continue to turn and expose the interlobe area to an outlet port. The compressed vapor is routed through the outlet port to the condenser.

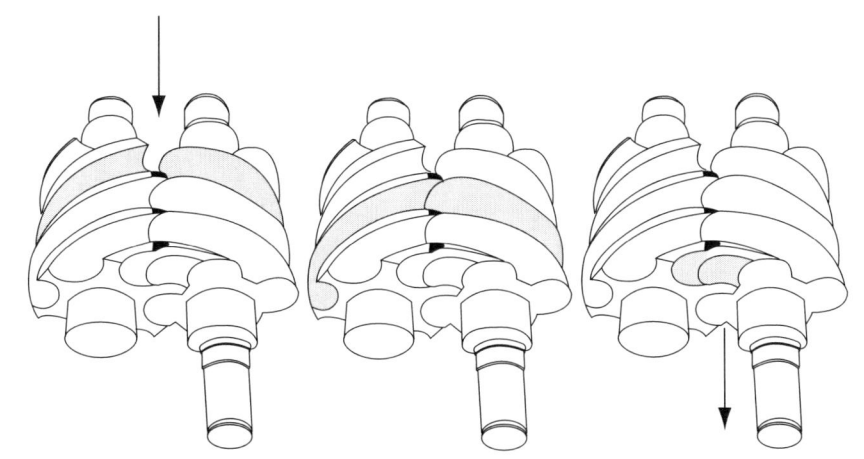

FIGURE 1-9. *Screw compressor operation*

Screw compressors are of either the direct-drive open type or the semi-hermetic type. They are highly rated for performance. Their rotating action makes them virtually vibration-free, even at high speeds and capacities. The screw compressor is usually limited to high-tonnage applications. It is widely applied to industrial refrigeration and air conditioning systems (35 to 750 tons.)

Scroll compressors

Figure 1-10 shows a *scroll* compressor. Scroll compressors are hermetic, positive-displacement compressors. A scroll compressor consists of two interlocking spirals, as shown in Figure 1-11. The refrigerant is compressed between a stationary scroll and a rotating scroll. Scroll compressors have fewer moving parts than reciprocating compressors. They provide smooth operation and tend to self-compensate for wear. Scroll compressors are 10 to 15% more efficient than reciprocating compressors.

Centrifugal compressors

Reciprocating, rotary, scroll, and screw compressors increase the pressure of suction vapor by squeezing it. Centrifugal compressors use kinetic displacement. They use a high-speed impeller to increase vapor pressure by accelerating movement of the refrigerant molecules. The impeller draws suction vapor into its center. Its high speed forces the vapor to the outside of the impeller. There it is forced into the smaller volume of a diffuser tube, increasing the vapor's pressure. These compressors work well with low-pressure,

FIGURE 1-10. *Scroll compressor*

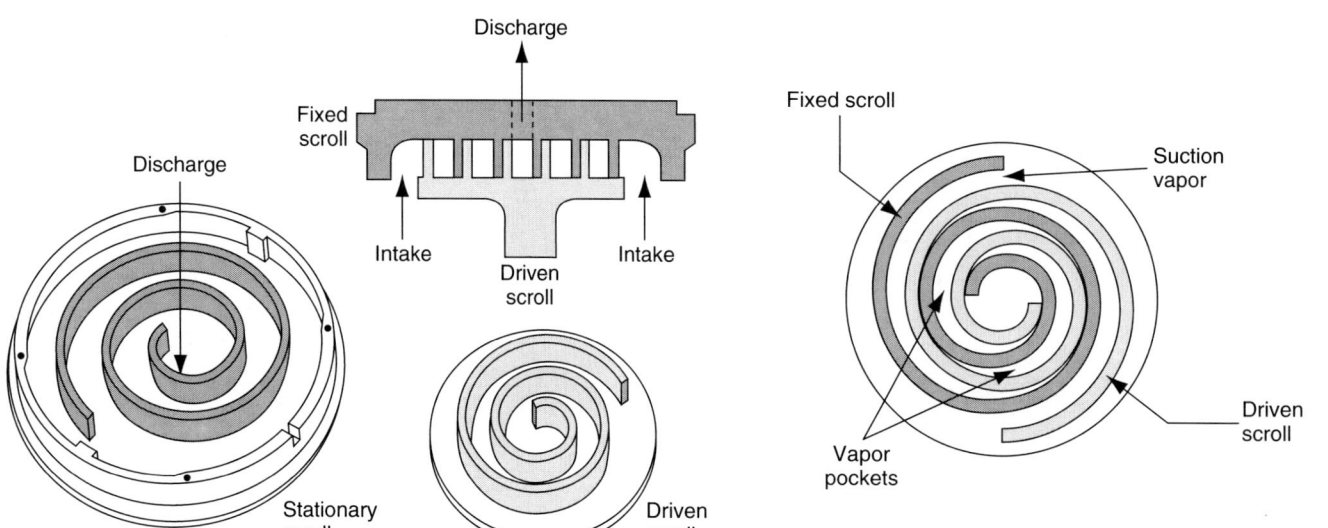

FIGURE 1-11. *Scroll compressor design*

high-volume refrigerants, because they handle large quantities of vapor. They are limited in their ability to increase pressure. Staging compressors by using several impellers in sequence allows for a greater increase in pressure. Even with the staging, a centrifugal compressor operates at pressures lower than positive-displacement compressors.

A centrifugal compressor has some major advantages. It has only a few moving parts. It rotates smoothly with little vibration. It can move a large volume of vapor with a compression ratio much lower than a positive-displacement type. It is limited to large, high-temperature applications, usually in industrial air conditioning systems (65 to 1,500 tons hermetic, up to 5,000 tons open-type). Centrifugal compressors, like screw compressors, are of the open direct-drive type or the semi-hermetic type. They are driven by electric motors and by gas or steam turbines.

Figure 1-12 shows how a centrifugal compressor is used in a standard compression refrigeration cycle. System water in the cooler is chilled as its heat is transferred to refrigerant at low temperature and pressure. As heat is removed from the water, the refrigerant vaporizes and is drawn into the compressor.

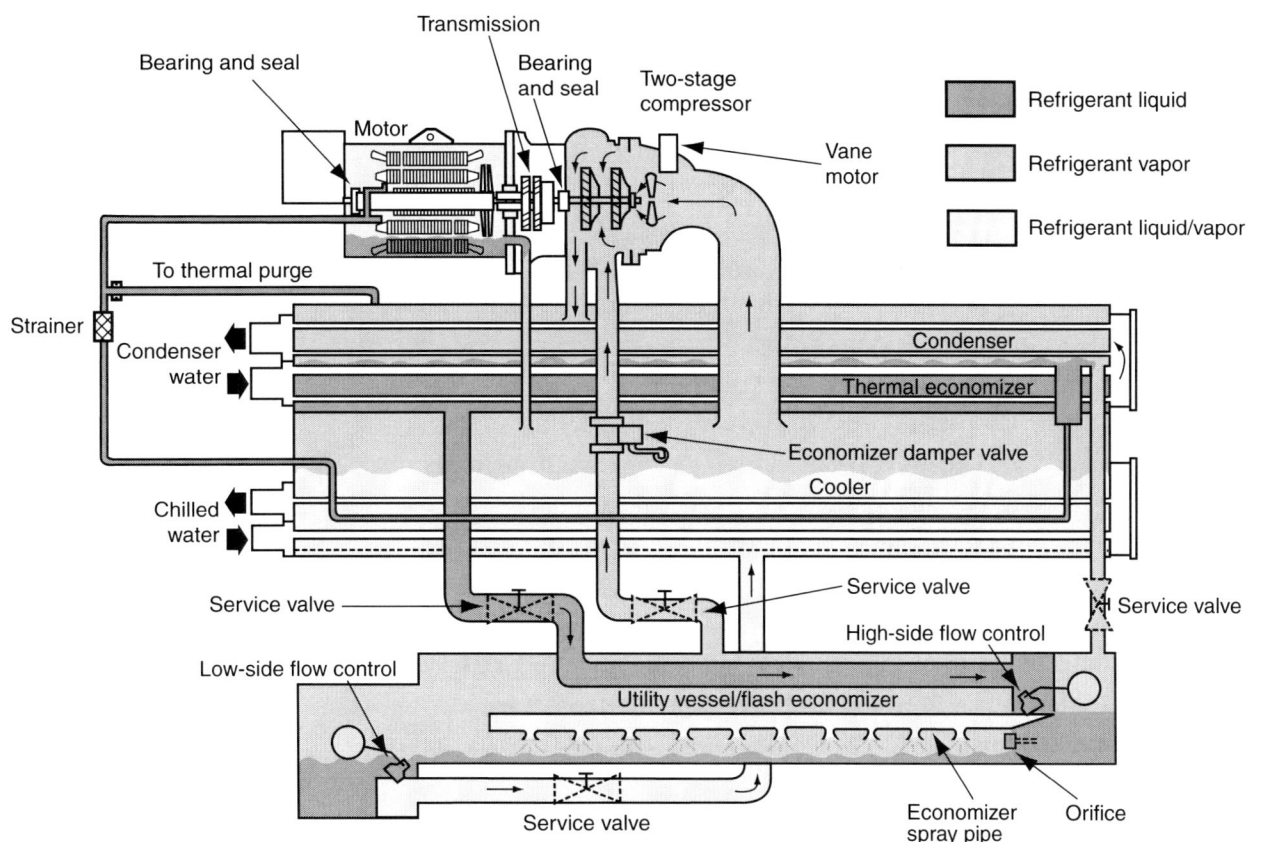

FIGURE 1-12. *Operation of a low-pressure chiller using a two-stage centrifugal compressor*

As the compressor raises the vapor pressure, the saturation temperature of the refrigerant rises above that of the condenser water. Refrigerant vapor is discharged directly into the condenser, where relatively cool condenser water removes heat from the vapor, causing it to condense again to liquid. The heated water leaves the system, returning to a cooling tower or other heat rejection device. As the refrigerant liquid leaves the condenser, it passes through a metering device where part of it vaporizes because of reduced pressure. The remaining liquid is cooled to the temperature at which the cycle began.

DIFFERENT COMPRESSOR TYPES HAVE IDENTICAL FUNCTIONS

All types of compressors must meet the same basic requirements. They are described in the following three points:

Point 1. They must create the required pressure differences. The evaporating portion of the system must be under low pressure, the condensing portion under high pressure.

The amount of pressure change required of a compressor is called the *compression ratio*. It is found by dividing the absolute discharge pressure by the absolute suction pressure. (Absolute pressures are gauge pressures + 14.7 psi.) For a discharge pressure gauge reading of 110 psig and a suction pressure gauge reading of 8 psig, the compression ratio is:

$$\text{compression ratio} = \frac{\text{absolute discharge pressure}}{\text{absolute suction pressure}} = \frac{124.7 \text{ psi}}{22.7 \text{ psi}} = 5.5$$

Absolute pressures are used to find compression ratios. Thus, 14.7 psi is added to the discharge and suction pressures.

Obviously, evaporating temperature with its corresponding suction pressure affects compression ratio. The lower the evaporating temperature/suction pressure level, the higher the compression ratio requirement. This is why low-temperature system compressors have extremely high compression ratios. Abnormally high discharge pressure can also cause high compression ratios.

Compressor manufacturers know that efficiency and reliability decline when compression ratios are high. Many of them have, as part of their service application criteria, set maximum compression ratios. Some are 9 or 9.5 to 1, others as low as 7 to 1.

Point 2. Pumping a sufficient volume of refrigerant is the second basic function of a compressor. Sufficient volume for a given refrigerant is determined by the evaporating temperature. As the temperature of the evaporator is lowered, more vapor volume must be circulated for efficient operation. It takes a larger compressor to handle a specific Btu load in a low-temperature application than in a medium-temperature application.

At a constant speed, a compressor pumps a constant volume, but its cooling capacity varies. For example, a compressor that produces 7½ tons of cooling at 40°F might produce only 3½ tons at 0°F. It might produce as little as 1 ton at –40°F. In this example, the speed of the motor has remained constant while the load has been reduced. A compressor at 40°F evaporator temperature has a high capacity and places a large load on the connected motor. In a system with a lower evaporator temperature, the same compressor would operate with reduced capacity. A smaller motor would drive it satisfactorily. Likewise, a motor able to drive a compressor operating at –40°F would be overloaded if the same compressor operated at +40°F.

Point 3. A compressor must accommodate the particular refrigerant used in a system. The design of a compressor is determined to a large degree by the refrigerant being used and the cooling requirements. Ammonia compressors of the reciprocating type, for example, run very hot. Therefore, they are designed with water jackets. Others may be designed for refrigerants that heat up to a lesser degree. They usually require only cooling fins cast into the housing and the cylinder head.

No single compressor can meet the requirements of all applications. A wide variety of types, models, and sizes is available. They are generally classified by manufacturers in the categories of refrigerant, capacity, and temperature range or evaporator pressure (suction pressure.)

COMPRESSOR EFFICIENCY

To function at full capacity, a system must have minimal loss of compressor efficiency. Losses can be caused by leakage and/or excessive friction between moving parts. For example, on a suction stroke, compressed vapor may leak back into a cylinder through a discharge valve. The result is wasted energy. Energy used to overcome friction also is nonproductive.

One measure of the efficiency of a compressor is its *volumetric efficiency*. The volumetric efficiency of a compressor is found by dividing the actual volume being pumped by the total calculated volume. For example, a one-cylinder reciprocating compressor has a total volume of 12 cubic inches (in^3) for each piston stroke. In operation, the compressor circulates only 6 in^3. Its actual volumetric efficiency is:

$$\text{actual volumetric efficiency} = \frac{\text{actual volume}}{\text{calculated volume}} = \frac{6 \text{ in}^3}{12 \text{ in}^3} = 50\%$$

For efficient operation, a high level of volumetric efficiency is essential. The level is affected by several factors. The first factor involves the *clearance volume*. This is the area left at the top of the cylinder between the piston and the valve plate. A larger clearance volume will allow more refrigerant to remain in the cylinder at the top of the stroke. This refrigerant will re-expand during the downstroke. No additional refrigerant will be able to enter the cylinder from the suction side until the leftover refrigerant has re-expanded to a pressure lower than the suction pressure. The compressor must pump against discharge pressure. As the discharge pressure increases, the amount of refrigerant left in the clearance volume of the cylinder will increase.

Lowered suction pressure will have the same effect as increased clearance volume or increased discharge pressure. Less refrigerant will enter the pumping chamber, reducing efficiency. Consequently, less refrigerant will be drawn in on the suction stroke.

Efficiency is a very broad term. It is only one element of a still broader term, *performance*. Performance incorporates "efficiency," "capacity," and "economy" of operation.

The *capacity* of a compressor is its Btu per cubic foot displacement. A given compressor is more efficient in terms of capacity if it has more Btu per hour capacity than one of equal displacement under the same conditions. *Economy* of operation is generally judged by the brake horsepower (bhp) per ton, or Btu per watt. The lower the bhp per ton and the higher the Btu per watt, the greater the economy of operation. Bhp per ton and Btu per watt are similar values. Bhp per ton involves only the compressor. Btu per watt involves both the compressor and the motor driving it. This makes the efficiency of the drive motor a factor.

OTHER FACTORS TO CONSIDER

The three elements of performance are efficiency, capacity, and economy of operation. They are the major factors in evaluating a compressor. In addition, the dependability should be considered carefully by the dealer, the purchaser, and the service technician. Replacing or repairing a compressor obviously has a cost factor. Compressor failure can lead to a loss due to spoilage, loss in sales, and loss of goodwill.

Hermetic compressors have a reputation for reliability. Small systems frequently use hermetically sealed compressors in a totally sealed system. This keeps the refrigerant and oil free from contamination. If no access is provided, leaks are rare except in case of physical damage to the system or components.

Compactness

The development of high-speed (3,500 rpm) hermetic compressors has reduced the size and weight of compressors, thus reducing the size and weight of equipment of equal capacity using slower compressors. The advantages of smaller and lighter equipment are numerous and obvious.

Flexibility

Flexibility is a factor that affects how many compressor models will cover a certain range. Open compressors offer the greatest flexibility. For example:

- Belt-driven models may be used for two or three different horsepower sizes.

- The displacement in cubic feet per hour may be changed. Simply vary the size of the motor pulley or the diameter of the flywheel. But they must not run at speeds above or below their design limits.

- Compressors may be used for both air-cooled and water-cooled condensing units.

- Compressors may be used with different refrigerants.

- Applications may involve variable degrees of suction vapor superheat.

Applying a given compressor at variable speeds has advantages, but may create a problem that is difficult to control at times. As the speed is changed, the amount of oil circulating with the system will change. This makes it difficult to determine the proper oil charge for proper lubrication under all conditions. On the other hand, a hermetic compressor is generally designed to operate at a fixed speed. Therefore, it has a fixed displacement and may be limited in temperature range and refrigerants used.

Serviceability

A compressor which can be serviced in the field has an advantage for the user and the service technician. This is especially important when a compressor failure occurs in commercial and industrial refrigeration and air conditioning applications. In a supermarket, for example, a compressor may serve a group of refrigerated cases. It cannot be out of service for very long. If it were, the merchant would have serious problems. The same is true for an air conditioning system that maintains close temperature and relative humidity levels. A prolonged shutdown of the system could stop operations or cause loss of business. Field serviceability is also important when equipment is installed in some remote location. It could be difficult for a service technician to get an exchange compressor.

APPLICATIONS

As noted, no compressor can give good performance in all conditions and applications. Compressors are generally designed, manufactured, and sold for specific applications, or a range of conditions. Some of these conditions are discussed below.

Suction pressure

Hermetic and semi-hermetic compressors are generally designed for a certain maximum suction pressure. As suction pressure increases, motor load also increases. At a certain point, the motor will reach maximum load. In this regard, compressors are generally designed for either high, medium, or low suction pressure range. One designed for the high-temperature range can often be used for medium- or low-temperature installations, but it will not have the capacity of a compressor designed for that particular range. It could be used for a medium or low suction range, but the motor would be lightly loaded. Reduced capacity would also result. Medium-temperature compressors can be used for low temperatures, but the motor would be lightly loaded and capacity sacrificed. A medium-temperature compressor should not be used for high-temperature applications, nor should a low-temperature compressor be used for medium-temperature applications. Overloaded motors will result.

Discharge pressure

Increased discharge pressure has several effects. It increases the load on the motor, reduces refrigerating capacity, and makes a compressor run hotter. In some cases, the displacement selected prevents operation above a certain limiting discharge pressure. For example, hermetic compressors may be designed for use in water-cooled units that operate at a low discharge pressure. If used with air-cooled condensers, a high ambient might result in an overloaded motor.

Belt-driven compressors are generally run at a slightly higher rpm on a water-cooled unit than an air-cooled unit. This assumes the use of the same suction pressure range, the same motor horsepower, and the same model compressor in both. The lower discharge pressure of the water-cooled unit allows a higher compressor speed for the same motor load. Excessive discharge pressures should be avoided whenever possible.

Superheat of suction vapor

Compressors and condensing units are usually rated at a given suction vapor temperature. (Don't confuse this with *evaporating temperature. Suction vapor temperature* is the actual temperature of superheated vapor entering the compressor at the suction shut-off valve.) Avoid too low a suction vapor temperature or too low a superheat of the suction vapor entering the compressor. Under such conditions, liquid refrigerant might enter the compressor. This causes stress on the compressor valves, wrist pins, rods, shaft, etc. It also causes excessive foaming of the oil in the crankcase and other damaging effects. The compressor will not reach its rated capacity.

Too high a suction vapor temperature will cause the compressor to run hot. In the case of suction-cooled compressors, motor cooling may not be sufficient. As a result, the motor may cycle on the protector. Motor life may be considerably shortened.

For best overall performance, the temperature of the suction vapor entering the compressor (not leaving the evaporator) should be controlled at a superheat of not less than 18°F. It should be superheated either in the evaporator or by a suction liquid-line heat exchanger. Suction lines should be insulated to protect them from superheating due to high ambient conditions or solar radiation. This causes a loss of refrigeration effect in the evaporator.

Maximum capacity in the evaporator comes from subcooling the liquid refrigerant and superheating the suction vapor in a heat exchanger. Avoid too high an actual suction vapor temperature, especially in compressors cooled by suction vapor. For best performance, the suction vapor temperature should not exceed 65°F. In suction vapor-cooled hermetic compressors used in low-temperature systems, avoid suction vapor temperatures higher than 40 to 50°F.

Discharge vapor temperature

Several factors affect the compressor discharge vapor temperature. They include suction pressure, discharge pressure, and superheat of suction vapor. It also varies with the characteristics of the system refrigerant itself.

Discharge vapor temperature for a given refrigerant depends on suction vapor temperature and compression ratio. The higher the compression ratio or suction

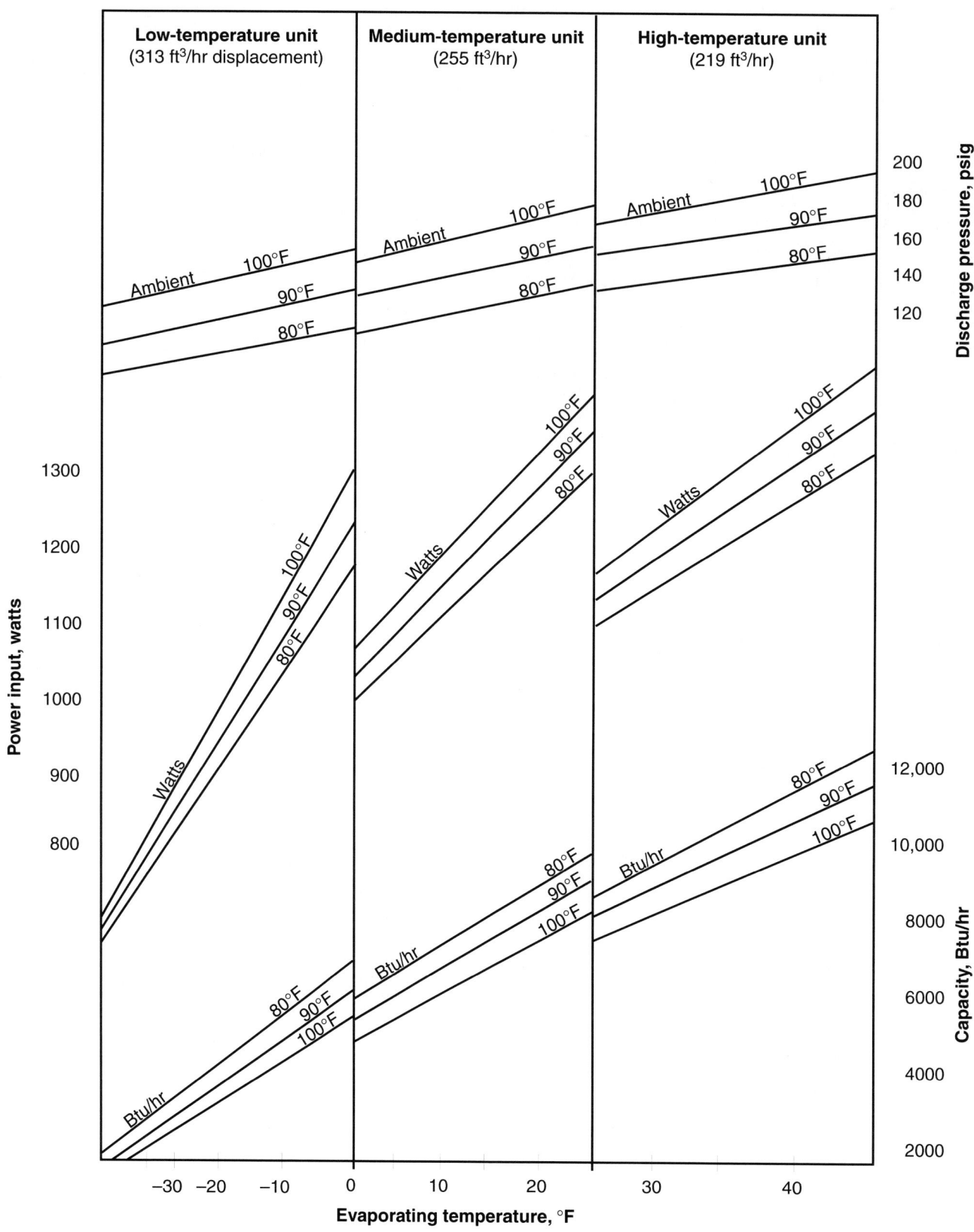

FIGURE 1-13. *Performance of a 1-hp air-cooled condensing unit*

vapor temperature, the higher the discharge vapor temperature. For a given suction pressure, the compression ratio and discharge temperature increase as suction pressure decreases. Thus, discharge temperature will run hotter in an air-cooled unit with low suction pressure than in a water-cooled unit with medium or high suction pressure. In general, this is true for the entire compressor.

Discharge-line temperature should never exceed 250°F. In fact, the lower the discharge-line temperature is, the better. High discharge vapor temperatures cause thinning of the oil, which impairs lubrication. There are more rapid chemical reactions if there is air or water in the system. Too high a temperature may cause oil breakdown, formation of acid, and shortened service life for the compressor.

CAPACITY VERSUS POWER INPUT

Obviously, you want to get maximum capacity from a compressor without overloading the motor. As stated before, capacity varies with suction and discharge pressures. Motor load also varies with these two factors. This can be shown by performance curves of a typical condensing unit. Figure 1-13 is a graphical representation of capacity (Btu/hr, also written Btuh), power input (watts), and discharge pressure (psig.) These factors are shown for three models of a 1-hp air-cooled condensing unit. They are low-, medium-, and high-temperature models. The capacity, power input, and discharge pressure are plotted against evaporating temperature for ambient temperatures of 80, 90, and 100°F. The power input curves are quite similar for all three models. But the capacity curves show a great change from one model or suction range to another. Displacements of these compressors were chosen to give the motor loads shown. In spite of increasing displacement from high- to medium- to low-temperature models, capacity actually decreases due to the increased compression ratio. As ratio of compression increases, the volumetric efficiency of any compressor decreases.

The curves also show that discharge pressure runs higher for the high-temperature model than for the other models. It also runs higher for the medium- than for the low-temperature model. This is because the condenser load varies with the capacity of the condensing unit. The higher the refrigerating capacity, the more heat the condenser has to dissipate. Therefore, with the same ambient, condenser surface, and volume of condenser air circulated, it must operate at a greater temperature differential. Discharge pressure goes up as the capacity becomes greater, while the efficiency is decreased.

The chart shows that the condenser load is less for the low-temperature model. It is still customary for manufacturers to supply the same condenser for low-, medium-, and high-temperature models. It is desirable to hold discharge pressure down as much as practical for low-temperature models in order to hold the ratio of compression low.

The performance curves in Figure 1-13 confirm the following conclusions:

- For a given model of condensing unit, as suction pressure increases, the capacity, power input, and condenser load all increase. This is why most condensing units are rated up to a maximum suction pressure or evaporating temperature.

- For a given model of condensing unit, as discharge pressure increases, power input increases and capacity decreases. Thus, the economy factor (Btu/watt) decreases as discharge pressure rises.

- For a given evaporating temperature or suction pressure, the medium-temperature model has more capacity than the high-temperature model. It also has a greater motor and condenser load. Similarly, the low-temperature model has greater capacity and motor and condenser load than the medium-temperature model. The reason is the greater displacement of the low- and medium-temperature models as compared to the high-temperature model. While increased displacement gives greater capacity, motor load must be considered when choosing equipment. In some cases, the model with less displacement might be selected to prevent the motor from overloading if the system is required to pull down frequently.

SELECTING A COMPRESSOR OR CONDENSING UNIT

Select a compressor or condensing unit according to the type best-suited to the application. It may be air-cooled, water-cooled, a combination air and water, an evaporative condenser type, or others. Consider the merits of the various types to ensure the best performance, economy of operation, and freedom from trouble and frequent maintenance. After selecting the condensing unit, the condensing medium temperature can be determined. It governs the discharge pressure of the compressor, thus affecting its capacity.

An air-cooled condensing unit is based in part on the average maximum ambient temperature. For a water-cooled unit, the maximum temperature of the water supply must be known. For a water-cooled unit using a cooling tower, or an evaporative condenser unit, the average maximum wet-bulb temperature will be a consideration. Figure 1-13 shows that air-cooled units are rated at given evaporating temperatures and ambient temperatures. Water-cooled units and evaporative condenser units are usually rated at given evaporating temperatures and given discharge pressures, or corresponding condensing temperatures. The latter also applies to ratings of compressors only.

CAPACITY REQUIREMENT

The compressor or condensing unit selected must have enough capacity to handle the load at average maximum conditions. For best overall performance, the condensing unit and evaporator capacities should have equal Btuh loads at design conditions. Obviously, the load and the desired number of operating hours per day must be known. The actual Btuh load times 24 hours divided by the daily operating time equals the capacity requirement for the condensing unit and evaporator:

$$\text{required capacity of the condensing unit} = \frac{\text{Btuh load} \times 24 \text{ hr}}{\text{hours of operation per day}}$$

To select the exact model of condensing unit, consider the design evaporating temperature. In general, for evaporating temperatures of 0 to –40°F, low-temperature models are used. Above 0°F but less than 25°F, medium-temperature models are used. Evaporating temperatures between 25 and 45°F require high-temperature models. These high-temperature models are used for air conditioning. Special models are available for temperatures above 45°F and heat pumps.

REVIEW QUESTIONS

1. How is the cooling effect in a mechanical refrigeration system produced?

2. What enables the refrigerant to be reused?

3. What is the primary purpose of a compressor?

4. Pressure produced by a compressor is measured in _____.

5. The two pressures involved in compressor operation are _____ pressure and _____ pressure.

6. What is the function of the compressor with regards to pressure?

7. Name another function that must be performed by the compressor.

8. List five types of compressors.

9. What characteristic defines an "open"-type compressor?

10. What is the major disadvantage of the open compressor?

11. Describe a semi-hermetic compressor.

12. What are the two main disadvantages of a hermetic compressor?

13. In a reciprocating compressor, the piston is connected to the crankshaft by a(n) _____.

REVIEW QUESTIONS

14. When does the suction valve close?

15. How do centrifugal compressors increase vapor pressure?

16. How is actual volumetric efficiency determined?

17. Name the three elements of performance that are the major factors in evaluating a compressor.

18. What happens to the motor load as suction pressure increases?

19. If the suction vapor superheat is too low, what could be the result?

20. What will happen if the suction vapor temperature is too high?

21. Minimum suction vapor temperature should be controlled at a minimum superheat of _____.

22. How can high discharge temperatures affect oil?

23. What happens to volumetric efficiency as the compression ratio increases?

24. How are air-cooled units rated?

25. What type of compressor should be used for temperatures above 0°F and below 25°F?

LESSON 2

Open-Type Compressors

INTRODUCTION

The refrigeration compressor is, without a doubt, the heart of the vapor/compression system. Compressors of the *open* type will be the subject of this Lesson. They vary by type (air-cooled or water-cooled) as well as by size (Btuh capacity).

Compressor selection is based on several factors. First, you must consider the pros and cons of water cooling versus air cooling. Second, calculate the anticipated total heat load accurately. Third, determine the desired evaporating and condensing temperatures. The compressor must also be applied and installed in a way that ensures satisfactory, efficient, long-term operation.

APPLICATION ADVANTAGES

Many different types of compressors are used to meet the varying applications of mechanical refrigeration. The open-type compressor is popular for many applications. It can be driven by an external motor, steam turbine, or internal combustion engine. The drive unit can be coupled to the compressor with belts and pulleys, or it can be connected directly.

For either drive method, the compressor shaft must extend through the crankcase of the compressor. This requires the use of a *shaft seal*. To prevent leakage of the refrigerant to the atmosphere, or air leakage into the compressor, a crankshaft seal must be provided. The seal of a reciprocating open compressor is on the low-pressure (or *suction*) side. If the seal leaks and the compressor crankcase is above atmospheric pressure (0 psig), refrigerant would leak out. If it is below atmospheric pressure, air and moisture would be drawn into the compressor.

Figure 2-1 shows several types of crankshaft seals that are in use. The requirements for a crankshaft seal are:

- It must not leak under pressure or vacuum when the shaft is idle or rotating.

- It must be self-adjusting to compensate for wear and for varying crankcase pressures.

- It must be self-lubricating, field-replaceable, and have a long life expectancy.

A shaft and seal are not needed on hermetic or semi-hermetic sealed-type compressors. This is because the motor is in the same housing as the compressor.

Each type has its advantages. One advantage of the belt-driven open compressor is that it can be very flexible. For example, its speed can be varied. Thus, one compressor can be used for two or three horsepower sizes of condensing units. Simply changing the size of the drive motor pulley in most cases increases compressor flexibility. It can be used with different motor sizes and speeds. It can be used for high-, medium-, or low-temperature applications.

There is another big advantage of an open-type compressor over the hermetic type. It can be used with motors made for odd voltages and frequencies, for which there are no hermetic compressors. This is particularly true in the case of direct current (dc) motors. A dc motor has a commutator and brushes, which cannot function in an atmosphere of oil and refrigerant.

The alternating current (ac) induction motor is used in hermetic and semi-hermetic compressors. It does not have a commutator or brushes and is suitable for operation inside the compressor housing, where it will be exposed to system oil and refrigerant.

Finally, the open-type compressor can be operated at low speed. This gives it a long life. Open-type compressors are always field-serviceable. A motor malfunction is easy to fix. Just loosen the belts or disengage the shaft coupling and replace it. If a motor burns out in a hermetic or semi-hermetic compressor, the entire system can become contaminated. The contaminants resulting from the motor burn-out must be cleaned up by filter driers in the suction and liquid lines, or the replacement compressor will fail. With an open compressor, however, the motor is *external* to the compressor and a resulting motor burn-out will not contaminate the system. Figures 2-2 and 2-3 on the next page show common types of open compressors.

APPLICATION CONSIDERATIONS

In most applications, performance is a major consideration. *Performance* can refer to capacity, efficiency, economy, and other factors. For a specific horsepower, or for a compressor used with a particular refrigerant, for example, you should select a compressor that produces the required Btuh *capacity*.

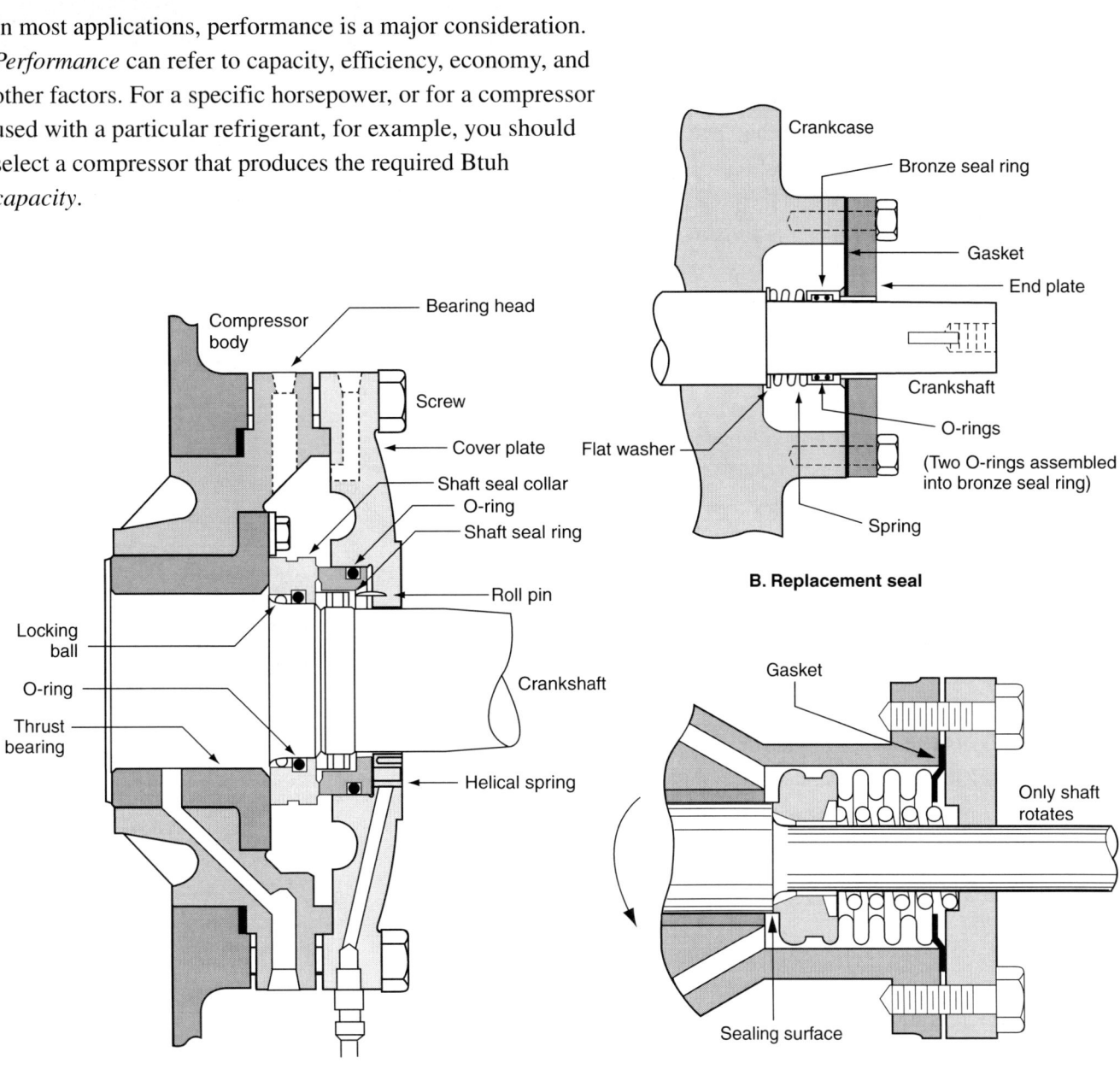

FIGURE 2-1. *Crankshaft seal construction for external-drive compressors*

The term *efficiency* is a very broad one. An efficient compressor has good capacity, even at low suction pressure and high compression ratio. Compressor efficiency is often judged by Btu per cubic foot (Btu/ft^3) of displacement. The more efficient compressor has greater Btu per hour capacity, per cubic foot of displacement, for a specific set of conditions.

Two factors normally are used to judge *economy* of operation. One is the brake horsepower (bhp) per ton factor. The other is Btu per watt of electricity consumed. The lower the bhp per ton factor and the higher the Btu per watt factor, the more desirable the compressor and the greater its economy of operation. These factors are similar, but bhp per ton involves only the compressor. Btu per watt involves both the compressor and its motor, since efficiency of the drive is a factor.

FIGURE 2-2. *Open-type belt-driven compressor*

Dependability is an equally important application consideration. It is a factor with great appeal to the installing company, the user, and the service technician. Do everything possible to match the correct compressor with the applied system. This is the best way to avoid problems leading to failure during operation. Compressor failure has many bad effects. First is repair cost, and then the cost of product loss due to spoilage. This, in turn, can mean loss of sales and good will. The value of these losses is hard to measure.

Physical *size* is also an important factor. This applies especially to self-contained fixtures and cabinets, and air conditioning. The smaller the compressor, the less space the complete condensing unit takes. Using compressors that run at higher speeds allows reduction in physical size.

FIGURE 2-3. *Open-type reciprocating compressor*

Flexibility is another factor in compressor application. Belt-driven compressors have an advantage here. They can be used for different horsepower requirements, as long as they operate within the design speed. You can change displacement in cubic feet per hour easily. Simply vary the size of the drive motor pulley or compressor flywheel diameter. Table 2-1 shows how you can operate the same compressor with 1½-, 2-, and 3-hp motors.

The speed at which the compressor will turn is determined by the ratio of the diameters of the motor pulley and the compressor flywheel. This can be determined from the following equation:

$$\frac{\text{compressor rpm}}{\text{motor rpm}} = \frac{\text{pulley diameter}}{\text{flywheel diameter}}$$

or:

$$\text{compressor rpm} \times \text{flywheel diameter} = \text{motor rpm} \times \text{pulley diameter}$$

Let's use the equation above to determine the motor pulley that must be used to run a compressor at 700 rpm, if the flywheel diameter is 12 in. and the motor speed is 1,725 rpm.

Application and horsepower	*Flywheel OD (in.) for 60 cycle	Motor pulley diameter (in.)	Compressor speed (rpm)	Displacement (ft³/hr)
Air-cooled				
1½ high	6½	3	740	283.5
1½ medium	6½	3⁷⁄₁₆	865	331.5
1½ low	6½	4¼	1,095	421.0
2 high	6½	3¹¹⁄₁₆	935	358.0
2 medium	6½	4¼	1,095	421.0
2 low	6½	5½	1,450	557.0
3 high	6½	5	1,310	502.5
3 medium	6½	6¹⁄₁₆	1,610	617.5
3 low	6½	8	2,150	826.0
Water-cooled				
1½ high	6½	3⁷⁄₁₆	865	331.5
1½ medium	6½	3¹¹⁄₁₆	935	358.0
1½ low	6½	4¾	1,235	474.0
2 high	6½	4½	1,165	447.0
2 medium	6½	5	1,310	502.5
2 low	6½	6½	1,730	663.0
3 high	6½	6¹⁄₁₆	1,610	617.5
3 medium	6½	7	1,870	717.0
3 low	6½	9	2,440	937.0

*Using two "B" belts

TABLE 2-1. *Compressor drives for belt-driven condensing units*

If compressor rpm × flywheel diameter = motor rpm × pulley diameter, then:

700 rpm × 12 in. = 1,725 rpm × pulley diameter
8,400 = 1,725 rpm × pulley diameter
8,400 ÷ 1,725 = pulley diameter
4.87 in. = pulley diameter
4.87 in. = approximately 4⅞ in.

Therefore, a motor pulley with a 4⅞-in. diameter would be required to drive this compressor at 700 rpm. From the equation above, it is obvious that if any three of the four variables are known, the fourth can be determined in the same manner.

Open-type compressors are flexible in other ways. They can be used for both air-cooled and water-cooled condensing units. They work with applications that involve varying degrees of suction vapor superheat. You can use them with different refrigerants. Open compressors are always used when *ammonia* (R-717) is the refrigerant. Pure ammonia is noncorrosive to all metals used in a refrigeration system. However, in the presence of moisture ammonia becomes corrosive to nonferrous metals like copper and brass. These metals are never used in an ammonia refrigeration system.

Remember, the hermetic and semi-hermetic compressors have motors *inside* the compressor housing. The motors have stator windings that are made of copper. The ammonia and moisture would quickly attack the copper motor windings and motor failure would result. Thus, open compressors must be used on systems that use ammonia as the refrigerant.

Operating an open-type compressor at various speeds has advantages. But consider a potential problem that may be hard to control. The problem is how to maintain good lubrication at all speeds if the amount of oil circulated changes.

Long compressor life is, of course, desired. Some compressors must run all day, every day. But this may be better than a cycling operation. When cycling, temperatures and oil viscosity change. For this reason, you may give up performance in some applications to be sure that the compressor will stand up under adverse conditions. These include liquid slugging, excessive discharge pressure, and periods of suction pressure above normal operating range.

SELECTING THE RIGHT COMPRESSOR FOR THE APPLICATION

Compressors are designed to operate satisfactorily up to a certain maximum suction pressure. As suction pressure increases, motor load increases. At some point, the motor will reach its maximum load. In this regard, compressors are usually designed for a certain range. There are *high-temperature* applications, *medium-temperature* applications, and *low-temperature* applications. For example, a high-temperature compressor would be used on an air conditioning application, as opposed to a low-temperature compressor, which would be found on a frozen food display case. A high-temperature range compressor may be usable in medium- or low-temperature installations. However, its capacity will not be that of one designed for the given range. The motor would be lightly loaded, resulting in reduced capacity. Compressors designed for medium- or low-temperature operation should not be used in higher-temperature applications. Overloaded motors will result.

Increased discharge pressure also increases the load on a compressor drive motor. This reduces refrigerating capacity, and makes a compressor run hotter. Check the displacement data for a particular compressor. Specifications may prohibit operation above a certain discharge pressure.

The same open-type compressor may be used in both air-cooled and water-cooled condensing units. The compressor in the water-cooled unit is usually run at a slightly higher rpm, if suction pressure range and motor horsepower are the same. A lower discharge pressure results from water cooling. This permits higher compressor speed without increased motor load. Always avoid excessive discharge pressures in any compressor application.

THE EFFECT OF SUCTION VAPOR TEMPERATURE ON COMPRESSORS

Compressors and whole condensing units are usually rated at a given *suction vapor temperature*. Don't confuse this with *evaporating temperature*. Suction vapor temperature is the temperature of the vapor entering the compressor at the suction service valve. For an air-cooled unit, the accepted standard is 80°F. For a water-cooled unit, it is 65°F. This is regardless of the evaporating temperature, which is saturated temperature corresponding to actual suction pressure at the suction service valve.

Always be sure that a superheated vapor is entering the compressor. Too little or no superheat might allow liquid refrigerant to enter the compressor. This could cause damage to valves, wrist pins, rods, shaft, etc. Another possible result is damage from excessive foaming of the oil in the crankcase. Also, the compressor will not maintain its rated capacity under these conditions.

Excessive suction vapor temperatures will cause a compressor to run hotter than normal. For best overall performance, control suction vapor at a superheat of not less than 30°F. Suction vapor temperature at the compressor inlet should not exceed 80 to 90°F.

Note: These values do not apply to hermetic or semi-hermetic compressors. They often use the low-temperature suction vapor to cool the enclosed motor. This is discussed in another Lesson.

THE EFFECT OF DISCHARGE VAPOR TEMPERATURE

Discharge vapor temperature has a great effect on compressor performance. It is affected by the other factors covered in this Lesson. They are *suction pressure*, *discharge pressure*, and *suction vapor superheat*. Also, discharge vapor temperature varies with the refrigerant used.

Discharge vapor temperature for a given refrigerant depends on suction vapor temperature and ratio of compression. The higher the actual suction vapor temperature, the higher the discharge vapor temperature. *Ratio of compression* is the absolute discharge pressure (psig plus 14.7) divided by the absolute suction pressure (psig plus 14.7). For a given suction pressure, ratio of compression and discharge vapor temperature will increase as discharge pressure increases. This is why discharge temperature—and the entire compressor—will be much hotter in an air-cooled unit at low suction pressure than in a water-cooled unit at medium or high suction pressure.

Compressors are designed for specific refrigerants and evaporating-condensing temperature ranges. These factors are not as critical with open-type compressors as with hermetic-type compressors. Still, you should consult the manufacturer before using a compressor for service outside its design range, or with a refrigerant other than the one specified.

COMPRESSOR INSTALLATION

You may have to install an open-type compressor for a number of reasons. It may be a replacement for a malfunctioning compressor. It may be to correct a previous misapplication of type, horsepower, or temperature range. It may be a component that is already a part of the applied condensing unit. Each reason requires attention to specific details. All require workmanship of the highest caliber.

Replacing a belt-driven open-type compressor requires careful alignment of the compressor flywheel and the drive motor pulley. It is also important to adjust belt tension to the manufacturer's specifications. Installing a compressor that is directly connected to the drive motor by a coupling is more complicated. Direct-drive compressors are usually in the larger-horsepower range (10 hp and up). The method of installation alignment will be covered in the manufacturer's instructions. These should always be followed. The following is a typical procedure. It is given here as an example of the instructions that you will have to follow. It points out the very precise operations required:

A direct-drive compressor with a flexible coupling usually has a drive package fastened to the compressor base. For field mounting, the compressor and motor are drilled and doweled in the field. This is done after alignment is correct. Dowel pins and shims are packed in the drive package with the coupling.

Drive couplings have a certain amount of flexibility. But precision alignment is still needed for long bearing life and smooth operation. Figure 2-4 shows a typical flexible coupling. To install and align it properly, follow this procedure:

1. Remove any dirt or burrs on the compressor and motor shafts. Clean the bores of both coupling hubs thoroughly. If needed, use emery cloth on the bore of the motor hub and the motor shaft. You want to have a sliding fit. Proper coupling assembly depends on the position of the motor hub on its shaft.

2. Carefully fit the keys to their respective hubs and shafts. Keys must bear on the sides and bottom of keyways. They should *not* bear on top.

3. Set the motor in position on the base. Place the compressor in its approximate position. Leave a space of 2¼ in. between shaft ends. Tighten the motor mounting bolts hand tight.

   Note: A minimum of 2¼ in. between shaft ends is required because this allows you to remove the coupling for repairs without moving the motor.

4. Install the key in the motor shaft. Slide the motor half of the coupling on the motor shaft.

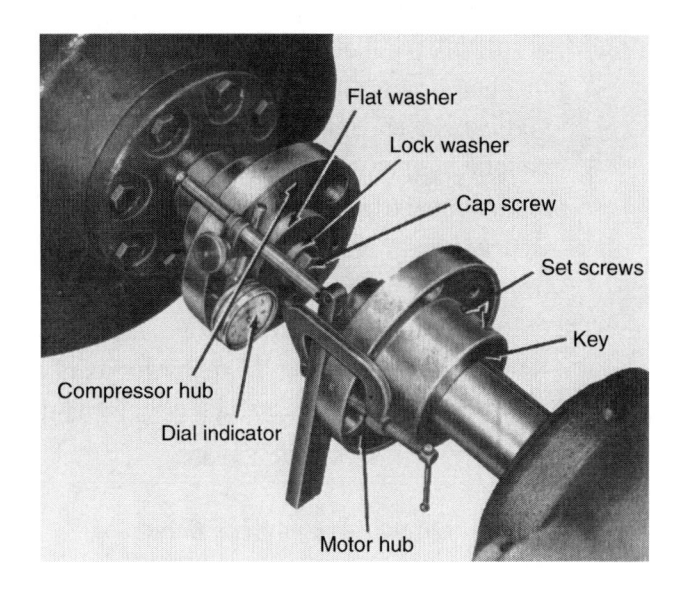

FIGURE 2-4. *Checking angular alignment*

5. Install the compressor half of the coupling, with key, on the compressor shaft. Draw the coupling half tight, using the cap screw, flat washer, and lock washer.

6. Position the motor hub of the coupling. The face of its flange should be approximately flush with the end of the motor shaft. Tighten its set screw on the key.

7. With a dial indicator or inside micrometer calipers, measure the distance between the faces of the two hub flanges. Measure at four points—both sides, top, and bottom. Adjust the position of the motor or compressor to get the same distance at all four points. Use shims as needed to secure this angular alignment.

8. To secure axial alignment, clamp a dial indicator to the motor hub. Its pointer should rest on the outside circumference of the compressor hub, as shown in Figure 2-5. Rotate the motor shaft and observe any fluctuations of the pointer. Adjust the position of the motor or compressor as needed. Keep adjusting until the pointer remains steady when the motor shaft is rotated one full turn.

9. Repeat steps 7 and 8 until both angular and axial alignments are correct.

    Note: The importance of correct alignment cannot be over-emphasized. Angular alignment ensures that the shafts are absolutely parallel. Axial alignment ensures that both shafts are in the same horizontal and vertical planes. You will not have correct coupling alignment unless both angular alignment and axial alignment are correct. Repeat steps 7 and 8 as many times as necessary to adjust either the compressor or the motor to obtain either alignment. Remember that moving the motor for axial alignment may destroy angular alignment and vice versa.

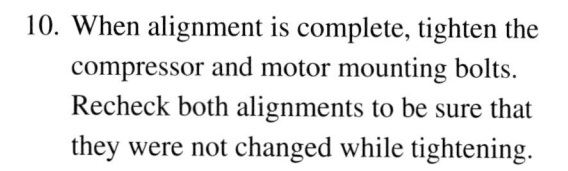

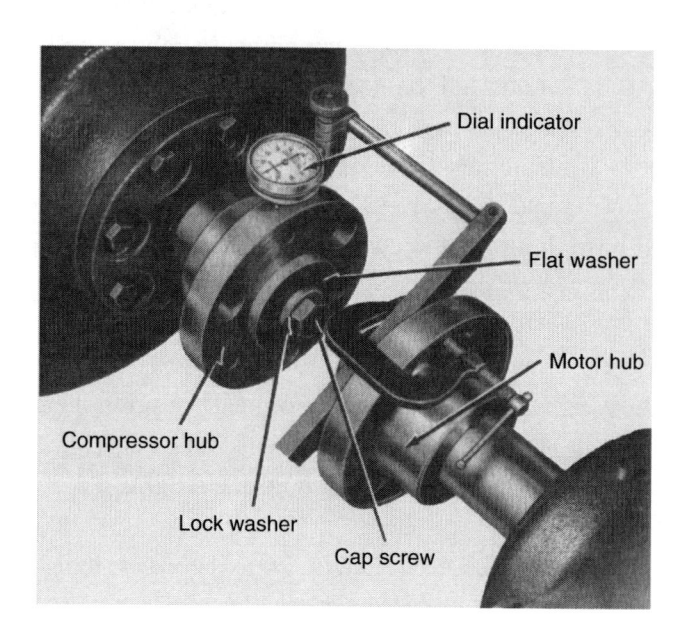

FIGURE 2-5. *Checking axial alignment*

10. When alignment is complete, tighten the compressor and motor mounting bolts. Recheck both alignments to be sure that they were not changed while tightening.

11. Remove the cap screw and washers that secure the compressor coupling hub to the shaft. Loosen the motor hub set screws. Slide the motor hub toward the motor frame. This allows space to assemble the coupling disks and center piece.

12. Rotate the motor shaft to line up the motor shaft and the compressor shaft keys 180° apart.

13. Be sure that the compressor shaft is extended toward the seal. The motor armature should be positioned at its magnetic center. This is determined by the position of the shaft relative to the motor end-bell when the motor is energized.

14. Bolt the flexible disks to the coupling hubs. Then bolt the center piece in place. Reinstall and tighten the compressor-side cap screw, flat washer, and lock washer.

15. Check to be sure that the motor hub is placed properly on the motor shaft. It should not exert any push or pull on the flexible disks. Then tighten the motor hub set screws.

16. Alignment is now correct. Both compressor and motor are bolted securely in place. Now they must be doweled to preserve the alignment. Drill and ream any two diagonally opposite mounting feet of the compressor and motor. Use the proper size drill and reamer for the dowel pins to be used. Drill these holes completely through the base. Ream them until the dowel pin drives tight when seated at its full depth.

REFRIGERANT CONNECTIONS

Open-type compressors may or may not have oil in them when they are shipped from the manufacturer. Make sure that you don't start a compressor with no oil or the improper oil. Always refer to the manufacturer's literature to determine the proper oil to use. This will vary depending on the compressor, the application, and the refrigerant.

It is important to ensure absolute cleanliness. Keep suction and discharge service valves closed during installation, and until final connections are made. In making discharge and suction connections, allow a long horizontal run before connecting into a header. Make it as long as practical. This absorbs the expansion and contraction of vertical connections. Clean the suction-line, liquid-line, and discharge-line piping as you install it. Conform to all code requirements. Follow proper installation procedures to prevent contaminants from entering the system.

On high-speed, compact open-type compressors, crankcase capacity is limited. Add enough oil to replace the oil that leaves the crankcase and circulates through the system. Large installations may use back-up compressors, or they may have compressors connected in parallel to handle varying load conditions. In such cases, *crankcase float valves* and an *oil receiver* are recommended. This ensures equal oil distribution to each crankcase. Figure 2-6 on the next page shows typical oil and refrigerant piping connections for this type of system. With such an arrangement, oil may be charged directly into an oil receiver. It acts as a reservoir, and keeps all crankcases filled to the proper level.

Oil receiver elevation is important. During operation, static head plus a small pressure difference forces oil into the crankcase. If a crankcase float were to stick open, and the compressor is stopped, the pressure would equalize. The oil in the crankcase and receiver would seek the same level. This level should be low enough to prevent damage to a compressor on subsequent start-up. Large, multi-cylinder compressors generally have a built-in crankcase float valve. Location and type may vary with different compressors. Figure 2-7 shows the function of a typical float valve.

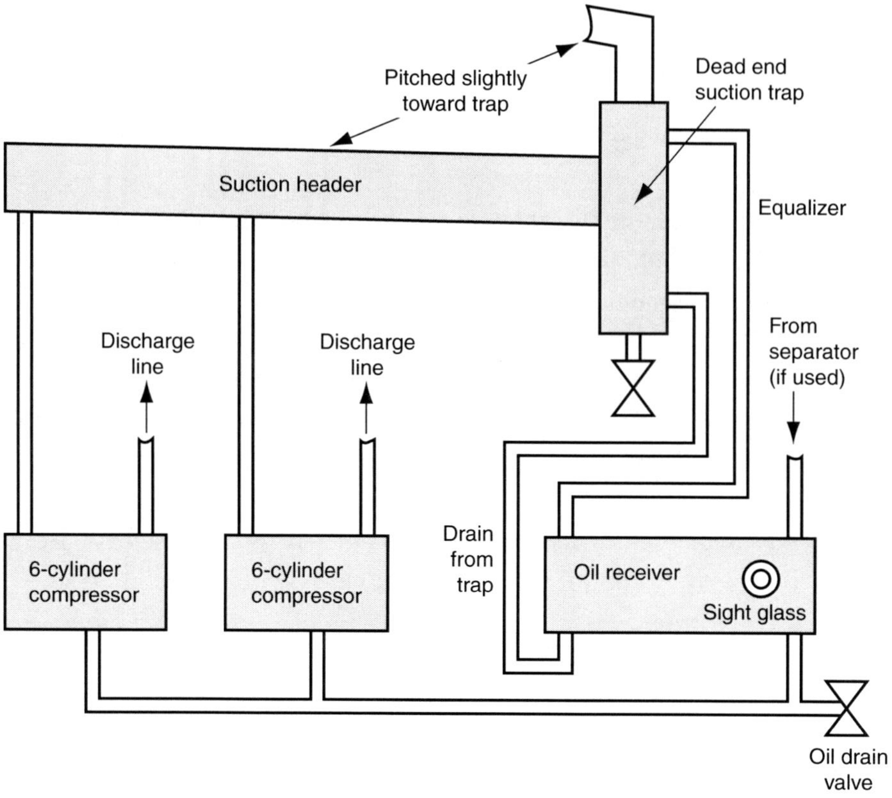

FIGURE 2-6. *Representative piping for parallel operation*

If a compressor has an oil pump, there is forced-feed lubrication of the shaft seal and all bearings. With some models, a pump provides hydraulic pressure for actuating an unloader mechanism for capacity reduction. To monitor oil pump operations and ensure safe compressor operation, an *oil pressure failure switch* is recommended on this type of system.

Electrically, the oil pressure failure switch is connected in series with the compressor starter holding coil. The low-pressure bellows on the switch is connected to a fitting in the compressor crankcase or head assembly. The high-pressure bellows is connected to the high-pressure gauge connection of the oil pump. When the system is placed in operation, the oil pressure failure switch can be adjusted for cut-in and cut-out points. This is done according to the instructions of the compressor and control manufacturers.

In operation, if the differential between the oil pressure and crankcase pressure drops to an unsafe level, indicating that the bearings are no longer getting sufficient lubricant, the time delay mechanism will be energized. If the differential pressure does not increase before the time delay period has ended, the compressor will be stopped to prevent damage. This type of safety control is usually a manual reset.

Remember that a compressor installed in an existing system is a component built to close tolerances. It will operate at moderately high speeds. To get good performance over a long period, take special care when you start the compressor for the first time. A new compressor may be connected to an old or existing refrigerant system. It is likely to collect foreign materials such as sludge, dirt, or chips. To prevent this, the compressor's suction and discharge service valves should not be opened immediately. Wait until the entire system (condenser, evaporator, compressor, and interconnecting piping) has been evacuated. Do this to accepted levels with a good vacuum pump. *Never* use the new compressor to evacuate a system.

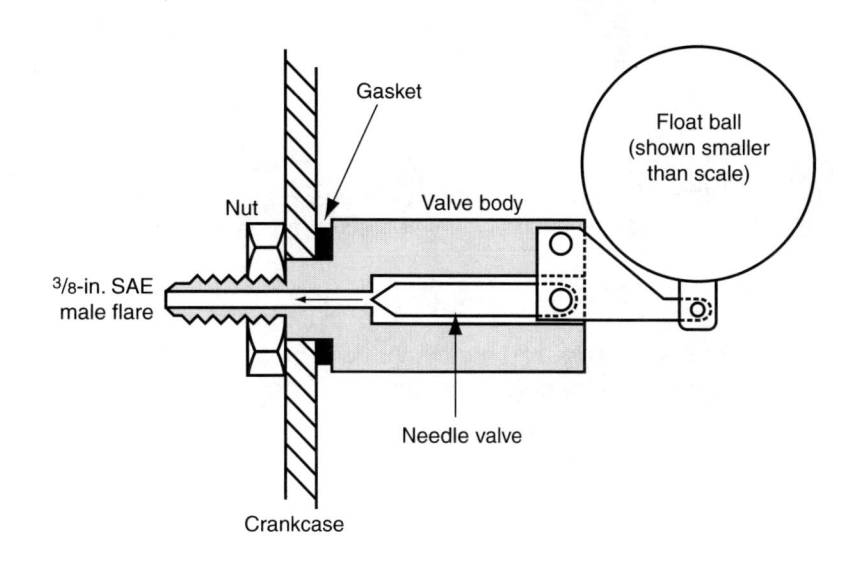

FIGURE 2-7. *Crankcase float valve*

REVIEW QUESTIONS

1. What is the heart of the vapor compression (refrigeration) system?

2. What important item does an open-type compressor employ (as opposed to a hermetically sealed compressor)?

3. How may an open-type compressor be adapted for high-, medium-, or low-temperature applications?

4. How is compressor efficiency often judged?

5. Why is it important to match a compressor correctly with the applied system?

6. How may the displacement (in cubic feet per hour) be changed with open-type compressors?

7. What problem is difficult to control when an open-type compressor is operated at various speeds?

8. Is compressor life shortened by continuous operation?

9. What effect does increased suction pressure have on the motor load?

10. What happens if a compressor designed for low-temperature operation is applied to a higher-temperature application?

11. What effect will increased discharge pressure have on the compressor drive motor load?

REVIEW QUESTIONS

12. When the same model of open-type compressor is used with both air-cooled and water-cooled condensing units, which is usually run at a slightly higher rpm?

13. Which application (air-cooled or water-cooled) would normally have a lower discharge pressure if run at the same speed?

14. How are compressors and condensing units usually rated?

15. If the superheat of the vapor entering the compressor is too low, what may result?

16. What is the equation for ratio of compression?

17. If satisfactory long-term operation is to be realized, what is necessary on open-type compressor installations?

18. Determine the size of the motor pulley required to run a compressor at 625 rpm, if the flywheel diameter is 16 in. and the motor speed is 3,450 rpm.

LESSON 3

Hermetic and Semi-Hermetic Compressors

TYPES OF COMPRESSORS

This Lesson deals with hermetic and semi-hermetic compressors. They have many advantages over open-type compressors, which were covered in the previous Lesson. Because of these advantages, they have replaced open-type compressors in many applications. There are five types of compressors used in mechanical refrigeration systems. They are:

- The *reciprocating* compressor has one or many pistons that travel back and forth to compress the suction vapor.

- The *rotary* compressor is available in both the *rolling piston* and the *rotary vane* types.

- The *scroll* compressor uses two spiral-shaped parts. One remains fixed while the other orbits against it.

- The *screw* compressor uses two screw-shaped rotors that mesh together to compress the refrigerant vapor.

- The *centrifugal* compressor has one or several high-speed impellers that compress the vapor by centrifugal force.

CAPACITIES AND APPLICATIONS

Reciprocating compressors

Open reciprocating compressors range in size from fractional up to about 150 tons. They are rugged compressors that are used in commercial and industrial refrigeration and large air conditioning applications.

Welded hermetic reciprocating compressors come in sizes ranging from fractional up to about 20 tons. They are non-serviceable units. They are found in household and commercial refrigeration, air conditioning, and heat pump applications.

Semi-hermetic reciprocating compressors are field-serviceable units ranging in size from fractional up to about 100 tons. They are found in commercial refrigeration, air conditioning, and heat pump applications.

Rotary compressors

Welded hermetic rotary compressors are available in sizes ranging from fractional up to approximately 5 tons. They are found in household appliances, in residential packaged or split-system air conditioning, and in heat pump applications.

Scroll compressors

Welded hermetic scroll compressors are available in sizes ranging from 2 to 10 tons. They are used in light commercial refrigeration and light commercial and residential air conditioning and heat pump applications.

Screw compressors

Screw compressors come in sizes ranging from 20 to 750 tons. They are typically used in large commercial and industrial refrigeration and air conditioning applications. Screw compressors are available in both the open and hermetic designs.

Centrifugal compressors

Centrifugal compressors are found in large commercial and industrial air conditioning and refrigeration applications. Sizes range from 100 up to about 10,000 tons. Like screw and reciprocating compressors, centrifugal compressors can be of either the open or hermetic design.

LESSON 3

COMPRESSOR OPERATION

Reciprocating compressors

Basically, a *reciprocating* compressor converts the rotary motion of the motor to reciprocating (back and forth) motion. This is done with a crankshaft and connecting rods. The connecting rod is connected to a piston that moves up and down in a cylinder. Figure 3-1 shows the path of refrigerant flow through the compressor. In Step 1, piston A has moved downward in the cylinder. This reduces the cylinder pressure and lets suction valve B open, allowing the low-pressure suction vapor to enter the cylinder. As the piston starts to move upward, the vapor pressure begins to increase in the cylinder. This will close suction valve B. As the piston moves toward the top of its stroke in Step 2, the vapor pressure is high enough to open discharge valve C. This allows the high-pressure, high-temperature vapor to leave the cylinder and flow to the condenser.

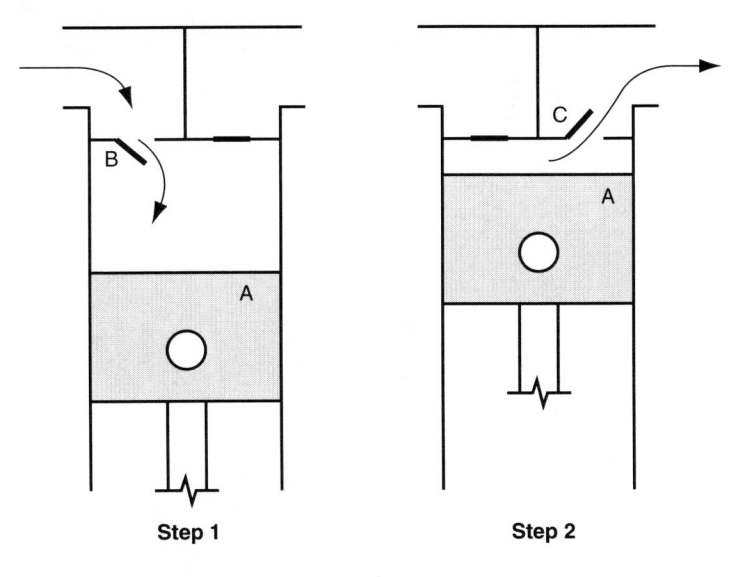

FIGURE 3-1. *Reciprocating compressor operation*

Rotary compressors (rolling piston)

Figure 3-2 on the next page shows a *rotary* compressor of the *rolling piston* type. Parts are identified in the drawing at the top of the illustration. As the rotor shaft rotates in Step 1, the attached eccentric traps suction vapor in the cylinder. The eccentric continues to rotate in the successive steps. The rotation reduces the volume of the trapped vapor and increases its pressure and temperature. By Step 4, the pressure in the cylinder is high enough to open the discharge check valve. High-pressure vapor will flow to the condenser. The stationary spring-loaded blade prevents the high-pressure vapor from flowing into the suction side of the compressor.

Rotary compressors (rotary vane)

Figure 3-3 on page 43 shows a *rotary vane* compressor. It has blades that rotate with the shaft. Centrifugal force keeps the blades extended against the walls of the cylinder. The extended blades trap the low-pressure suction vapor. As the shaft rotates, the volume of the trapped vapor is reduced, as shown in Steps 1 through 4. This increases vapor pressure and temperature until the pressure is high enough to discharge the vapor to the condenser in Step 4.

A. Identification of parts

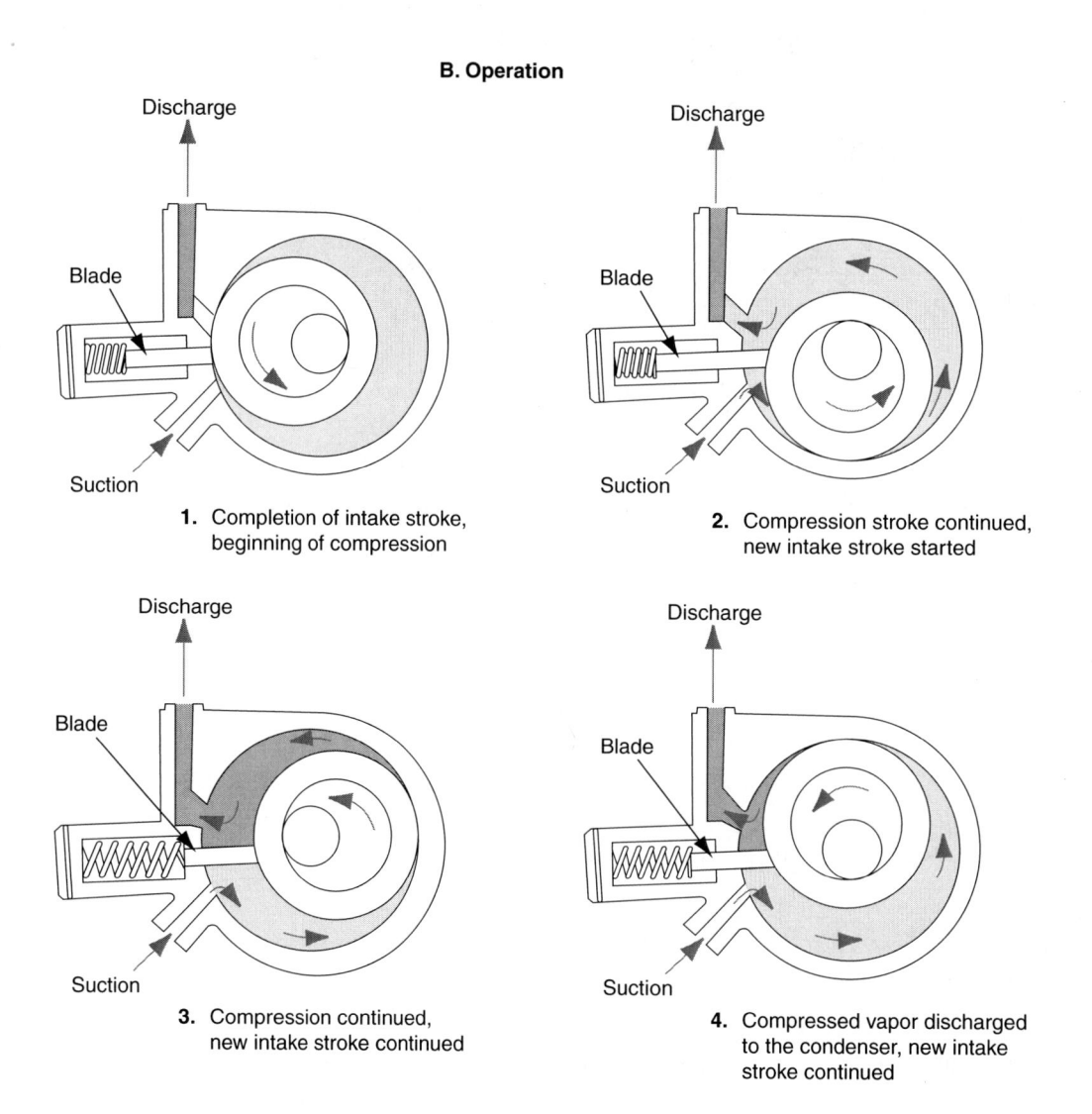

B. Operation

1. Completion of intake stroke, beginning of compression
2. Compression stroke continued, new intake stroke started
3. Compression continued, new intake stroke continued
4. Compressed vapor discharged to the condenser, new intake stroke continued

FIGURE 3-2. *Rotary compressor parts identification and operation*

Scroll compressors

Because of its higher efficiency, fewer moving parts, and quieter operation, the *scroll* compressor is replacing reciprocating models in many applications. The scroll compressor uses two spiral disks to compress the refrigerant vapor. Figure 3-4 shows how the stationary scroll (the piece on the left) and the moving scroll (on the right) fit together. The orbiting scroll, driven by the motor shaft, moves within the fixed scroll. This creates crescent-shaped pockets of vapor. As the orbiting scroll moves, it reduces the size of these pockets. The volume of the vapor decreases and the pressure increases. The suction vapor enters along the outer edge of the scroll. It is compressed as it is moved toward the center. Finally, it is discharged at the center of the scroll.

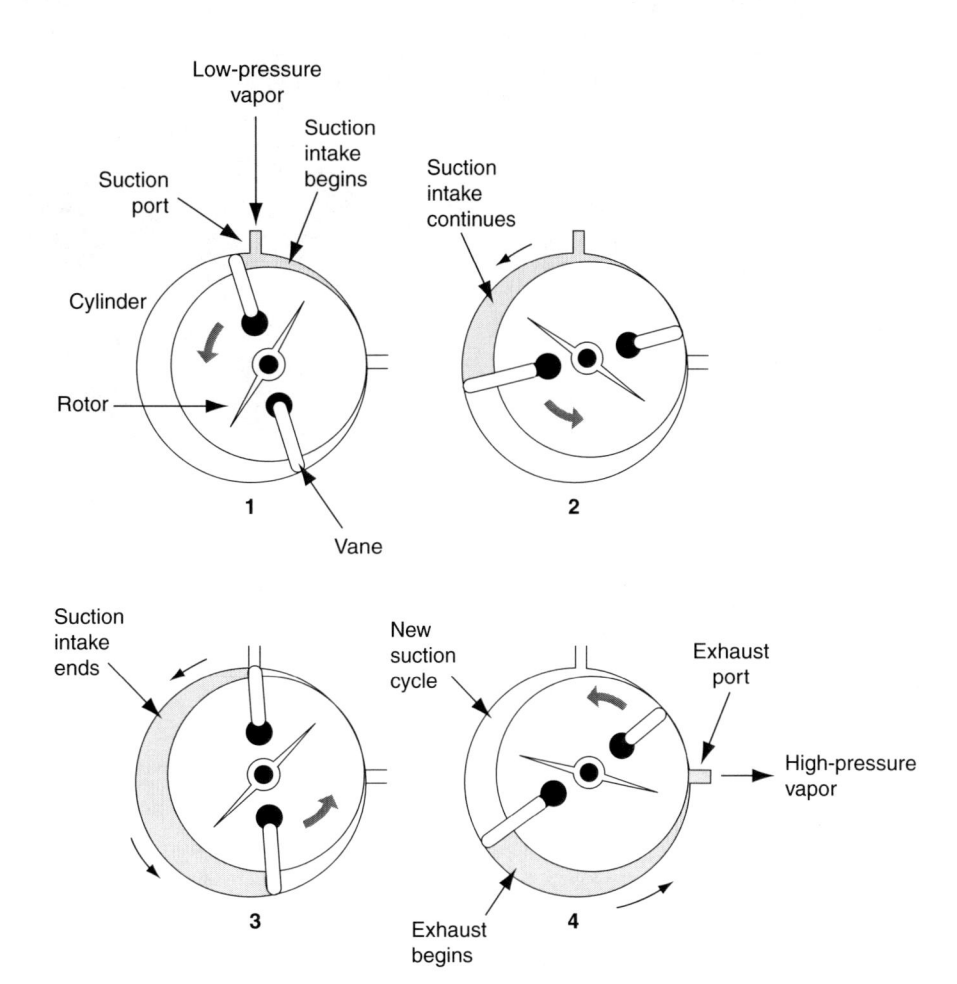

FIGURE 3-3. *Rotary vane compressor, with thick arrows showing the direction of rotation of the rotor and thin arrows showing the direction of refrigerant vapor flow*

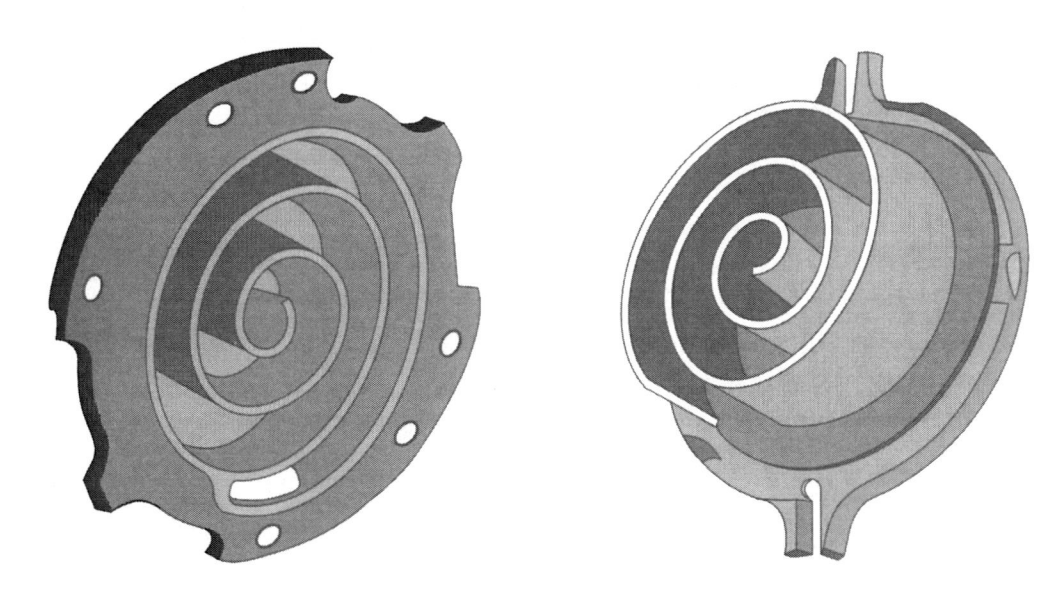

FIGURE 3-4. *Two halves of a scroll compressor*

Screw compressors

The *screw* compressor uses two *helical* (screw-shaped) rotors. One is a male thread and the other female. Their shapes allow them to compress refrigerant vapor as the threads of the two rotors mesh. The male thread is driven by the compressor motor and then drives the female rotor. Figure 3-5 shows a helical rotary screw compressor.

Centrifugal compressors

Figure 3-6 shows a cutaway view of a centrifugal compressor. The impeller of a centrifugal compressor is driven at high speeds, between 3,000 and 20,000 rpm. Suction vapor flows into the center of the high-speed impeller. Centrifugal force hurls the vapor through the radial blades to the outer edge, where its pressure has increased a small amount. Most applications require a greater pressure rise than one impeller can produce, so more than one impeller is used. When more than one stage (impeller) is used, the discharge from one stage goes into the inlet of the next stage. The centrifugal compressor is relatively simple in operation and has few moving parts. There are no valves, pistons, or cylinders. The only wearing parts are the main bearings.

HERMETIC AND SEMI-HERMETIC COMPRESSORS

Figure 3-7 shows a typical *hermetic* compressor. The hermetically sealed compressor has no protruding crankshaft or shaft seal. This is a major advantage over the open-type compressor, because it eliminates a source of leaks. Also, it is smaller, more compact, and less susceptible to vibration. Its drive motor is lubricated continuously and it has no belts that need adjustment or replacement.

A variation of the hermetic compressor is the accessible or *semi-hermetic* type. It combines the sealed-system qualities of the hermetic type and the serviceability and

FIGURE 3-5. *Helical rotary screw compressor*

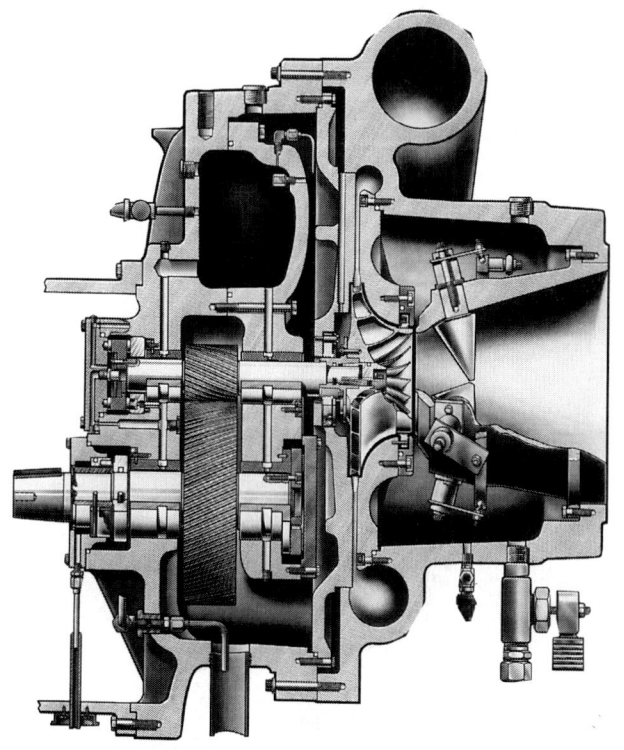

FIGURE 3-6. *Hermetic centrifugal compressor*

ruggedness of the open type. Figures 3-8 and 3-9 on the next page show such compressors. The motor and compressor are completely contained within a casting that is bolted together. You can disassemble the compressor for troubleshooting and service, while the system stays sealed from the atmosphere. The bolted casting also makes it easier to rebuild the compressor.

The drive motor for a hermetic or semi-hermetic compressor is enclosed in the crankcase. Heat generated from motor losses has to be picked up and removed somehow. This can be done in four ways:

- by passing suction vapor through or around the stator winding to pick up motor heat, which is carried by the refrigerant to the condenser, where it is dissipated to the cooling medium (either air or water)

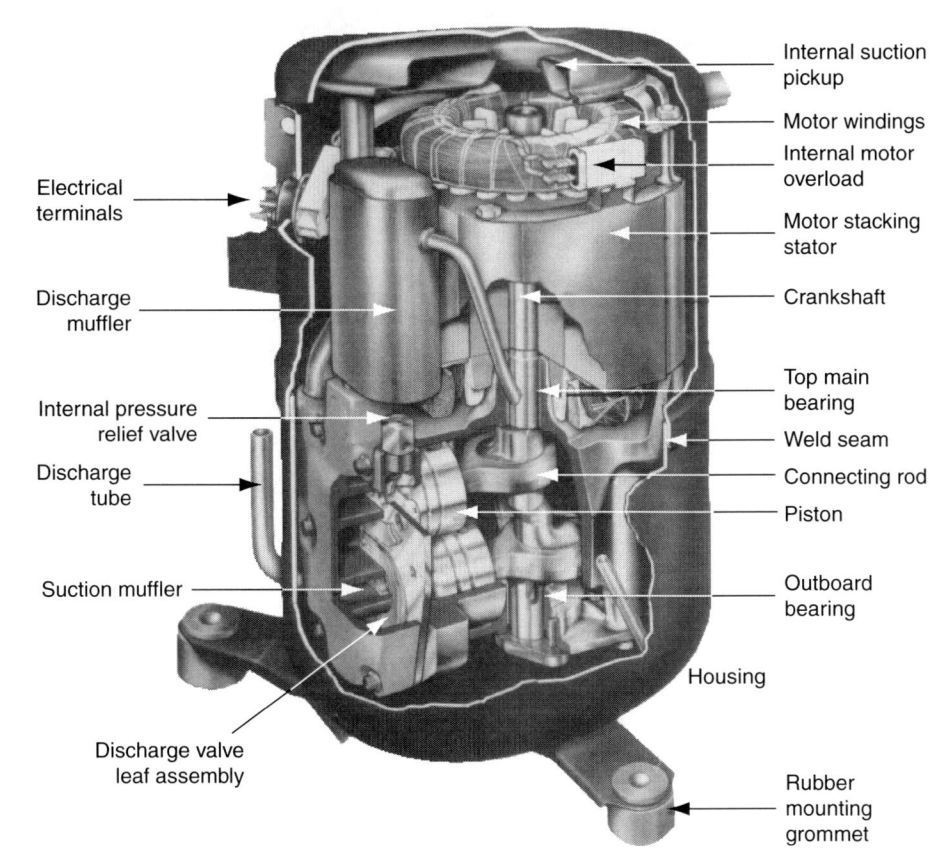

FIGURE 3-7. *Cutaway view of suction-cooled hermetic compressor*

- by blowing air over the motor housing to dissipate the heat

- by a combination of the above

- by a water jacket around the motor, or by applying a water coil to the motor housing (water is circulated through it to pick up the motor heat).

Suction cooling is very effective if the compressor operates at high suction pressure. A large amount of refrigerant is circulated for the amount of heat to be picked up. As a result, there is little superheating of the suction vapor as it passes through or around the motor. At very low suction pressures, suction cooling has a disadvantage. There may be excessive superheating of the vapor before it goes under compression. More heat is added under compression, and discharge vapor temperature can reach dangerous levels. This can contribute to oil breakdown and rapid chemical reactions in the case of air and moisture. Also, there can be an overall increase in compressor temperature, which can cause oil thinning and impaired lubrication. Thus, hermetic compressors in low-temperature applications often use supplementary cooling. A fan is used to blow air over the compressor housing. An auxiliary fan can be used—or, on an air-cooled unit, the compressor can be put in the path of the air off the condenser.

Water cooling of the hermetic motor is often built into water-cooled condensing units. Water going to the condenser is first circulated around the motor housing. It picks up motor heat and dissipates it in the same way in which condenser heat is dissipated. The demands of the condenser are much greater than the amount of water required to cool the motor. As a result, the temperature of the water passing around the motor rises only slightly. In general, motor heat will be only 5 to 10% of the total heat. Water-cooled hermetic or semi-hermetic compressors have water jackets, or water coils around the compressor/motor shell or housing.

Like open-type compressors, hermetic compressors are designed to operate within specified suction pressure ranges. Many of the considerations for open-type compressors also apply to hermetic or semi-hermetic compressors. With a hermetic compressor, some limitations are even more important. A hermetic type of a given horsepower has a fixed speed—

FIGURE 3-8. Combination suction and air-cooled semi-hermetic compressor

FIGURE 3-9. Water-jacketed semi-hermetic compressor

and therefore, a fixed displacement. You cannot change the capacity or the temperature application range by changing motor pulleys or compressor flywheels. You must calculate application requirements accurately before you select a hermetic compressor. For example, consider an internally spring-mounted hermetic compressor designed for high or medium temperatures. It will always run excessively hot in a low-temperature application. This invites high discharge temperatures, impaired cylinder lubrication, and ultimate motor failure.

Hermetic compressors designed for water-cooled units with relatively low discharge pressures should not be applied to air-cooled units. An overloaded motor could result from the higher discharge pressures that would prevail. Excessive discharge pressures with hermetic compressors should be avoided. This is done by adequately sizing the condenser, and by maintaining it properly.

Also, avoid too high a suction vapor temperature, or too low a superheat of the suction vapor entering the compressor. Low superheat invites the presence of liquid refrigerant in the compressor. This has a number of damaging effects. High suction vapor temperature results in an excessively hot-running compressor. In the case of a suction vapor-cooled type, insufficient motor cooling is possible. Under this condition, a hermetic compressor may cycle on its motor protector. This would considerably shorten its service life.

If the suction vapor superheat is too low, check the operation of the metering device. Make sure that it is not overfeeding liquid refrigerant. If this is not the case, installing a suction/liquid line heat exchanger will increase suction superheat. It is imperative that superheated vapor enter the compressor. If the suction vapor temperature is too high, check the metering device again. It could be starving the evaporator coil. Insulating the suction line will reduce suction vapor temperatures. High suction vapor temperatures will cause high compressor discharge temperatures. Do not allow the discharge temperature to exceed 225°F. (Measure the temperature 6 in. away from the compressor on the hot vapor line.) Temperatures higher than 225°F will cause compressor failure due to lubrication problems.

There is no hermetic or semi-hermetic compressor that can perform well in *all* conditions and applications. In the selection process, always consider the manufacturer's allowable range of evaporating temperatures for a particular model. It is the most important criterion for avoiding premature failures.

CAPACITY VERSUS POWER INPUT IN COMPRESSOR APPLICATIONS

In the application of a hermetic compressor, the goal is maximum capacity without motor overload. Capacity varies with suction and discharge pressures.

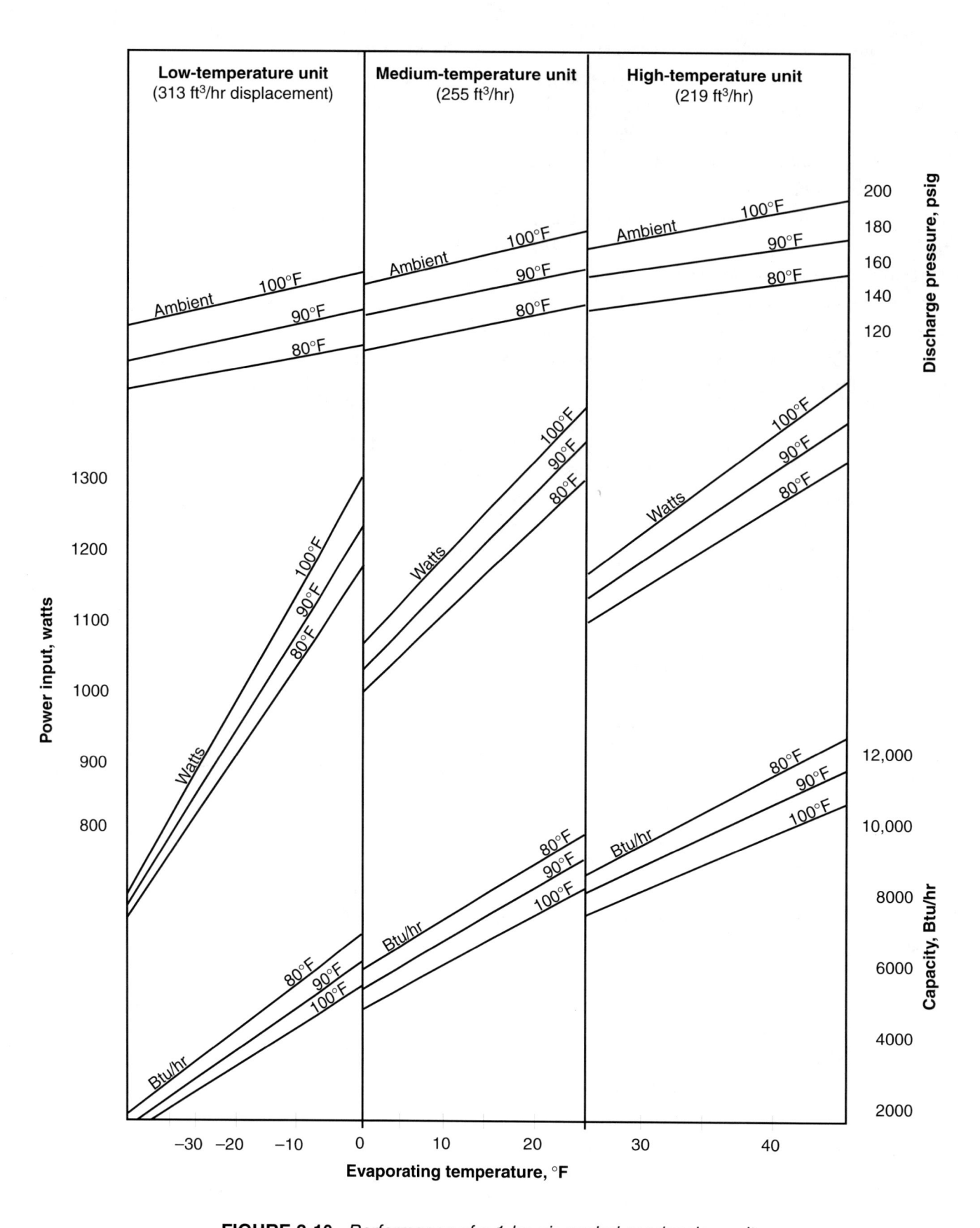

FIGURE 3-10. *Performance of a 1-hp air-cooled condensing unit*

LESSON 3

The hermetic motor load varies with these same factors. The performance curves of a typical condensing unit with a hermetic compressor clearly show this. Figure 3-10 provides information about three models (low-, medium-, and high-temperature) of a 1-hp air-cooled condensing unit with a hermetic compressor. The graphs show capacity (Btuh), power input (W), and discharge pressure (psig) for each model. Capacity, power input, and discharge pressure are plotted against evaporating temperature for ambient temperatures of 80, 90, and 100° F.

You can see that power input curves are quite similar for all three models. But capacity curves show considerable change from one suction range to another. Displacements of the compressors were selected to give the motor loads shown. In spite of the increasing displacement, capacity actually decreases. Why? As suction pressure lowers, the ratio of compression increases. As the ratio of compression increases, volumetric efficiency is reduced.

Figure 3-10 also shows that compressor discharge pressure runs higher for the high-temperature model than for the others. It is also higher for the medium-temperature model than for the low-temperature model. This occurs because the condenser load varies with the capacity of the compressor. The greater its capacity, the more heat the condenser has to dissipate. Therefore, with the same ambient, the same amount of surface, and the same volume of air circulated, a condenser must operate at a greater temperature differential. Compressor discharge pressure increases as capacity becomes greater.

The condenser load is less for the low-temperature model. Condenser load is less for compressors designed for low-temperature applications. Yet, the same condenser is usually used for low-, medium-, and high-temperature models. It is desirable to maintain as low a discharge pressure as practical for low-temperature models. This is also done to maintain the lowest possible compression ratio.

From Figure 3-10 you can draw the following conclusions:

- As suction pressure increases, so does capacity, power input, and condenser load. This is why most cooling units are rated up to a limiting suction pressure or evaporating temperature.

- As discharge pressure increases, power input increases, but capacity decreases. The Btu/watt economy factor also decreases.

- For a given evaporating temperature or suction pressure, a medium-temperature hermetic motor/compressor will have more capacity than a high-temperature model. However, the motor and condenser load will increase proportionately. Similarly, under the same conditions, a low-temperature hermetic motor/compressor will have greater capacity than a medium-temperature model. And, again, it will have higher motor and condenser loads. The reason is that the lower-temperature models have greater displacement than the higher-temperature models. Although increased displacement results in higher capacity, consider the increased motor load when selecting equipment. The model with a hermetic compressor with less displacement could be a wiser selection. The motor would operate safely during severe operating conditions, or if frequent pulldown conditions exist.

EQUIPMENT SELECTION

You must consider several factors in selecting a hermetic compressor/condensing unit for a specific application. First of all, decide what type of unit is best-suited to the application. It may be air-cooled, water-cooled, combination air-water, an evaporative condenser type, or some other type. Study manufacturers' product publications closely. They frequently provide helpful information on the relative merits of the various types. Then consider the other factors that ensure the best performance, economy of operation, and freedom from trouble and excessive maintenance.

After selecting the type of unit, determine the temperature of the condensing medium. It governs the discharge pressure of the compressor, thus affecting capacity. For an air-cooled hermetic unit, you need to know the average maximum ambient temperature. For a water-cooled unit, determine the maximum temperature of the water supply. For a water-cooled unit connected to a cooling tower, or for an evaporative condenser, you must know the average wet-bulb temperature.

As Figure 3-10 shows, air-cooled hermetic condensing units are rated at given evaporating and ambient temperatures. Water-cooled and evaporative condenser units are usually rated at given evaporating temperatures and discharge pressures, or at corresponding condensing temperatures. The latter also applies to ratings of compressors only.

CAPACITY REQUIREMENT

The compressor/condensing unit must have enough capacity to handle the application load at average maximum conditions. For best overall performance, capacity should be about equal to the Btuh load at design conditions. Obviously, you must know the load and also the planned hours of operation per day.

A simple formula will give you the capacity requirements of the application. Multiply the actual Btuh load by 24. Then divide by desired hours of daily operation:

$$\text{required capacity of condensing unit} = \frac{\text{Btuh load} \times 24 \text{ hr}}{\text{hours of operation per day}}$$

After you determine Btuh capacity requirements, the next step is to find the evaporating temperature and suction pressure. This will depend on the differential for which the evaporator is selected. For example, assume that a cooler will operate at 38°F. The evaporator is selected for a 15°F differential. The evaporating temperature will be 23°F (38 – 15). At 23°F, R-134a has a saturation pressure of 20.6 psig.

From this evaporating pressure you must subtract the pressure drop through the suction line. Assume the pressure drop to be 2.0 psig. The compressor will operate at a suction pressure of 18.6 psig (20.6 – 2.0). This corresponds to a 20°F evaporating temperature. So, the application has a design evaporating temperature of 23°F, but the compressor must have the required Btuh capacity at 20°F evaporating temperature. The compressor will operate at the pressure corresponding to this temperature because of the pressure drop through the suction line.

So far in this Lesson, you have looked at the conditions of evaporating temperature and ambient or condensing temperature. This is usually enough to enable you to select the unit for an application. However, in some cases, other factors affect the capacity requirement. Actual suction vapor temperature is an example.

You are not likely to find a hermetic compressor/condensing unit that meets exact capacity requirements. Usually you will select a unit with a little more or a little less capacity than the actual Btuh requirement. In most cases, this simply means slightly more or less running time. For example, assume an application with a 12,000-Btuh load, and running time of 16 hours per day. The actual capacity requirement would be:

$$\frac{12{,}000 \text{ Btuh} \times 24 \text{ hr}}{16 \text{ hr}} = 18{,}000 \text{ Btuh}$$

Now assume that you have a choice between two pieces of equipment. One has a rated capacity of 15,000 Btuh. The other, the nearest larger size, is rated at 24,000 Btuh. Both ratings are at the application's design conditions. Using the smaller unit, running time would be:

$$\text{hours of operation per day} = \frac{\text{Btuh load} \times 24 \text{ hr}}{\text{unit capacity}}$$

$$\frac{12,000 \text{ Btuh} \times 24 \text{ hr}}{15,000 \text{ Btuh}} = 19.2 \text{ hours per day}$$

With the larger unit, running time would be:

$$\frac{12,000 \text{ Btuh} \times 24 \text{ hr}}{24,000 \text{ Btuh}} = 12.0 \text{ hours per day}$$

It is more practical to choose the smaller unit. It will operate 19.2 hours per day, assuming that the load is based on average maximum conditions.

To select the exact model (temperature range) of hermetic unit, you must consider design evaporating temperature. In general, for evaporating temperatures of 0°F or lower, low-temperature range compressors are used. For evaporating temperatures above 0°F but lower than 25°F, medium-temperature models are used. For evaporating temperatures above 25°F, high-temperature models are needed. Some manufacturers rate hermetic compressor units for two ranges. They might be rated as *high and medium* or as *medium and low*. In such cases, the compressors are actually designed for the higher temperature range. They simply operate in a lightly loaded condition at the lower range.

There can be an advantage to having a hermetic compressor/condensing unit operate at a suction pressure or evaporating temperature below its design range. Assume that you want an air-cooled condensing unit (compressor) with a capacity of 7,200 Btuh at 20°F evaporating temperature. Ambient temperature is 90°F. You calculate that a ¾-hp unit would not have sufficient capacity. From Figure 3-10, you find that the 1-hp medium-temperature model has a capacity of about 8,300 Btuh. This is well above the required capacity. But Figure 3-10 also shows something else. A 1-hp high-temperature model operating at 20°F evaporating temperature has a capacity of about 7,400 Btuh. This more closely matches your requirement. In this case, it is preferable to use the high-temperature model, even though the application is in the medium-temperature range.

In spite of this example, remember this: It is not always recommended to apply high- or medium-temperature hermetic compressors to low-temperature applications. This applies to hermetic and semi-hermetic compressors of the suction vapor-cooled type. The reason for this is that inadequate motor cooling and high discharge vapor temperatures may result. Follow the recommendations of the manufacturer in this regard.

MOTOR LOAD—A CRITICAL APPLICATION FACTOR

Motor load also governs which exact model of hermetic compressor is best for an application. As you observed in Figure 3-10, motor load increases as suction pressure increases. Now, assume a low-temperature application in which a prolonged pulldown is frequent. Contrary to what was just said, it might be best to use a hermetic unit in the medium-temperature range (that is, if the compressor manufacturer gives approval for the change).

Recall that low-temperature hermetic units are not usually designed for continuous operation at evaporating temperatures above 0°F. This corresponds to a 6.5 psig suction pressure for R-134a. However, on some automatic defrosting systems, the compressor may operate at a 30-psig suction pressure. This would be either during the defrosting period (with hot gas defrost systems), or immediately after. Depending on the evaporator design and the defrost method used, the compressor could be seriously overloaded. Application calculations may show the possibility of such frequent motor overload in a low-temperature hermetic unit. This should make you question whether to select a low-temperature model, or a medium- or high-temperature model.

In selecting a hermetic condensing unit or compressor, follow the manufacturer's recommendations about motor cooling. For air-cooled equipment, you need adequate volume and velocity of air over the motor. For water-cooled equipment, enough water must circulate to provide proper heat dissipation. Suction vapor-cooled hermetic compressors are generally limited to high- and medium-temperature applications. In some cases, you must supplement suction vapor cooling with forced convection air cooling. Be sure of the manufacturer's recommendations. Make serious inquiry rather than gamble on a misapplication.

COMPRESSOR INSTALLATION

As with open-type compressors, there are generally two reasons for installing a hermetic compressor. One is as the replacement of a malfunctioning component. The other is as an integral part of an assembled condensing unit. Replacement may be needed because of a motor-compressor burnout. This usually means that moisture and acid from the motor windings have traveled through the system. You must remove this moisture and acid. Otherwise, the windings of the new motor-compressor will also be attacked and soon fail. To replace the compressor:

1. First close the suction and discharge service valves, if it has them. Then recover the refrigerant charge from the compressor using approved recovery equipment. Next, unbolt the service valves from the body of the compressor. The suction and discharge lines may be directly connected

to the compressor. If so, recover the refrigerant from the system before removing the suction and discharge lines from the compressor. Remove the electrical wiring from the terminals of the compressor. Remove the motor hold-down nuts or bolts and lift the compressor from the condensing unit. *Caution: Do not allow any of the contaminated oil or sludge from the system to get on your skin or in your eyes. Serious acid burns can result. Wear protective clothing, gloves, and eye protection.*

2. If the condensing unit is water-cooled, disconnect the water line and blow out the condenser with compressed air (do *not* use oxygen) or nitrogen. (Water in the condenser might freeze and burst the water tubes when refrigerant is recovered from the system.)

3. Recover refrigerant from the system or from that part of the system that will be opened.

4. Install the new compressor and reinstall the connecting lines.

5. Install a new liquid-line filter-drier of adequate size. Install a large suction-line filter-drier for temporary operation.

6. Pull a deep vacuum using a two-stage vacuum pump and hold this vacuum at 500 microns.

7. Proceed to charge the system until the proper refrigerant charge has been introduced. *Caution: Never start a compressor when it is under a deep vacuum. The compressor motor windings could be damaged.*

8. Operate the system for 48 hours. Then check the oil for acids using an acid test kit. If the oil is discolored or acidic, change both filter-driers, and put the system back in operation. Repeat this procedure every 48 hours until the oil tests good.

9. When the system is clean and the compressor oil tests good, remove the suction-line filter-drier and install a suction-line filter. The suction-line *filter* will have a lower pressure drop across it than the *filter-drier.*

After performing an installation, check for refrigerant leaks. Carefully check the compressor, refrigerant lines, and all other components affected. The time required in leak detection is well spent. It pays dividends by avoiding future troubles. This is especially true in applications where normal operating suction pressure will be at a vacuum. In such cases, a leak could result in air and moisture getting into the system.

REVIEW QUESTIONS

1. Does the centrifugal compressor utilize a piston and valves to compress the refrigerant vapor?

2. What type of compressor is found in large applications up to 10,000 tons?

3. Which compressor relies on pistons and valves to compress the refrigerant?

4. List the two different types of rotary compressors.

5. Which compressor is replacing the reciprocating compressor in some applications because it has higher efficiency, fewer moving parts, and is quieter in operation?

6. Which compressor utilizes two helical rotors to compress the refrigerant vapor?

7. What is the most outstanding advantage of the hermetically sealed compressor over the open type?

8. What advantage does the semi-hermetic compressor have over the hermetic type?

9. Name some of the results of high compressor discharge temperatures.

10. How are these disadvantages overcome in compressors that are employed in low-temperature applications?

11. How are these disadvantages overcome in water-cooled hermetic compressor systems?

REVIEW QUESTIONS

12. What percentage of overall heat dissipated from the system comes from the compressor motor?

13. Why do some compressor limitations take on added importance in a hermetic compressor of a given horsepower?

14. When a hermetic compressor designed for high or medium temperatures is applied to a low-temperature system, what is the resulting effect?

15. What will result if a compressor designed for use with a water-cooled condenser at normally low discharge pressure is applied to an air-cooled system?

16. What problem does low superheat invite?

17. What is the ultimate goal in the application of a hermetic compressor?

18. In general, what evaporating temperatures do low-temperature compressors use?

19. In general, at what evaporating temperatures do medium-temperature compressors operate?

20. Is the condenser load greater or less for compressors designed for low-temperature applications than for compressors designed for high-temperature applications?

21. When discharge pressures increase, power input increases. What happens to capacity?

REVIEW QUESTIONS

22. As suction pressure increases on a compressor, three other important factors also increase. What are they?

23. For a given evaporating temperature or suction pressure, which will have the greater capacity—a medium-temperature compressor or a high-temperature compressor?

24. When selecting equipment for a specific application, what ambient temperature must you consider for air-cooled equipment?

25. When you consider a water tower for a water-cooled unit, what average temperature is very important?

LESSON 4

Refrigeration System Accessories

INTRODUCTION

The word *accessories* probably makes you think of the extra options you add on to your car. They are not essential for driving, but are convenient or attractive. A refrigeration system can also have accessories. In a refrigeration system, accessories are more than just attractive add-ons, but they *are* optional. The system can operate without them.

However, in some applications these accessories should be used in order to *ensure* proper and safe system operation. Since they are commonly used, you should know their functions and operating principles. This Lesson covers such controls and other devices.

CONDENSING WATER REGULATORS

Two-way regulators

Water passes through a water-cooled refrigerant condenser in response to condensing pressure. The condensing water regulator controls the amount of water. In a vapor cycle refrigeration system, it maintains a condensing pressure level that loads—but does not overload—the compressor motor. It automatically adjusts to correct for changes in temperature or pressure of the water supply. It also reacts to changes in the quantity of refrigerant vapor that the compressor sends to the condenser.

Operation. The condensing water regulator consists of a valve and an actuator linked together, as shown in Figure 4-1. The actuator usually is a combination of a metallic bellows and an adjustable spring. It connects to the high side of the system to sense condensing pressure. For large water flow capacities, a small condensing water regulator is used for pilot operation of a diaphragm-type main valve.

After the compressor starts, condensing pressure begins to rise. When it reaches the pressure setting of the regulator spring, the bellows begins to move. It gradually opens the valve disk from its seat. The regulator continues to open as condensing pressure rises. At some point there is a balance between water flow and the heat rejection requirement. At this point, condensing pressure is stabilized. When the compressor stops, water flow continues through the regulator. This causes condensing pressure to drop gradually, which closes the regulator. It is fully closed at a pressure typically 7 psi below the opening pressure.

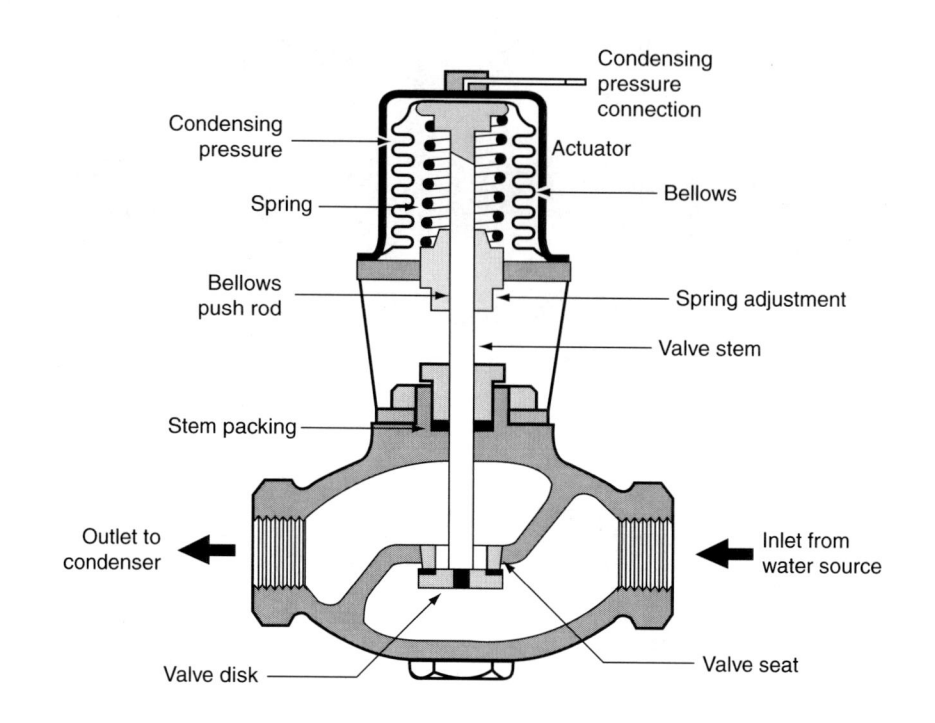

FIGURE 4-1. *Two-way condensing water regulator*

Selection. Selection of a condensing water regulator is based on three factors:

- type of refrigerant

- required water flow rate

- available water pressure drop across the regulator.

One standard bellows operator may handle any of several refrigerants. But special springs or bellows may be required for very high-pressure or very low-pressure refrigerants. This is the case with ammonia (R-717).

A combination of water and ammonia will corrode nonferrous metals like copper or brass. Therefore, a stainless steel bellows must be used instead of a brass bellows.

The water flow rate required depends on several factors:

- condenser performance data

- water temperature

- amount of heat that the water must collect

- allowable leaving water temperature.

The opening of the valve will correspond to the pressure rise above the regulator opening point. For a given opening, the flow rate through the regulator depends on the available water pressure drop across the valve seat. To find available water pressure drop for the required flow rate, add together condenser water pressure drop, pipe line pressure drop, and static head losses. Deduct the total from the pressure of the water at its supply point.

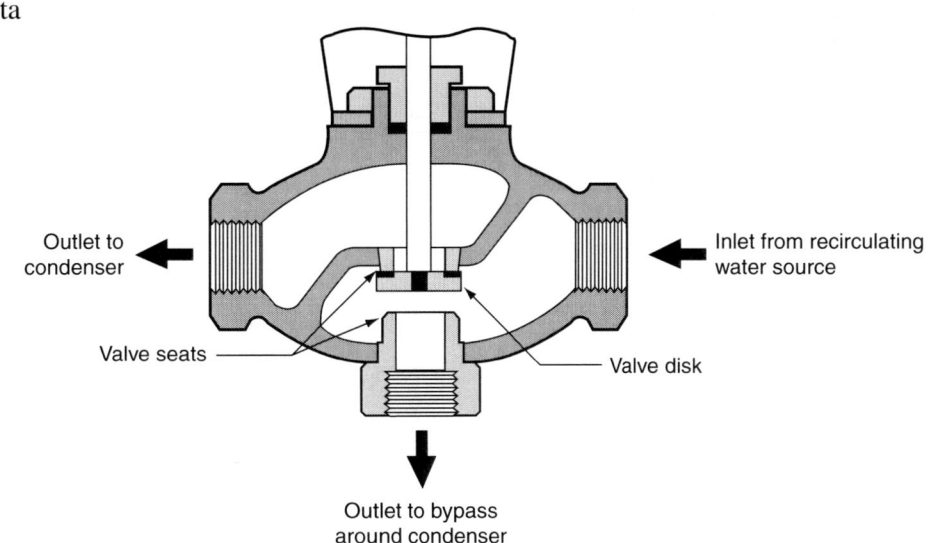

FIGURE 4-2. *Three-way condensing water regulator*

Consult manufacturers' data when choosing a condensing water regulator. Select the condensing water regulator that is best-suited for the application on the basis of maximum required flow rate and minimum available pressure drop.

Application. Avoid oversizing a regulator. It encourages hunting. Two-way condensing water regulators cause problems if used in recirculating cooling tower systems. The throttling action of the valves during cold weather reduces pump and tower circulation. This is undesirable for that equipment.

Three-way regulators

Some tower systems need individual condensing pressure control. In these cases, you should use three-way condensing water regulators. These are similar to two-way regulators, but have an additional port, as shown in Figure 4-2. It opens to bypass water around the condenser as the port that controls flow to the condenser closes. Thus, the tower decking or sprays and the circulating pump have a constant water supply. Yet the water supply to individual condensers is modulated for condensing (head) pressure control.

Three-way regulators must be supplemented in cooling tower systems that operate in freezing weather. An indoor sump is usually required, and a temperature-actuated three-way water control valve. The valve diverts all of the water leaving the condenser directly to the sump when the water gets too cold.

Almost all water supplies contain either scale-forming chemicals or foreign particles, or both. These can cause considerable wear on the condensing water regulator valve stem and seat. To prevent such damage, a water strainer should be installed ahead of the regulator.

CHECK VALVES

Check valves are useful in refrigerant lines where pressure reversals could cause an undesired reverse flow. The valve, which permits flow in one direction only, is usually opened by some of the pressure drop that causes flow in the line. It closes when there is a reversal of pressure. It also closes when the pressure drop across it is less than the minimum opening pressure drop in the normal flow direction.

Conventional check valve design is usually of the piston type. The globe pattern is employed in large sizes. In-line designs are commonly smaller than the 2-in. size. Either design may be used with closing springs. The heavier springs give reliable and tight-closing, but need greater pressure drop for the check to open. The in-line check design does not permit a manual opening stem. Conventional check valves may open at a drop of less than 1 psi. However, they may not be reliable at temperatures below –25°F. This is because light-closing springs may not overcome the viscous oil.

Special refrigeration check valves are available. Excess flow checks close only when the flow exceeds a maximum desired rate. Electrically lifted checks require no pressure drop to remain open. Remote pressure-operated checks are normally open, but close when supplied with a higher-pressure source of refrigerant.

Applications. Check valves in compressor discharge lines prevent refrigerant flow from the condenser to the compressor during the off cycle. They also prevent flow from an operating compressor to an idle one. While a 2- to 6-psi pressure drop is tolerable, check valve design must resist pulsations of the compressor and temperature of discharge vapor. They must be bubble-tight to prevent accumulation of liquid refrigerant at compressor discharge valves or in the crankcase.

In liquid lines, check valves prevent reverse flow through the unused expansion device on heat pump systems. They also prevent backup into the low-pressure liquid line of a recirculating system during a defrost period. While a 2- to 6-psi pressure drop is usually acceptable, the check valve seat must be bubble-tight.

A check valve may be useful in the suction line of a low-temperature evaporator. It can prevent transfer of vapor to a lower-temperature evaporator on the same suction main. In this case, the pressure drop must be less than 2 psi. Also, the valve seating must be reasonably tight, and the valve must be reliable at low temperatures.

Normally open, pressure-operated check valves are often used to close suction lines, vapor legs, or liquid legs in gravity recirculating systems during defrost. In hot gas defrost lines, check valves may be used in the branch hot gas lines connecting individual evaporators. They prevent cross-feed of refrigerant during the cooling cycle when the defrost operation is not taking place. In addition, check valves are used in the hot gas line. They are placed between the hot gas heating coil in the drain pan and the evaporator. This prevents pan coil sweating during the refrigeration cycle. Tolerable pressure drop is typically 2 to 6 psi. Seating must be nearly bubble-tight, and seat materials must withstand high temperatures.

Check valves should be sized for the pressure drop that ensures that they will be wide open at the desired flow rate. This prevents chatter or pulsation.

SAFETY RELIEF DEVICES

A safety relief device prevents the pressure of refrigerant from rising above a safe limit. They can be used with a storage vessel, or with a system component such as a receiver or water-cooled condenser. They function when operating or high-limit controls fail, and when the vessel is exposed to excessive heat.

Three general types of relief devices are common:

- fusible plug

- rupture member

- pressure relief valve.

The *fusible plug* is a fitting filled with an alloy that has a low melting point. The alloy will soften and "blow" at a predetermined temperature. That temperature corresponds to the safe saturation pressure of refrigerant in the vessel or system. The *rupture member* contains a thin disk of metal designed to rupture at a certain pressure. Neither the fusible plug nor the rupture member reseal after opening. Consequently, all of the refrigerant is discharged from the storage vessel or protected part of the system should they open. The relief device then would have to be replaced.

The *pressure relief valve* is a pressure-actuated valve held closed by a spring or other means. It automatically relieves at a predetermined pressure. The pressure relief valve is adjustable— but, once set, the valve is sealed to prevent tampering. It is important that relief settings not be adjusted in the field. If the seal is broken, the valve should be replaced with a correctly adjusted and sealed valve. The setting should be 25% above maximum system operating pressure (MSOP). This safety factor gives enough spring force on the valve seat to keep a tight seal, yet allows for other factors that cause settings to vary.

A pressure relief valve will usually close about 10 to 20% below its operating pressure. Relief valves are factory set within a few pounds of their stamped setting. But this may vary as much as 10% after a period of storage or service.

Relief devices must vent directly to the outside atmosphere in many cases. This applies to the discharge of toxic refrigerants or large amounts of non-toxic refrigerants. The outside wall or roof opening must be the size of the discharge pipe. The only exception is for ammonia. It can be vented into a tank of water. The tank must be large enough to dilute the ammonia sufficiently to make it inoffensive.

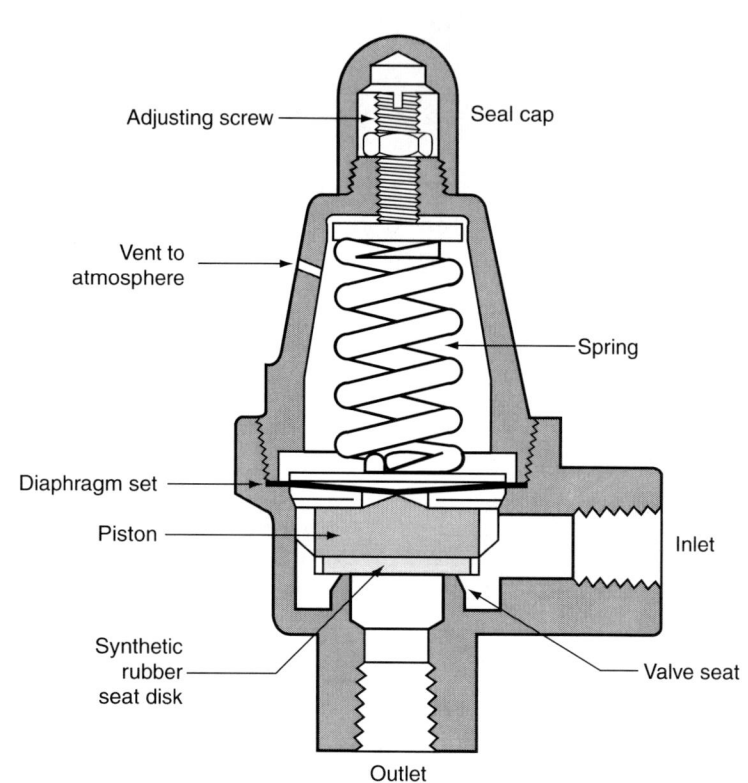

FIGURE 4-3. *Diaphragm-type relief valve*

Diaphragm-type relief valves

Figure 4-3 shows a *diaphragm*, or *bellows-type*, relief valve. It is indirectly spring-loaded. System pressure acts on a diaphragm that lifts the piston from the valve seat. It is especially suitable for high side-to-low side discharge in a refrigeration system.

"Pop" safety relief valves

The most popular relief valve is the directly spring-loaded or "pop" type, shown in Figure 4-4. Pressure above the spring setting first causes refrigerant to seep through. When there is enough flow to pop the piston open, it allows full discharge. The pop-type relief valve has its advantages, which include simple design, low initial cost, and high discharge capacity. By contrast, the diaphragm type has high initial cost and relatively low discharge capacity.

There are limits on the length of discharge pipe from a safety pressure relief valve. The limits are based on pipe size and relief valve discharge capacity in pounds of air per minute. Table 4-1 on the next page gives these limits for a 300-psig pressure setting. Relief valve seats may be metal, plastic, lead alloy, or synthetic rubber. The latter two are very popular. They have greater resilience that means probable reseating tightness. Valves with lead alloy seats may have an emergency manual reseating stem. The seating surface is reformed by tapping the stem lightly with a hammer.

Relief valves are designed to reclose as the pressure is reduced. However, it is very unlikely that the valve will reseal. Most manufacturers recommend replacement. Failure to reseal tightly is generally due to an accumulation of dirt and foreign matter that attaches to the valve seat disk while the valve is discharging. For this reason, it is impossible to predict the reliability of the relief valve resealing after it has discharged in service. This condition also allows the relief valve to seep refrigerant after reclosing, but not necessarily reseal.

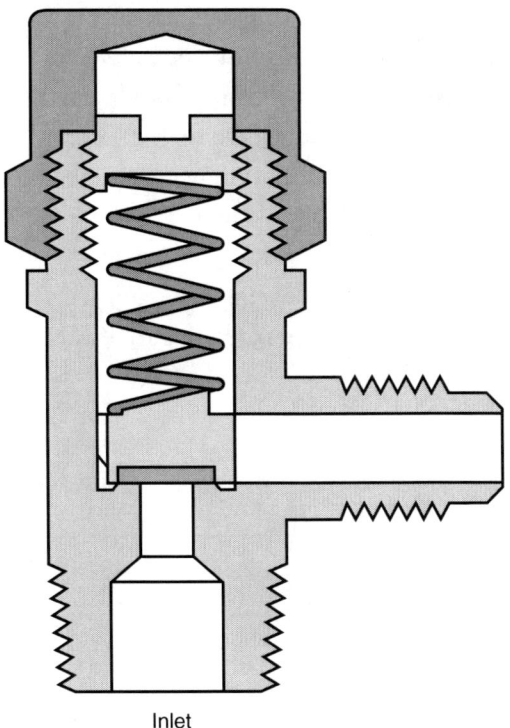

FIGURE 4-4. *Pop-type safety relief valve*

All valves must comply with the ASME Code for Unfired Pressure Vessels. Discharge rates are certified by the National Board of Boiler and Pressure Vessel Inspectors. A code symbol is stamped on relief valves indicating this certification. It includes the letters "UV" in a clover leaf design. The letters "NB" are stamped directly below this symbol. The pressure setting and capacity are also stamped on the valve.

The exact number, location, and type of relief devices required are set forth in detail in the American Standard Safety Code for Mechanical Refrigeration. Local codes vary somewhat in this respect, and should also be considered in designing an installation. For the most part, the selection of relief devices depends on the size and type of system.

RAC

The discharge capacity of the relief device must keep vessel pressure from rising more than 10% above design working pressure. The capacity of a relief device is measured at 10% above its stamped setting. Therefore, the setting cannot exceed the design pressure of the vessel.

DISCHARGE OIL SEPARATORS

A discharge oil separator removes oil from the discharge vapor coming out of the compressor. It does so immediately after the vapor leaves the compressor. Oil is separated from the refrigerant by reductions in velocity, changes in direction of flow, and impingement on baffles, mesh pads, or coarse screens. Their use reduces the amount of oil reaching the low side. They help maintain oil volume in the compressor oil sump. They also muffle the sound of vapor flow.

Figure 4-5 shows a small separator with inlet and outlet screens and a high-side float valve. A space below the float valve collects dirt or sludge. When enough

Relief device capacity (in lb of air per min)	Soft copper tube OD ⅜ in.	½ in.	⅝ in.	Schedule 40 pipe ½ in.	¾ in.	1 in.	1¼ in.	1½ in.	2 in.
2	49	262							
4	12	65	221						
6	5½	29	98	173					
8	3	16	55	97					
10	2	11	35	62	254				
12	1½	7	25	43	176				
14	1	5½	18	32	130				
16	1	4	14	24	99				
18		3	11	19	78				
20		2½	9	16	63	212			
25		1½	5½	10	41	136			
30		1	4	7	28	94			
35			1	3	5	21	69		
40			2	4	16	53	209		
45			1½	3	13	42	165		
50			1½	2½	10	34	133		
60			1	1½	7	24	93	200	
70				1½	5	17	68	147	
80				1	4	13	52	113	
90				1	3	10	41	89	
100					2½	8	33	72	252
125					1½	5½	21	46	161
150					1	4	15	32	112

TABLE 4-1. *Maximum length of discharge piping (in ft) for 300-psig pressure setting*

oil accumulates, it raises the float ball. The oil then passes through a needle valve and returns to the low-pressure crankcase. When the oil level in the separator falls, the float valve closes. This prevents the release of hot vapor to the crankcase. Insulation and even electric heaters may be added to the separator. This keeps the refrigerant in the separator from condensing under low-temperature conditions. There is a wide variety of horizontal and vertical flow oil separators. They use one or more elements such as centrifuges, baffles, wire mesh restrictors, or cylindrical filters.

Select an oil separator using one of two criteria. One is the rating for *system capacity*. The other is *compressor displacement volume*. Remember that compressor capacity increases when suction pressure is increased or when condensing pressure is decreased. Therefore, select the oil separator on the basis of system capacity at the compressor's lowest compression ratio.

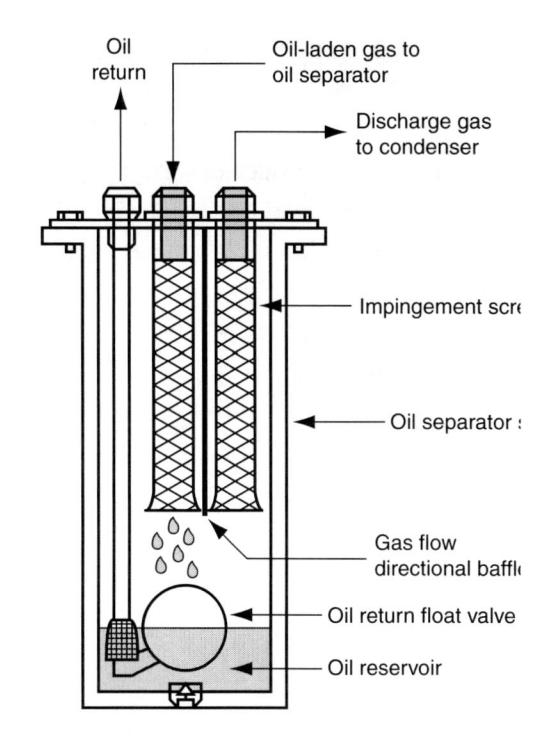

FIGURE 4-5. *Discharge-line oil separator*

Some refrigerants, such as ammonia (R-717), do not mix with the compressor oil. This type of system will function more efficiently with an oil separator. Any oil carried out of the compressor will be trapped by the separator and returned to the compressor crankcase. It is important to remember that oil separators are not 100% efficient. Some oil will get through the oil separator and out into the system. In the case of nonmiscible refrigerants, oil drains have to be placed in the low points of the system. Oil drains should be placed at the bottom of all receivers, evaporators, accumulators, and other vessels containing liquid ammonia.

Oil separators can be very valuable as a means of reducing oil fouling in the evaporator. This is especially true with flooded systems, low-temperature systems, and systems with long runs of piping or other factors that tend to cause oil return problems.

LIQUID LEVEL INDICATORS AND MOISTURE INDICATORS

Liquid level indicators are otherwise known as *sight glasses*. They are usually a glass bull's-eye in the side connection of what looks like a tee fitting. They are installed in the liquid line between the receiver and the expansion valve. They are important because they enable you to detect a shortage of refrigerant in a system or *flash gas* in the liquid line. Flash gas is caused by excessive pressure drop in the liquid line or insufficient subcooling of the liquid refrigerant. This causes the refrigerant to boil off in the liquid line, which reduces the capacity of the system and can eventually damage the expansion valve. The flash gas can be detected in the liquid-line sight glass as bubbles.

When there is a shortage of refrigerant, the level of liquid in the receiver is low. This allows some vapor to escape into the liquid line. The vapor is carried along as bubbles in the liquid. When the bubbles reach the sight glass, they can be seen through the glass bull's-eye. You will not ordinarily see bubbles in an adequately charged system. However, it *is* normal to have bubbles appear in the sight glass for a few minutes when the compressor is first started. One type of liquid level indicator has two bull's-eyes, opposite each other. A light held under the bottom glass makes it easy to see any bubbles through the top glass. Sight glasses are also available that have built-in moisture indicators.

The moisture indicator is a chemical that will change color if there is moisture in the system. For example, a moisture indicator used on an R-22 system will be green if the system is dry and will turn pink if wet. For accurate indication, the liquid-line temperature should be close to 75°F. The moisture indicator also serves the purpose of a liquid-line sight glass for indicating a flash gas or refrigerant undercharge. Moisture indicators are covered in more detail in the next Lesson.

DISCHARGE MUFFLERS

Piston operation creates pulsations that can cause objectionable noise in the compressor discharge vapor line. If noise is an important consideration, a muffler can minimize the pulsations. Figure 4-6 shows a typical example of a discharge muffler. The perforations in the muffler chamber have a dampening effect on the pulsations of the discharge vapor. The muffler should be as close as possible to the compressor discharge connection. It is usually installed vertically to provide efficient oil movement. Some mufflers, when mounted horizontally, must be positioned correctly to prevent trapping oil. An oil separator is also an effective muffler—so an oil separator and a muffler are not used in series.

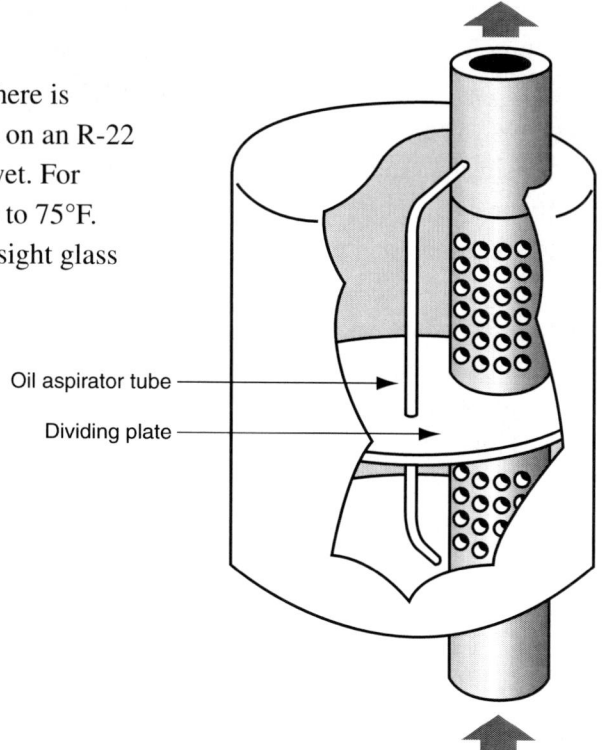

FIGURE 4-6. *Hot gas muffler*

COMPRESSOR LUBRICATION PROTECTION CONTROLS

Early refrigerant compressors had large bores. Their compression ratios were lower than present-day types. They operated at much lower speeds. Lubrication was not a critical problem. But then came high-speed compressors. They had very close tolerances between moving parts, and bearings that carried heavy loads. Proper lubrication became a major concern. Pressure-feed systems similar to those in automobile engines were designed. They normally provided adequate lubrication for all moving parts.

The next problem was protecting the compressor if the forced lubrication system failed. Compressor lubrication problems are different from those in an auto engine. Auto engine crankcase pressure, even if not always at atmospheric pressure, varies only slightly. It needs only one pressure measurement. Also, the engine is always attended. It's easy to monitor lubrication with a gauge or a light on the dashboard.

The refrigeration compressor is quite different. Lubricating oil pressure must be monitored in conjunction with varying crankcase refrigerant pressures. When the compressor starts, oil pressure should increase while crankcase pressure decreases. The two pressures remain about the same only if the lubrication system malfunctions.

Lube oil protection control solves this monitoring problem. The type of control shown in Figure 4-7 measures the different but related pressures and monitors the difference. It responds to change in a predetermined differential by opening the control circuit to the compressor motor. This is called *pressure differential monitoring*.

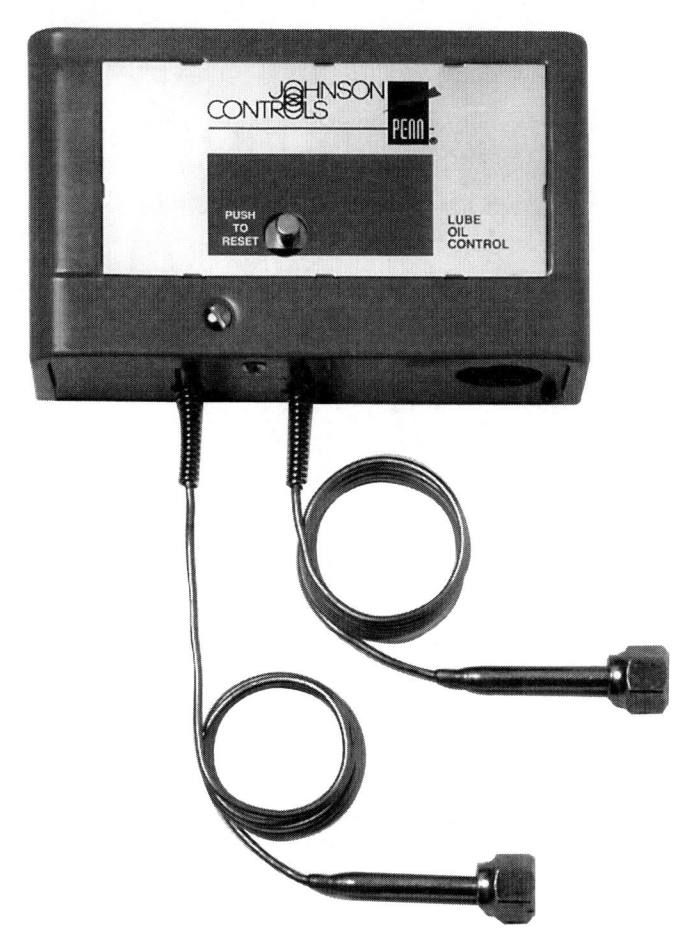

FIGURE 4-7. *Lube oil protection control*

The oil pressure monitoring control has two capillary tubes. The high-pressure capillary connects to a tapping specified by the compressor manufacturer. It senses oil pressure. The low-pressure capillary measures crankcase pressure. It connects to a suitable tapping in the crankcase and *not* to the gauge port of the suction service valve. Control switch contacts are wired in series with the compressor control circuit. Built-in time-delay components prevent nuisance shutdowns while pressures are stabilizing on start-up. A typical example of the lube oil protection control in a systems control circuit is shown in Figure 4-8 on the next page.

The control shown in Figure 4-7 is not adjustable. It is factory-set to the compressor manufacturer's specifications. However, some controls may be adjusted after installation. To adjust these types of controls, one pressure gauge goes in the oil pump circuit, wherever recommended by the compressor manufacturer. The other pressure gauge goes in the tapping in the suction service valve body. Then start the compressor and note the oil pressure and crankcase pressure. Soon the oil pump will reach its maximum speed and output. At this point there will be a differential between oil pressure and crankcase pressure. This difference is the value sensed by the control. Adjust the control to meet the specified requirements of minimum differential that will ensure compressor lubrication. The control is now set to shut down the compressor if there is any sign that the lubrication system is not working.

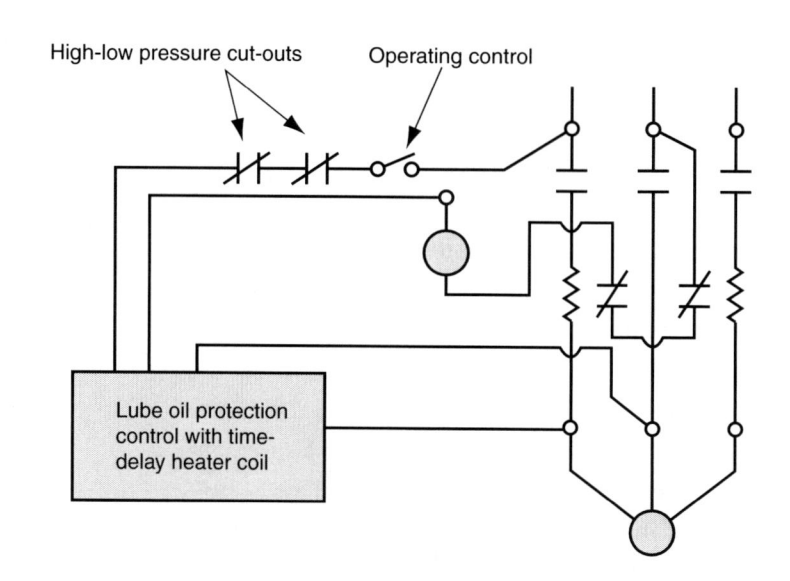

FIGURE 4-8. *Example of arrangement of control in system control circuit*

STRAINERS AND FILTERS

Many problems in refrigeration systems result from foreign matter in the system. Dirt, pieces of solder, and pipe compound get into the system during installation. No matter how much the system is cleaned, this material is seldom removed completely. It is carried through the system by the refrigerant. If it reaches either the expansion valve or the solenoid valve, it will interfere with their operation. Therefore, there should always be a strainer in the liquid line. It should be ahead of the expansion valve or solenoid valve, whichever is the next downstream device. Figure 4-9 shows typical liquid-line strainers.

VIBRATION ELIMINATORS

When installing a compressor, you discover that it must be located close to a wall and other equipment. This makes it necessary to pipe discharge and suction

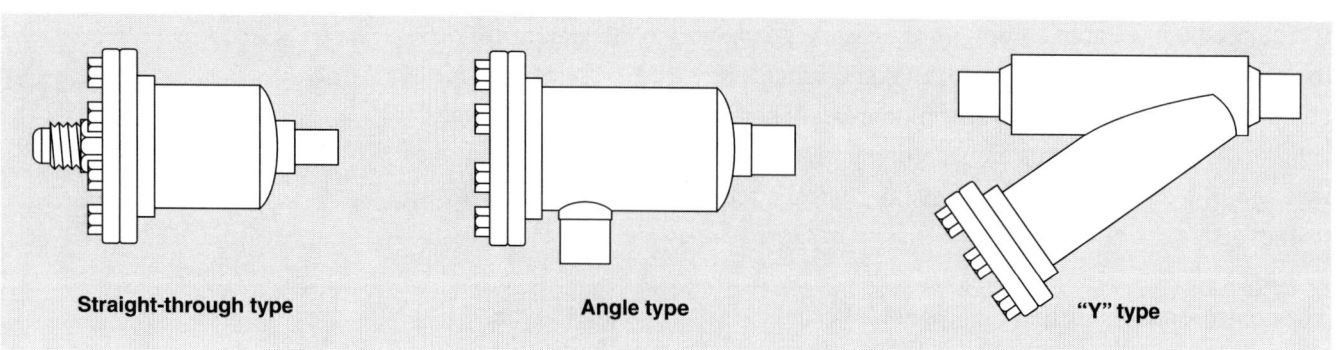

FIGURE 4-9. *Different types of strainers*

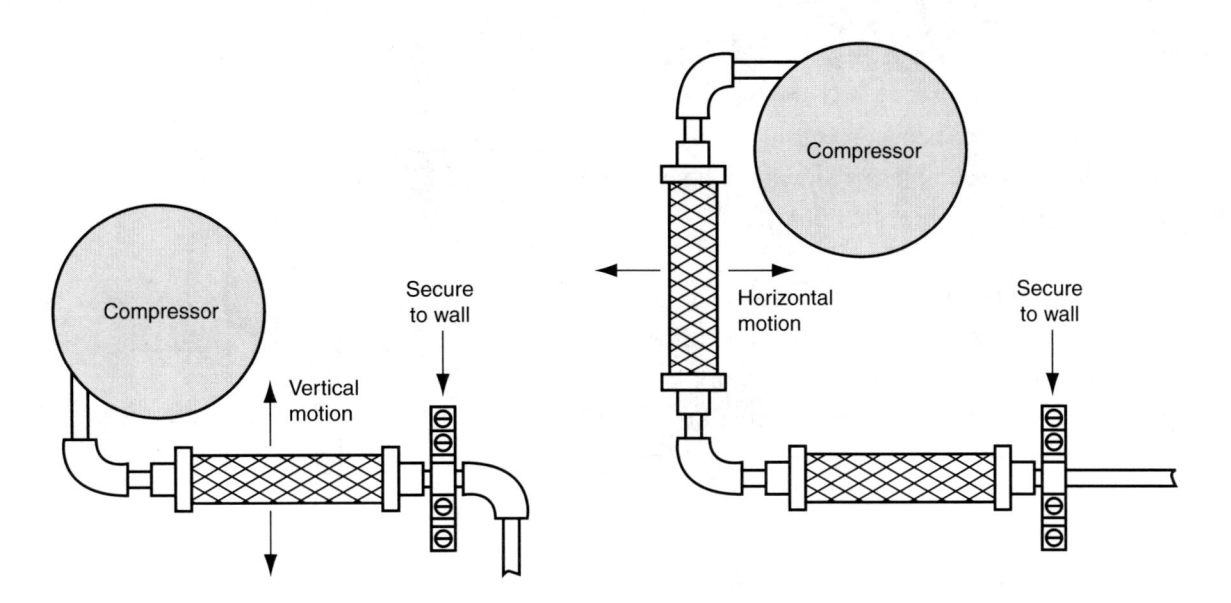

FIGURE 4-10. *Installation of vibration eliminator*

lines from the compressor to vertical supports with short lengths of tubing and 90° ells. Rigid connections at the compressor are prone to crack or break from vibration and stress. The cause may be discharge vapor pulsation or compressor movement because of high torque.

There is a simple way to prevent line breakage from these causes. Install *vibration eliminators* in both suction and discharge lines. They should be the same size as the lines. Install the vibration eliminators parallel with the drive shaft on the compressor. Install them in a vertical position only if necessary because of conditions. It is important not to stretch, twist, or compress the eliminator during installation. The sight method of installing vibration eliminators is illustrated in Figure 4-10.

A typical vibration eliminator has rigid copper ends to connect to the compressor and the system. Between the ends is a length of flexible tubing. It is covered with woven brass mesh for strength. The compressor may move because of torque. The piping may move because of discharge vapor pulsation. The vibration eliminator will absorb either movement. Thus, it prevents damage to both compressor piping and system piping.

SUCTION-LINE ACCUMULATORS

A defective expansion valve, refrigerant overcharge, or extremely low load may permit liquid refrigerant to reach the compressor from the evaporator. Because liquids are not compressible, the pistons and valves can suffer damage from such "slugs" of liquid.

RAC

To prevent this, you can put a *suction accumulator* in the suction line between evaporator and compressor. An accumulator usually has its own metering device (to feed liquid back to the compressor slowly without damage) or a heater (to evaporate the liquid).

Trapped oil may build up in the bottom of the accumulator after the refrigerant evaporates. Accumulators therefore have an oil return line leading from the bottom of the trap. Accumulators are especially important in heat pumps, truck refrigeration systems, and hot gas defrost systems.

Figure 4-11 shows a cross section of a typical suction-line accumulator. It has a U-tube for passage of refrigerant *vapor* back to the compressor. The metering port at the bottom of the tube allows oil to return back to the compressor. The metering port is small enough that any liquid refrigerant entering will be boiled off before it reaches the compressor.

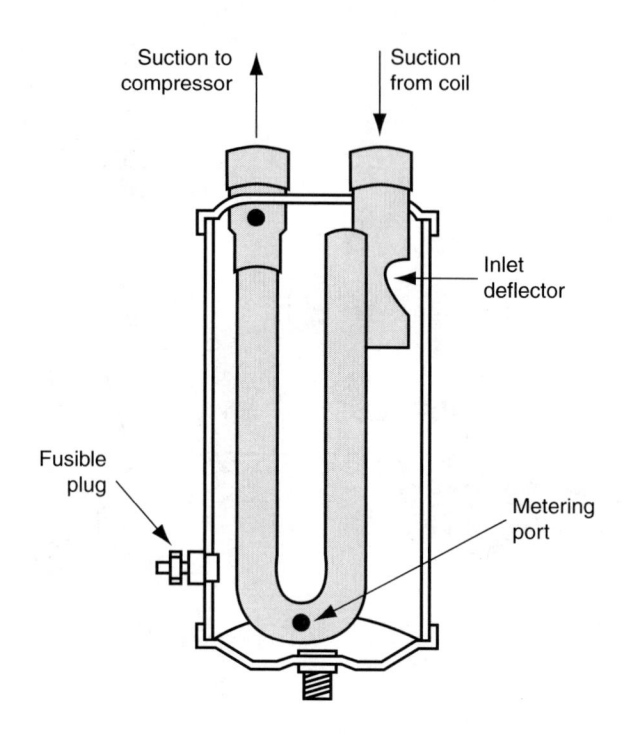

FIGURE 4-11. *Typical suction-line accumulator*

Figure 4-12 shows an accumulator with a built-in heat exchanger to heat and evaporate the liquid. The heat given off by the liquid in the liquid line will help boil off any liquid refrigerant trapped in the accumulator. Also, the liquid refrigerant in the liquid line will gain additional subcooling. Both accumulators come with either horizontal or vertical shells.

SUCTION-LINE HEAT EXCHANGERS

A suction-line accumulator simply protects a refrigeration compressor. But a heat exchanger improves performance in all phases of the cooling cycle. At the same time, the expansion valve works better if the liquid refrigerant is subcooled several degrees below condensing temperature.

A heat exchanger uses the heat in liquid refrigerant flowing toward the expansion valve to superheat refrigerant vapor going to the compressor. Look at the heat exchanger in Figure 4-13. The liquid line is wrapped around the suction line. Thus, warm liquid in the outer line heats the cold vapor in the inner one.

To obtain optimum heat transfer and reduce thermal shock, heat exchangers are usually piped in a counterflow configuration. Observe the flow of refrigerant in the heat exchanger shown in

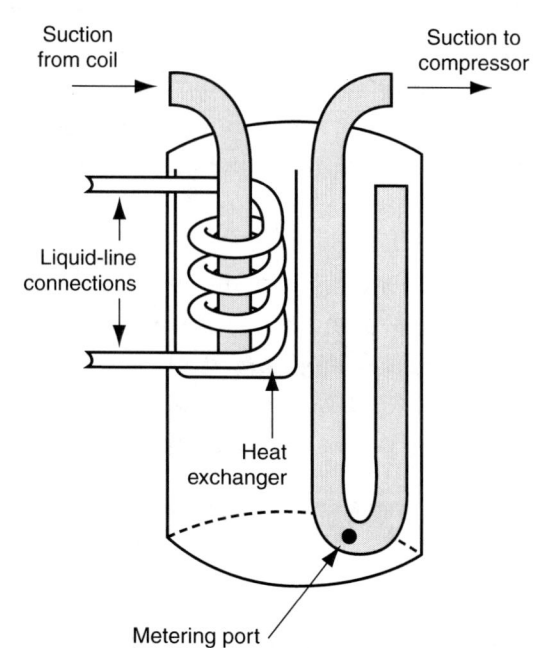

FIGURE 4-12. *Suction-line accumulator with heat exchanger*

Figure 4-13. Notice the higher-temperature entering liquid is entering on the same end as the higher-temperature leaving vapor. Also, the lower-temperature leaving liquid is leaving on the same end as the lower-temperature entering vapor.

A heat exchanger should be as close to the evaporator as possible. The thermostatic expansion valve remote bulb should be at the outlet of the evaporator, and never located downstream from the heat exchanger.

A heat exchanger improves system performance noticeably. It reduces loss of refrigeration effect to surrounding air. It reduces *sweating* and dripping from the suction line. However, a heat exchanger will increase pressure drop in the suction and liquid lines.

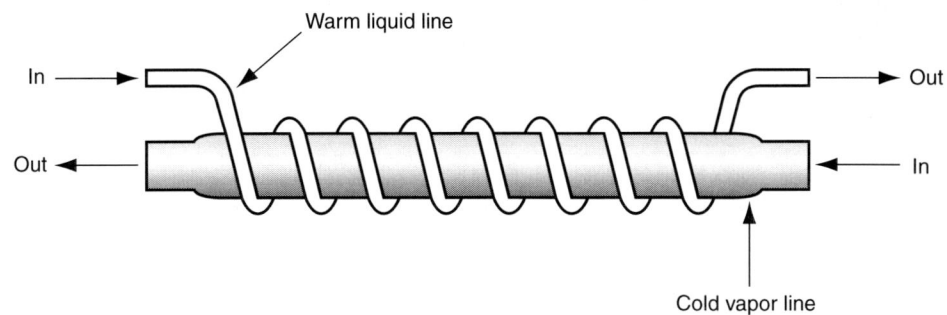

FIGURE 4-13. *Heat exchanger for suction line*

A heat exchanger is most helpful in commercial and low-temperature systems that have a wide temperature difference between suction vapor and subcooled liquid. It is less useful in air conditioning, where this difference is fairly narrow. A good heat exchanger will soon justify its initial cost. It improves energy efficiency by the increased refrigeration effect that results from subcooled refrigerant.

Take precautions when installing a heat exchanger. Watch the heat exchanger's performance closely to make sure that it doesn't trap oil. Also, the amount of superheating that takes place should be limited. Heat exchangers are not generally recommended for systems that use R-22. The additional superheating of the suction vapor can result in excessive discharge temperatures.

RECEIVERS

An evaporative condenser, air-cooled condenser, or tube-in-tube condenser that does not provide subcooling needs a *receiver* to collect the condensed refrigerant used by the system. The receiver, located between the condener and the expansion valve, stores the entire refrigerant charge if the system is pumped down. It is usually nothing more than a steel tank with proper shut-off valves and a safety relief device.

Ordinarily, a receiver is not needed in systems with shell-and-tube condensers. Such condensers usually have ample volume to store the refrigerant charge from the entire system. But if this is not the case, a separate auxiliary receiver should be used. The auxiliary receiver should be valved off and not used except when the system is pumped down.

Large receivers should have a sight glass so that you can check the refrigerant level easily. Figure 4-14 shows a typical gauge glass for receivers. A good liquid level gauge should have top and bottom ball checks and valves. This can prevent the escape of refrigerant, should the glass be broken. The liquid supply line leaving the receiver should exit at the bottom of the receiver. If it must exit at the top of the receiver, it should extend all the way to the bottom.

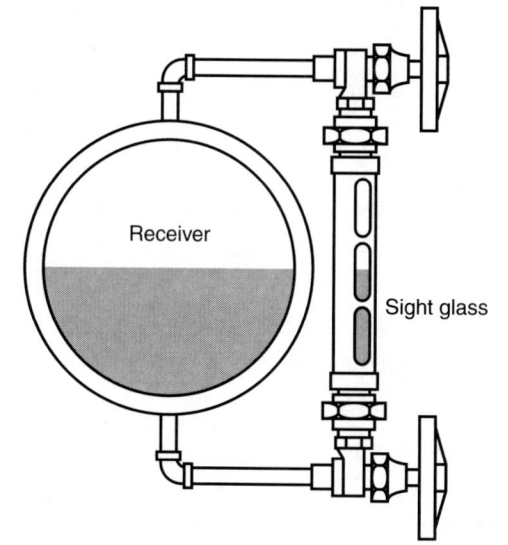

FIGURE 4-14. *Typical gauge glass for receivers*

REVIEW QUESTIONS

1. How does a condensing water regulator respond to an increase in condensing pressure?

2. Does a check valve allow flow in more than one direction?

3. Name three types of commonly used safety relief devices.

4. Does a fusible element respond to pressure or temperature?

5. Should relief devices be adjusted in the field?

6. What important precaution should you take when discharging toxic refrigerants?

7. What refrigerant may be discharged into a tank of water if enough water is available?

8. What are the two disadvantages of a diaphragm-type relief valve?

9. What two types of relief valve seats are more popular because of their resilience and better reseating qualities?

10. What limits the maximum pressure setting for a relief device?

11. What is the function of a discharge oil separator?

12. For what purpose may an electric heater be used in a discharge oil separator?

REVIEW QUESTIONS

13. Where should you install a sight glass for checking liquid refrigerant?

14. List two conditions that would cause bubbles to appear in a sight glass.

15. How does a moisture indicator react to moisture in the system?

16. What device is used to reduce noise caused by compressor discharge pulsations?

17. Where should a discharge muffler be located?

18. A lube oil protection control is sensitive to the difference between _____ pressure and _____ pressure in a refrigeration system.

19. Why does the lube oil protection control have built-in time delay components?

20. Which portion of the liquid line is the best location for installing a liquid-line strainer?

21. In what refrigerant line is the accumulator located?

22. Where is the receiver located?

LESSON 5

Desiccants and Driers

FOREWORD

The goal of this Lesson is to make clear the difference between desiccants and driers. In the refrigeration industry, a *desiccant* is defined as a solid substance that can remove moisture from refrigerant. The refrigerant may be in either vapor or liquid form. In order to remove moisture from the refrigerant, the desiccant is placed in a device that is installed in the refrigerant piping system. The term *drier* refers to both the container and the desiccant, combined into a single unit. All references in this text are in accordance with these definitions.

To maintain dry refrigeration systems, the refrigeration industry turned to desiccants used successfully in the chemical industry. Several gave good results, and were accepted for refrigeration system application. Others were used for years in the belief that they had good desiccant properties. Careful testing eventually proved otherwise and they were discarded.

Activated alumina and the zeolites (molecular sieves, microtraps) are the desiccants most widely used now. Silica gel, once common, may still be found in some applications. Others, including calcium chloride and calcium oxide, were used in small quantities but for various reasons have been discontinued.

PROPERTIES OF A DESICCANT

The primary property that the desiccant contained within the drier must have, obviously, is the ability to remove moisture and acids. However, several secondary properties are also important and should be considered when you are choosing a desiccant. Various general properties that a drier manufacturer must provide are described here.

Adsorption of water

This is the ability of a desiccant to attract moisture in a refrigerant and to reduce the moisture to a low level. ARI Standard 710-86 established an EPD (end-point dryness) of 5 ppm (parts per million). If a desiccant cannot attain this, it is not good enough for use with refrigerants. The moisture level of 5 ppm can be reached with activated alumina, silica gel, and the zeolites. This level is needed for low-temperature units, particularly those using R-12, which has a very low moisture solubility characteristic.

Capacity

Capacity is generally defined as moisture-holding ability. A desiccant must pick up and hold the moisture found in the average installation for which it is designed. Capacity varies with different desiccants. Driers contain varying amounts of different desiccants according to the capacity required. Table 5-1 illustrates the moisture capacity of various desiccants in an R-12 system. These data depend on the moisture solubility of the refrigerant.

Grams of moisture per 100 grams of desiccant at 125°F liquid temperature (R-12)		
Activated alumina	Silica gel	Molecular sieve
4	3	16

TABLE 5-1. *Moisture capacity of desiccants*

Speed

A desiccant must act rapidly. It must reduce moisture to a sufficiently low level in one pass through the drier. Refrigerant leaving the drier with excess moisture can freeze at the expansion valve or capillary tube in a system operating at low temperatures.

Effects of oil

A desiccant's efficiency, capacity, and speed should not be seriously affected by oil or other substances normally found in a system. (See the section called "Hydrophobic Behavior of Desiccants" later in this Lesson.)

Effects of temperature

A desiccant's efficiency, capacity, and speed should not be seriously affected by an increase in temperature. Desiccants have greater moisture capacity at lower temperatures. In general, they work better in a cold location than a hot location. Low temperatures allow desiccants to remove more moisture from a system. This prevents such problems as freezing at the expansion device and the other problems associated with moisture in a system.

Permanency

A desiccant must retain its characteristics during storage, and over its working lifetime in a system.

Drying of liquids or gases

Desiccants should be able to dry refrigerant in either the liquid or vapor phase. All refrigerants can be dried effectively in either phase. In some cases, however, more time is required to dry vapor. This is because of less intimate contact between vapor and desiccant. Further, drying vapor in the suction line takes more desiccant. It also takes a larger shell to handle proper flow and still maintain a low pressure drop.

Corrosion

A desiccant must remove moisture to a level below that causing corrosion. The corrosion level for water in a system is higher than the level that causes expansion valves and capillary tubes to freeze up. Therefore, any desiccant that eliminates freeze-ups will also prevent corrosion problems.

Chemical reactions

A desiccant must not react chemically with oil, refrigerant, or materials of construction. It must not react with substances such as methyl alcohol, which might be added to the system, or with the moisture it absorbs.

Stability

It is important for the desiccant to remain in its original solid state. Under no circumstances should it dissolve or become a sticky mass. A desiccant that dissolves would pass out of its shell and cause problems by plugging expansion valves or capillary tubes. A soft, pliable desiccant could easily plug or restrict flow through the drier shell.

A desiccant particle cannot shrink or expand. Shrinkage could result in unfilled areas within the drier shell. Expansion could bulge the shell's sides. Either case would cause restricted flow of refrigerant.

Dusting

A desiccant must not form any dust, either in storage or in use. Dust may produce restrictions in the desiccant itself. Or, it may escape into the system to cause restrictions and/or wear of moving parts.

Hazards

A desiccant must not be explosive, either in storage or in use. None of the popular desiccants now in use are hazardous in any way. Some used in the past were hazardous, but they have been eliminated. The manufacturer is responsible for selecting desiccants safe for use in air conditioning or refrigeration systems. The service technician generally does not need to be concerned about this point.

Reaction with moisture

A desiccant should not react chemically with moisture to produce dangerous or corrosive products. It must not react with either refrigerant or oil, for these same reasons.

HOW DESICCANTS WORK

Desiccants pick up and hold moisture either by adsorption or absorption. *Adsorption* is sometimes referred to as a physical process. *Absorption* refers to a chemical action. To help understand the first process, let's look at the physical makeup of silica gel and activated alumina.

Silica gel is a special form of silica acid or silicon dioxide. Manufactured as a jelly-like material, it was once widely used. Upon drying, silica gel loses part of its water to form a hard, glass-like substance. During the drying process, it develops a surface of tiny tubes, called *capillaries*, that fill the entire structure. Activated alumina has this same structure throughout its granules. Both of these desiccants always contain some water in the walls of the tubes. It cannot be removed without destroying their structure and ruining the desiccant. This moisture is usually called *moisture of constitution*.

These desiccants pick up and hold moisture by the physical process of adsorption. Molecules of water stick to the inner walls of the capillaries much like a stamp sticks on an envelope, as shown in Figure 5-1. Only a limited number of stamps may be stuck on any envelope. Similarly, a limited number of molecules of water will stick to the walls of a capillary. But the amount of surface of many capillaries is tremendous. The size of the water molecules is very small. Thus, a relatively large amount of water may be picked up and held by either silica gel or activated alumina, without even wetting the solids.

SOME COMMON DESICCANTS

A brief description of the most common desiccants follows. All of these desiccants have proved their worth in use. The order of listing is alphabetical. It does not show relative worth.

FIGURE 5-1. *Water molecules adsorbed on capillary walls, magnified many times*

Activated alumina

Activated alumina is a white, hard solid. It dusts only slightly when used in loose granular form. It will not dissolve in water. Depending on the type of aluminum, it is either a non-gel or gel-type desiccant. It takes up moisture by adsorption. It is available in the following forms:

- *granular* (8 to 14 mesh, a commonly used type)

- *ball* (white colored)

- *tablet* (pure white, not in general use)

- *solid core*. Granular activated alumina can be readily molded to form a porous core. This provides filtration as well as drying ability. Molecular sieves may be mixed with the activated alumina for increased moisture capacity, as shown in Figure 5-2.

Silica gel

Silica gel is a glass-like solid. It dusts very little when used in loose form. It does not dissolve in water. It is a gel-type desiccant. It takes up moisture by adsorption. Although silica gel is no longer a common desiccant, it is available in three forms:

FIGURE 5-2. *Filter-drier containing activated alumina, molecular sieve, and activated carbon within a molded block*

ALCO CONTROLS

- *granular* (8 to 14 mesh, a commonly used type)

- *pellets* (a form now in use under the name Sovabead®, with drying ability equivalent to the granular type

- *solid core*. Granular silica gel is bound as a molded porous core. Molecular sieve in ball form may be mixed with the silica gel.

Molecular sieves (zeolites)

The newest type of desiccant, molecular sieves are well-accepted by the industry. They are a tan or gray solid. They do not dissolve in water. Moisture is held by adsorption. They are available from a number of manufacturers in either granular or spherical form. This desiccant has a very low dependence on moisture solubility in the refrigerant. Figure 5-3 shows an example.

It is interesting to note that of all the desiccants tried over the years, only those that remove moisture by adsorption are still in use today. This is evident in examining the illustrations of driers as supplied by the major manufacturers.

CAPACITY AND EFFICIENCY

Moisture-holding *capacity* refers to the amount of moisture that a desiccant can hold. *Efficiency* is its ability to dry refrigerant to a low moisture content. This is generally known as *end-point dryness* (EPD). Both values are measured with moisture in equilibrium between desiccant and refrigerant.

FIGURE 5-3. *Molecular sieve filter-drier*

The phrase "in equilibrium" may require some explanation. As an example, suppose that a desiccant with no moisture is placed in a cylinder. In the cylinder is some refrigerant containing 25 ppm of moisture. The desiccant will pick up moisture from the refrigerant. As the refrigerant circulates through the desiccant, it continues to pick up moisture. It will also begin to give up some of the moisture previously collected. The moisture content of the refrigerant is reduced and the amount of moisture in the desiccant is increased. As this happens, the speed at which the moisture is collected by the drier will be reduced. At the same

LESSON 5

time, the amount of water being released by the desiccant is increasing. When the amount of water being released equals the amount being collected, the moisture contents of the refrigerant and the desiccant are said to be "in equilibrium." A certain quantity of moisture in the desiccant is in equilibrium with a definite amount of moisture in the refrigerant.

The unit of measure for end-point dryness, parts per million (ppm), can be explained as follows. The moisture in a refrigeration or air conditioning system is not measured in quantities such as ounces, glasses, pints, or quarts. Generally, the amount is so small that it is related to a million parts of refrigerant. "Parts per million" means the number of parts of moisture compared to one million parts of refrigerant on a weight-by-weight basis. Another description will give you some idea as to proportions. One drop of water in a 125-lb cylinder of refrigerant would be equal to 1 part per million.

ARI Standard 710-86 makes practical use of these terms. Most manufacturers now rate their driers in accordance with this standard. By so doing, they list a drier's capacity in drops at a specific end-point dryness. For R-12, an end-point dryness of 15 ppm is used. For R-22, an end-point dryness of 60 ppm is used. To further help the service technician, most manufacturers also list the capacity of their units at two different temperatures. Temperatures specified by the ARI standard are 75°F and 125°F. Both refer to liquid-line temperatures.

Examining the moisture capacity of a drier at various liquid-line temperatures shows an important characteristic of most adsorbent-type desiccants. As liquid-line temperature increases, the desiccant's moisture capacity decreases. This is shown in Figure 5-4.

Figure 5-4 raises a good question: "What is the effect of high temperature on a desiccant that has been in a system for some time and is fairly saturated with moisture, if the system is operated only in relatively cool weather?" The answer is that a sudden hot spell causes the moisture to leave the desiccant and freeze up the expansion valve or capillary tube. This occurs only if a desiccant is saturated with moisture at a low temperature and is then suddenly warmed. It cannot retain as much moisture at high temperature as it does at low temperature. Fortunately, it is rare for a drier to be completely saturated. Usually, the desiccant contains only a small amount of moisture compared to its total capacity. Thus, an increase in condensing temperature will not cause it to give up moisture. A desiccant must be very dry if it is to dry a

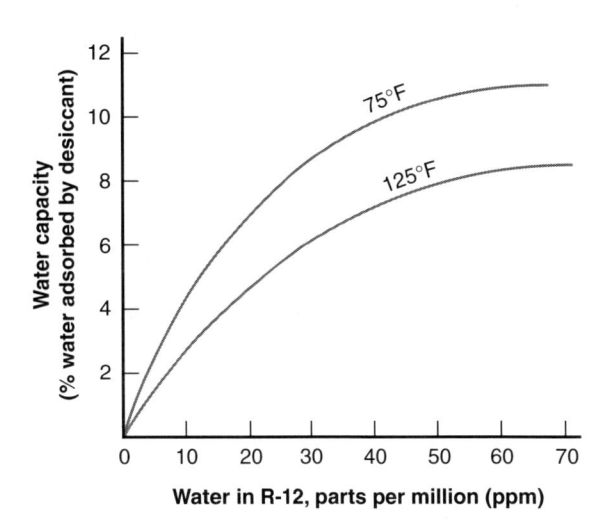

FIGURE 5-4. *Moisture equilibria curves, showing the effect of temperature on adsorption-type desiccants*

refrigerant, and as it adsorbs moisture, its capacity for further adsorption is reduced.

Figure 5-5 shows the difference in water capacity between a desiccant applied to R-12 and one applied to R-22. They are at a specified temperature and an EPD of 15 ppm. For R-12, water capacity is about 6.2%. For R-22, it is about 3.5%. Thus, a desiccant in equilibrium with R-12 will hold roughly 1.8 times more water than with R-22, both considered at an EPD of 15 ppm.

Different EPDs are used in the ARI Standard 710-92 for R-12 and R-22. Thus, water capacities must be stated at these points. At an EPD of 15 ppm for R-12, desiccant capacity is about 6.2%. At an EPD of 60 ppm for R-22, it is about 7.2%. Use of different end-point drynesses for these refrigerants is justified, since R-22 can tolerate more water in solution than can R-12. The hazard from freezing at expansion devices is less acute with R-22 than with R-12. For example, at –40°F, the amount of water soluble in R-12 is 1.7 ppm. In R-22, it is 120 ppm. Water capacity is relevant only for a specified end-point dryness, at a specified temperature, and for a particular refrigerant. ARI Standard 710 was established for this reason.

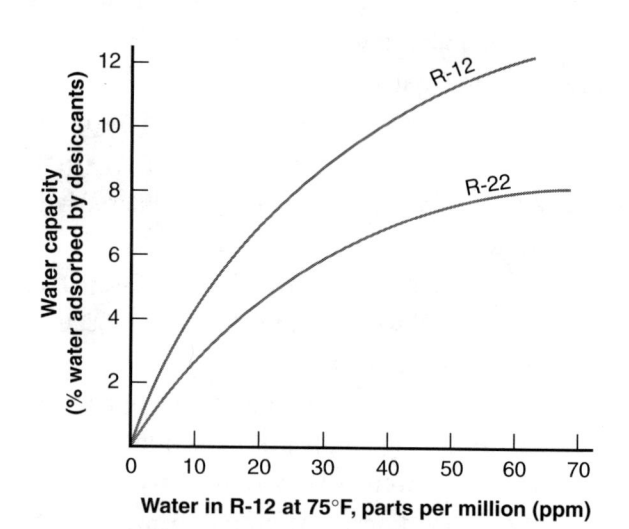

FIGURE 5-5. Moisture equilibria curves for R-12 and R-22

MIXED DESICCANTS

The use of mixed desiccants is a recent industry trend. This is primarily confined to filter-driers with molded porous cores, but there are several loose fill and spring-loaded bead types also available. A large volume can be achieved by mixing a low-capacity desiccant with one of much higher capacity. The mixed desiccant can be molded to provide a relatively large filtering area. Therefore, with a solid core, it combines high water capacity with good filtration properties. Usually, spring-loaded bead-style driers provide the best filtration.

Note that a desiccant, whether alone or mixed with one or more others, arrives at its own characteristic end-point dryness. This differs for each desiccant at each temperature and for each refrigerant. When two or more desiccants are mixed and brought to equilibrium in a refrigerant, each comes to its own characteristic capacity, as shown in Figure 5-6.

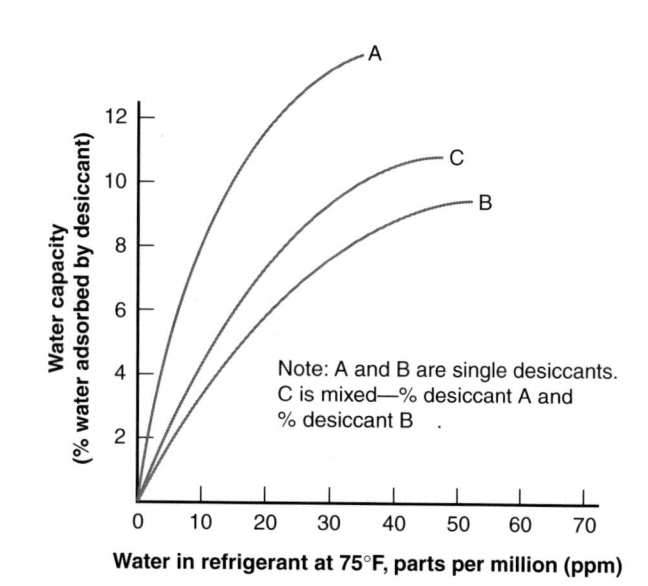

FIGURE 5-6. Moisture equilibria curves for single and mixed adsorption-type desiccants

SOLID-CORE DESICCANTS

Molded porous cores consist of one or more standard desiccants, held together by a binder. The nature and amount of binder varies with the manufacturer. The binder is not a desiccant, so its amount is held to a minimum. The binder is selected for its ability to remain stable when used with any of the common refrigerants. Also, it must not affect the moisture adsorption ability of the desiccants. Obviously, the core must meet all the requirements of a desiccant since it is subject to the same use. It must have sufficient strength to resist breakage during normal handling. Molded porous core driers are rated according to ARI Standard 710-86.

The geometry of cores fits a fairly set pattern, but changes do appear. The usual core is a cylindrical block. It has an axial hole either part way through it or running its full length. With the full-length hole, a metal plate is fixed at the inlet so that refrigerant flows through the core with no by-passing. Cores are designed so that the refrigerant mixture passes through a uniform bed of desiccant. This prevents channeling and ensures uniform filtering and moisture removal. The drier is so constructed that refrigerant contacts the core uniformly on its outer surface. It then passes along the axial hole and through a thin auxiliary filter. Pressure drop across the core and filtering characteristics are controlled by desiccant particle size.

Filtering action is sometimes provided by using a core of non-desiccant material. The core is filled with, or surrounded by, molecular sieve. This type of drier is shown in Figure 5-3 on page 82.

The position of a drier with a molded porous core is less critical than for one that uses loose-fill desiccant. This is because the core does not lose its shape when placed on its side. All types of driers must maintain the proper direction of flow. This is generally marked by the manufacturer by an arrow or some similar indication.

MOISTURE CAPACITY

ARI Standard 710-86 sets the required desiccant moisture holding capacity of a drier or filter-drier. This standard calls for an actual moisture capacity test. The test must be done in accordance with ASHRAE Standard 63-95. The capacity of the drier depends on temperature, the desiccant, and the refrigerant. Thus, all of these factors are important and must be considered. These standards require a rating for R-12 and R-22 at 75 and 125°F. As mentioned before, end point dryness for R-12 is 15 ppm. End point dryness for R-22 is 60 ppm. Capacities are stated in drops of water held by the drier at each of these four rating points.

Other refrigerants used today require separate rating points. Most equipment manufacturers now list capacities for refrigerants other than those shown in ARI Standard 710-86.

CORRECT POSITION—HORIZONTAL OR VERTICAL?

The actual position of the drier in an operating system is no longer very important except in loose-fill filter-driers. In these driers, desiccant settling may be a problem, so position should be vertical. Another exception is suction-line filter-driers, where an upright position is preferred, with feed at the top. Actually, this has little to do with the desiccant. It is mainly concerned with oil return, and avoiding oil trapping. In summary, driers have been installed in almost every conceivable position. In most cases they have worked fairly well.

DIRECTION OF FLOW

For years, driers were designed for refrigerant flow in one direction only. It is important to install these driers so that the refrigerant flows in the right direction. An arrow or some other designation shows the proper flow direction. As heat pumps became popular, manufacturers began to design driers for flow in either direction. This was necessary because refrigerant flow changes directions on a heat pump when the reversing valve operates.

REACTIVATION OF DESICCANTS

To understand reactivation of desiccants properly, consider the process in two distinct categories. One is the method used with sealed-type driers, which are non-refillable. The other is the method of handling the refillable-type drier.

With a sealed-type filter-drier or one with a replaceable molded porous core, one word sums up reactivation. That word is *don't*. There are many reasons. First, the days of placing a filter-drier in the oven to drive out existing moisture are long gone. Each type of desiccant requires different reactivation procedures. Unless they are adhered to, the service technician is wasting time. Further, in some cases, relatively high temperatures are required for reactivation. The service technician is not likely to have the equipment required.

Even assuming that the proper equipment is available, there are still serious drawbacks. Assume that ovens are capable of proper temperature, and that moisture might be driven off. This still does not remove oil or solid contaminants left in the molded porous cores. In some cases, the temperatures might actually cause the oil to break down. Then the so-called "reactivation" process would further contaminate a system, rather than help clean it up.

LESSON 5

Also remember that manufacturers of quality filter-driers are set up to provide complete reactivation at minimum cost. The cost of reactivation in the field could be excessive, considering a technician's time and the cost of heat energy.

There are still a number of refillable desiccant driers in use today. The desiccant for these must be bought in bulk. If the material is not received in factory-guaranteed containers, reactivation is necessary. Remember that various desiccants require different activation temperatures. Consult the supplier for times and temperatures, and other handling recommendations.

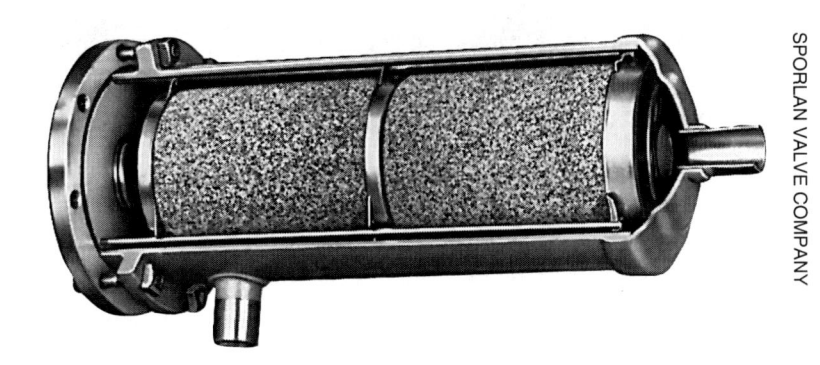

DRIERS

FIGURE 5-7. *Cutaway view of a drier with a replaceable core*

The next part of this Lesson is on *driers*. Remember the earlier definitions. A *desiccant* is a substance that can remove moisture from refrigerant. It is placed in a device that is installed in the refrigerant piping system. The term *drier* refers to the container and the desiccant combined into a single unit.

REPLACEABLE-CORE FILTER-DRIERS

In the refrigeration and air conditioning industry, sealed filter-driers generally are used in small-tonnage systems. Commercial and industrial systems have become larger and larger. This has created the need for a much larger filter-drier. Larger equipment is often handled on a preventive maintenance basis. As a result, customers wanted a filter-drier that could be serviced without taking it out of the refrigerant piping. They did not want loose-fill desiccants because of their basic disadvantages. To meet these needs, large filter-driers with replaceable molded porous cores were developed. Examples of replaceable-core driers are shown in Figures 5-7 and 5-8.

SELECTING A DRIER

Historically, it was found that keeping a system dry avoided expansion device freeze-ups and corrosion. This raised a logical question. How large a drier should be used? The answer was usually arrived at by guesswork, based on

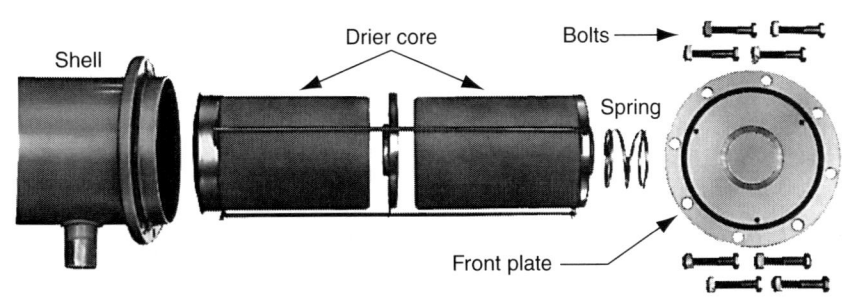

FIGURE 5-8. *Interior parts of a replaceable-core filter-drier*

a certain weight of desiccant per ton of refrigeration, but without knowing how much moisture was in the system. The service technician could only hope that the drier had the capacity to remove all the moisture. If one drier did not do the job, the technician simply replaced it with a second, and perhaps even a third.

Based on available information and much practical experience, a series of driers evolved. These worked out well due to two things. First, the amount of desiccant in the drier was usually more than needed to dry the average system. Second, it was simple to install a second or even a third drier if one was not enough.

Today, the selection of the proper size drier is much more scientific. We now have ARI Standard 710-86, which provides for an accurate testing method. It also specifies how driers should be rated. Thus, all manufacturers using the ARI standard publish ratings in the same format. The service technician can now select a drier based on very realistic data.

ARI Standard 710-86 specifies moisture capacity at two specific temperatures and flow rates at a 1-lb pressure drop across the drier. Everyone follows this same arrangement, and comparisons are easy. The service technician can choose a drier knowing it will do the intended job.

Some manufacturers go one step beyond the standard. They publish data per ARI, but also make selection *recommendations* for the service technician. They make selections on the basis of commercial temperature equipment, original equipment manufacturers' air conditioning equipment, and field built-up and field replacement. The recommendations provide for some dirt in the system. This means that the filter-drier can pick up a lot of dirt and still have enough flow to maintain system capacity.

A drier's location and the ambient temperature around it should be considered, if possible. In most cases, installation locations are limited. There may be little choice but to put the filter-drier at the condensing unit or in the refrigerated space.

Rating data on filter-driers show us that drier size varies according to the type of equipment and refrigerant. If R-12 and R-22 systems had to be dried to the same end-point dryness, R-12 would require a larger drier. ARI Standard 710-86 requires an R12 system dried to a 15-ppm EPD. An R-22 system needs to be dried to only a 60-ppm EPD. Further, an R-12 system circulates more refrigerant than an R-22 system. Both points considered, an R-22 system requires a smaller drier than an R-12 system, assuming all other factors to be equal.

The size of a drier in original equipment can be accurately selected. The manufacturer can determine—within certain limits—the amount of moisture in the system. However, it is quite different for a service technician working on a unit in the field. The service technician has no way of determining the amount of water in a system without extensive lab testing. For this reason, a good service technician will install a drier of adequate flow capacity and a moisture-liquid indicator (if there was none). This provides a visual check on refrigerant flow and dryness.

Air and moisture can enter a system any time it is opened for service. So it is good practice to install a larger drier than normally required for the system's flow capacity. This provides extra desiccant to ensure a good drying job. Most manufacturers' selection recommendations for field replacement take this into account. The moisture-liquid indicator is important because it tells you if the system was dried adequately by the first drier. If not, there may be enough moisture left to cause problems. The moisture indicator indicates the presence of moisture before a freeze-up can occur. If moisture is still present, the drier must be replaced a second time and possibly a third. It also helps avoid loss of product if the installation is a low-temperature refrigerated case.

A drier should also be a good filter. Filter area is especially important if it appears that there are solids or semi-solids (sludge) in the system. The larger the filter area, the wider the distribution of the solids and semi-solids. Only a thin layer will build up on the core surface. For a given amount of filtered material, the depth will be inversely proportional to the area it covers. Resistance to flow of refrigerant increases with the depth of filtered material. Thus, the filter area should be as large as possible.

Where the filter area is small, a relatively small amount of dirt or sludge can reduce flow and bring the system operation below its rated capacity. A drier with a large filter area has only a slight flow decrease as it collects dirt. It can handle more sludge or solids and still keep its rated flow capacity. If sludge or a high contamination level is suspected, a larger drier should be selected. Since no one can be sure of the level of contaminants in a system, a drier with a large filtering area should always be selected.

An oversize filter-drier placed in the suction line will remove material such as sludge and acids from burned-out systems. These are sometimes replaceable-core types. Special units designed for suction-line filter drying are now available. In both cases, sludge is filtered out and acid products adsorbed by the desiccants.

LOCATION OF THE DRIER

In the past, common sense dictated the location of the drier unit. For the service technician, the best location is almost always in the liquid line, just ahead of the expansion valve or capillary tube. This makes sense, since those are the areas where moisture and dirt cause problems. Elsewhere, a drier does not give immediate protection from freeze-ups and plug-ups. Aside from the liquid line, there is only one other practical location for a filter-drier, and that is the suction line. Both locations have advantages and disadvantages. They will be covered in the following paragraphs.

Liquid-line location

Advantages. Installed in the high side, the filter-drier is ahead of the expansion valve or capillary tube. It is the location most acceptable to everyone, including the original equipment manufacturer and the service technician. Installation in the liquid line (or high side) has a number of advantages. First, moisture is removed just ahead of the metering device. This limits the chances for a freeze-up. Second, the filter-drier also removes solid contaminants. This avoids plugging up the expansion device.

In the liquid line, the filter-drier handles only liquid refrigerant. There usually is ample pressure to ensure proper flow rate. This in turn helps keep the filter-drier size within economic limits. Further, liquid has excellent contact with the desiccant for drying purposes. Low end-point dryness can be achieved readily and rapidly.

Disadvantages. Warm liquid causes the filter-drier to operate hot. This reduces the efficiency of the desiccant. The higher the temperature of the liquid refrigerant, the lower the moisture capacity of the filter-drier. This is also noted in ARI Standard 710-86, which treats moisture capacity under two conditions, 75°F and 125°F. Manufacturers' literature on filter-driers shows that the moisture capacity of a unit at 75° liquid temperature is higher than at 125°F. Remember that filter-drier manufacturers have considered this. To compensate for reduced capacity at higher temperatures, they simply add more desiccant to their filter-driers.

There have been attempts to increase the filter-drier's moisture capacity by putting it in the refrigerated space. Results have been excellent in freezers and other low-temperature units, provided there are long runs of liquid line in the same refrigerated space.

There is only one real disadvantage to using a filter-drier in the liquid line. It concerns the loose-fill filter-drier installed with liquid feed at the bottom. In this case, pulsations of refrigerant may lift and drop the desiccant in a loosely packed unit. This in turn forms excessive dust or powder. It may plug the outlet screen or even cap tubes under certain conditions.

Suction-line location

Advantages. A filter-drier in the suction line is usually only for clean-up after a motor burnout or compressor failure. In this location it can remove acids, moisture, and solid contaminants. This keeps them from circulating into the new compressor and causing a repeat burnout.

Disadvantages. It was once thought that putting a filter-drier in the suction line would make the desiccant more efficient because of lower temperatures. But tests show that this is not the case. In some cases, a filter-drier in the suction line has less capacity than it would in the liquid line. Consider an R-12 system as an example. A filter-drier in the suction line has only one-eighth the moisture capacity it would have in the liquid line. In an R-502 system, it has only one-fourth the capacity it would have in the liquid line. Only in R-22 systems does a filter-drier have roughly the same capacity in both suction-line and liquid-line locations.

A filter-drier installed in the suction line must be substantially larger than a drier installed in the liquid line, where only liquid is involved. It must handle the system's total flow capacity of vapor, yet cause only a minute pressure drop. The larger filter-drier also means greater cost.

Another factor is the potential for solid contaminants to cause restriction in the filter-drier. This could result in an excessive pressure drop in the suction line, which, in turn, could cause a severe reduction in system capacity. Further restrictions would result in added pressure drop. Actual compressor failure is possible if refrigerant flow is restricted too much.

It is true that a suction-line filter-drier will protect the compressor from contaminants. But it cannot protect the expansion device or other system accessories from moisture or dirt. Anything in the high side could reach the expansion device. Trouble could develop from the very beginning.

For all these reasons, suction-line filter-driers are recommended primarily for clean-up after a motor burnout. Even then, a new liquid-line filter-drier should be used in conjunction to protect both high side and low side.

THE DRIER AS FILTER

Every drier is a filter to some degree. Driers with molded porous cores are very good filters. The entire surface of the core has an exceptionally good filtering characteristic. Even the loose-fill drier acts as a filter to some extent. It has screens, filter pads, or porous metal cones or disks to retain the loose granular desiccant in the shell. A screen or diffuser plate at the inlet holds the loose desiccant in place. This also filters out large particles suspended in the refrigerant. The granules, unless quite large, also provide some filtering action.

Some granular desiccant driers have a porous or screen cone cylinder or dispersion tube. They generally present more filtering surface than flat filters. With today's filter-drier design, a straight filter in the liquid line is not needed when there is a filter-drier in the high side. But there is good reason to have a suction-line filter immediately ahead of the compressor. This applies even on a new system, particularly one with long refrigerant lines. It protects the compressor from any solids left in the low side during fabrication. A filter in this location will protect the new compressor. Remember that a suction-line filter has no moisture-, acid-, or sludge-removing capabilities. If a system might contain such material, a full suction-line filter-drier should be installed instead. Figures 5-9 and 5-10 show typical examples.

FIGURE 5-9. *Cutaway view of a suction-line filter*

HYDROPHOBIC BEHAVIOR OF DESICCANTS

Some years ago, a manufacturer found a peculiar condition in used solid-core desiccant driers returned from the field. Drops of water placed on the desiccant were not absorbed, even after an hour or more. The desiccant repelled the water instead of immediately absorbing it, as would normally be the case. This condition came to be known as "hydrophobic behavior." *Hydrophobic* means "water-hating." The manufacturer feared that something in the use of the driers in the field had destroyed the desiccant's ability to absorb water. An investigation was made. Refrigeration oil was found to be the source of hydrophobic behavior. This same behavior was later found in other desiccants and even on filter pads from driers.

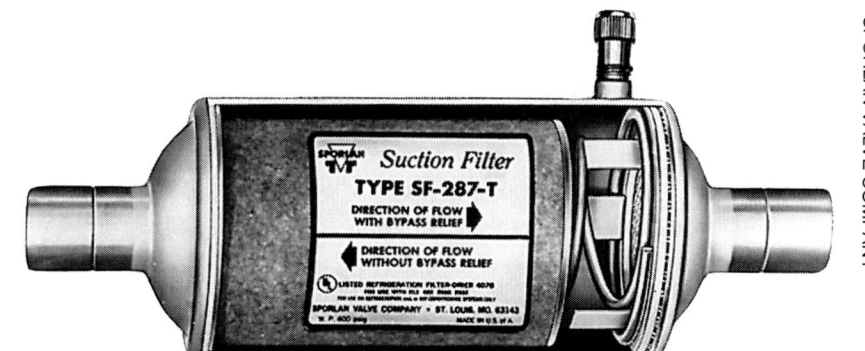

FIGURE 5-10. *Suction-line filter with bypass relief feature*

When heated, either with or without air present, refrigeration oil darkens and gets more viscous. If heated enough and then allowed to saturate the desiccant, the oil causes the desiccant to become hydrophobic.

A check was made of driers from machines known to pump oil excessively. It supported the conclusion that oil produced hydrophobic desiccants. In almost every case, the desiccant from these driers was hydrophobic.

Continued testing of hydrophobic desiccants showed something else. The desiccant was definitely hydrophobic when drops of water were put on it, but it was found to have lost little of its ability to dry refrigerant when used normally in the refrigerating system.

Occasionally, a drier is found installed in a system that contains methyl alcohol. The alcohol was added to the system in the field as a drying agent to prevent free moisture in the system from freezing. Strangely enough, some of these systems develop freeze-ups after methyl alcohol is added. At first, there was no explanation for these peculiar results. Then tests proved that a desiccant can also adsorb methyl alcohol. In fact, it prefers it over water. In a system that contains both methyl alcohol and water, the desiccant may take up only alcohol. This leaves the moisture to freeze the expansion valve or capillary tube.

If alcohol content is kept below 1%, it will not cause corrosion. The water that remains in the system can cause serious corrosion. The only sensible thing is to remove the moisture with a drier.

Note: Most compressor manufacturers do not recommend the use of alcohol with their equipment. In many cases, they will void a warranty if alcohol is found. This is because polyester insulation, now used in many hermetic compressors, is damaged by alcohol. This causes a corrosion problem—and an insulation problem as well. Check with the compressor manufacturer before adding alcohol for any reason.

COLOR ADSORPTION BY DESICCANTS

Some leak detectors use colored oil for their operation. The oil is forced out through a leak at a point in a system above atmospheric pressure. Oil colored red or some other distinctive color is easily seen. The color will show up around the location of the leak. One drawback to this approach is that silica gel and activated alumina can remove leak indicator coloring matter from the refrigerant stream. In time, the indicator becomes useless. Time is required to adsorb the coloring, so there is some immediate use for this type of leak indicator. Incidentally, silica gel adsorbs red coloring matter to form a beautiful ruby-like solid.

RAC

MOISTURE INDICATORS

Moisture indicators show whether a system is wet or dry. They are used by both service technicians and equipment manufacturers. A typical example is shown in Figure 5-11.

The moisture indicator element is usually part of a sight glass, so it serves two functions. The indicator element contains a chemical salt. It causes the element to change color if there is moisture in the liquid refrigerant. The elements are calibrated to change color according to the safe and unsafe levels for moisture. Remember that the safe limit for moisture varies with each type of refrigerant. Therefore, color change points in the moisture indicator also vary. With R-12, the indicator should change color at around 10 to 15 parts per million. With R-22, it should change at about 50 to 60 parts per million.

All moisture indicators operate on the principle of relative saturation of moisture to refrigerant. This, in turn, is based on temperature of the refrigerant. So consider temperature when evaluating the color of the indicator. Remember also that the moisture indicator only shows if there is more or less than a certain amount of moisture in a system. How *much* less does not matter, since the system is safe. The moisture indicator also does not show how much excess water is present. It shows only that the system has excess moisture and that steps must be taken to remove it.

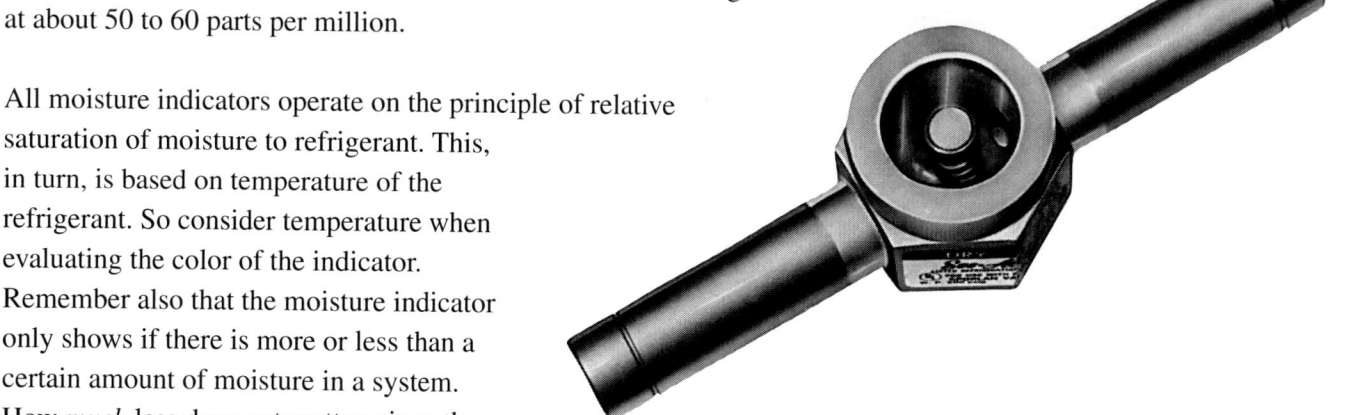

FIGURE 5-11. *Typical liquid-line moisture indicator*

SPORLAN VALVE COMPANY

Some manufacturers use one element in the moisture indicator. Others use two, one for R-12 and another for R-22. Both types seem to satisfy their users.

The moisture and liquid indicator is installed in the liquid line, either upstream or downstream from the drier. For moisture indicators, the actual location is not important. The entire charge of refrigerant will come to equilibrium. Therefore, the indicator gives true moisture indication in either location.

Location becomes important only when you are troubleshooting. If the indicator is downstream from the filter-drier, two things can cause bubbles or vapor in the viewing glass. One is a shortage of refrigerant, and the other is a partially plugged filter. If the indicator is installed ahead of the filter-drier, bubbles or vapor definitely show a shortage of refrigerant.

94

REVIEW QUESTIONS

1. Define a *desiccant*.

2. What term is given to the container and desiccant combined in a single unit?

3. Name the two most widely used desiccants today.

4. Why is a drier installed in a refrigeration system?

5. What determines the capacity of a drier?

6. Why must a desiccant act rapidly?

7. Will a desiccant do a better job in a cold location or a hot location? Why?

8. What is the criterion for stability of a desiccant?

9. How should a desiccant react with water?

10. What is the difference between absorption and adsorption?

11. Why are molecular sieves occasionally mixed with activated alumina?

12. Describe silica gel.

13. The only type of desiccant in use today is the type that removes moisture by _____.

REVIEW QUESTIONS

14. What is the term used to express the moisture capacity and efficiency of desiccants?

15. How is this measured, and how is the unit of measurement explained?

16. What will occur if a drier that has operated only in cool weather is saturated with moisture and is suddenly exposed to a hot spell?

17. At –40°F, what is the amount of water that is soluble in R-22?

18. When desiccants are held together by a binder, what is the moisture removal capability of the binder?

19. What is the path of refrigerant flow through a core drier?

20. What standard determines the moisture-holding capacity of a drier?

21. In what position should liquid-line driers be placed?

22. Why were larger replaceable-core filter-driers developed?

23. ARI Standard 710-86 specifies flow rates through a filter-drier at a pressure drop of _____.

24. Will an R-22 system require a larger or smaller filter than an R-12 system of the same size?

25. How can a service technician check for moisture in a system?

REVIEW QUESTIONS

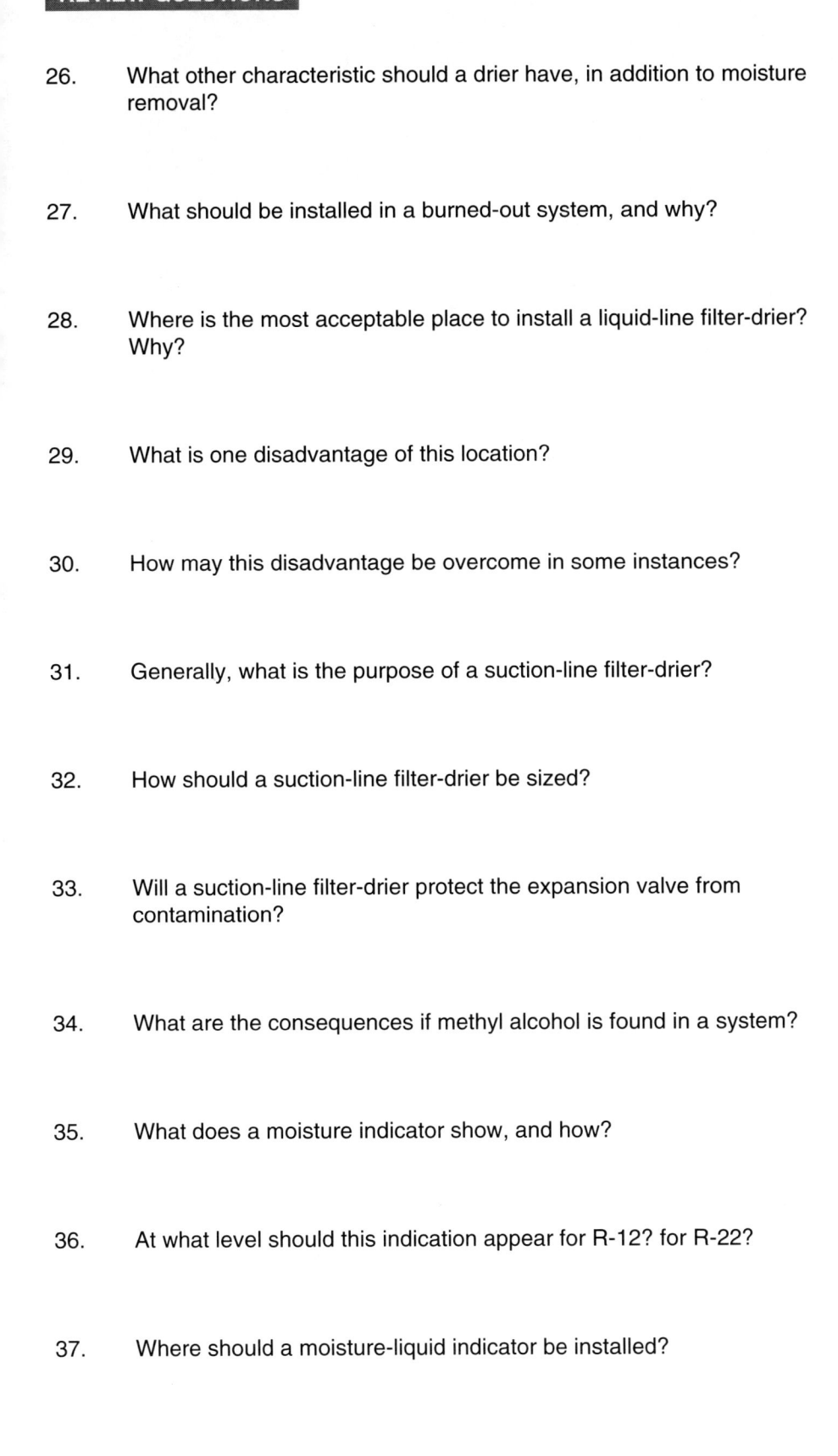

26. What other characteristic should a drier have, in addition to moisture removal?

27. What should be installed in a burned-out system, and why?

28. Where is the most acceptable place to install a liquid-line filter-drier? Why?

29. What is one disadvantage of this location?

30. How may this disadvantage be overcome in some instances?

31. Generally, what is the purpose of a suction-line filter-drier?

32. How should a suction-line filter-drier be sized?

33. Will a suction-line filter-drier protect the expansion valve from contamination?

34. What are the consequences if methyl alcohol is found in a system?

35. What does a moisture indicator show, and how?

36. At what level should this indication appear for R-12? for R-22?

37. Where should a moisture-liquid indicator be installed?

LESSON 6

Air-Cooled Condensers

CONDENSERS

The refrigeration cycle can be defined in very simple terms. It is the process of removing heat from where it isn't wanted and releasing it somewhere else. In operation, the refrigeration cycle uses several heat-exchanging components. They contribute to the final disposal of the absorbed heat. One of these heat exchangers is the refrigeration condenser. It is the final outlet for the heat removed from the refrigerated product or occupied area.

The *condenser* is the component in a refrigeration or air conditioning system that removes and rejects heat from the high-temperature, high-pressure vapor. The heat in the vapor comes from three sources:

- the heat absorbed in the evaporator

- the heat picked up in the suction line

- the additional heat of compression, caused by compressor operation.

Heat-laden vapor from the evaporator enters the compressor on the suction stroke. On the compression stroke, its temperature increases greatly. At the compressor discharge valve, as it opens, vapor temperature can be close to 300°F. The temperature drops rapidly as the vapor enters the discharge line. For the purpose of this discussion, let's assume that the vapor is 220°F in the discharge line. The compressor forces this superheated vapor through the discharge line into the condenser. The condenser cools the refrigerant in three stages:

- the vapor is cooled to saturation temperature (desuperheated)

- the vapor is condensed to a liquid (latent heat removed)

- the temperature of the condensed liquid is reduced below its saturation temperature (subcooled).

Saturation temperature, or condensing temperature, is that at which a vapor is condensed into a liquid.

The condenser removes the heat in the vapor in two steps. First, it transfers it to the walls of the condenser tubes. Then, the heat moves from the tubes to the cooling medium. In this case, the medium is air. A condenser's heat transfer capacity depends on a number of factors:

- its surface area

- the temperature difference between the cooling medium and the refrigerant vapor

- the velocity of the refrigerant vapor through the condenser

- the rate of flow of the cooling medium over or through the condenser

- the material used in producing the condenser

- the cleanliness of the heat transfer surface.

In general, the physical characteristics of a condenser are fixed. The basic primary variable is the temperature difference between the refrigerant vapor and the condensing medium.

THE AIR-COOLED CONDENSER

An *air-cooled* condenser is a coil of metal tubing that acts as a heat exchanger. The tubing may be copper, aluminum, or steel. Hot refrigerant vapor flows through the tubing. Cooler air passing over the coil absorbs heat from the refrigerant. Plate-type fins are attached to the coil to increase the surface area for heat transfer. There are two basic types of air-cooled condensers:

- *natural-draft* condensers

- *forced-air* condensers.

LESSON 6

In the natural-draft condenser, the tubing may be arranged in rows, as shown in Figure 6-1A. Heat transfers from the coil to the air by natural convection. In the forced-air type, fans or blowers force air over the coils, as shown in Figure 6-1B. The air-cooled condenser functions on a simple principle. It increases the sensible heat content of the cooling medium—air. In other words, the cooling air is increased in temperature by a certain number of degrees. This rise in air temperature is caused by the heat being removed from the condensing refrigerant.

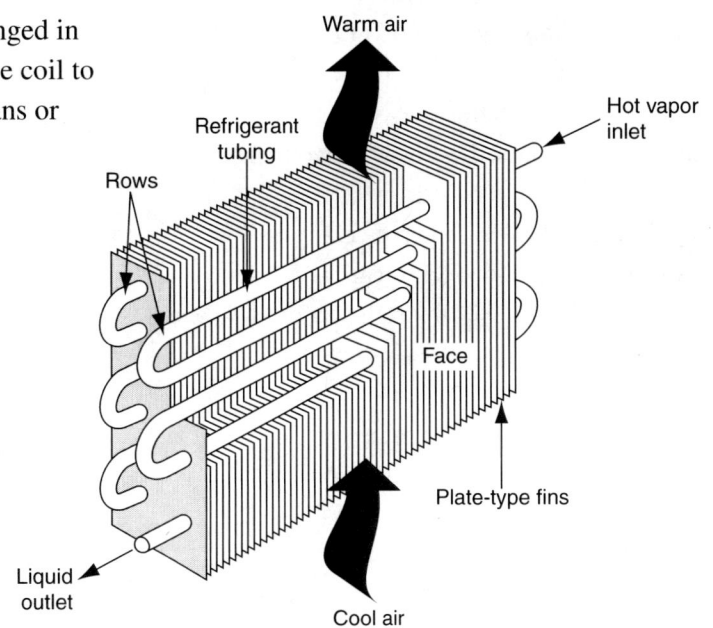

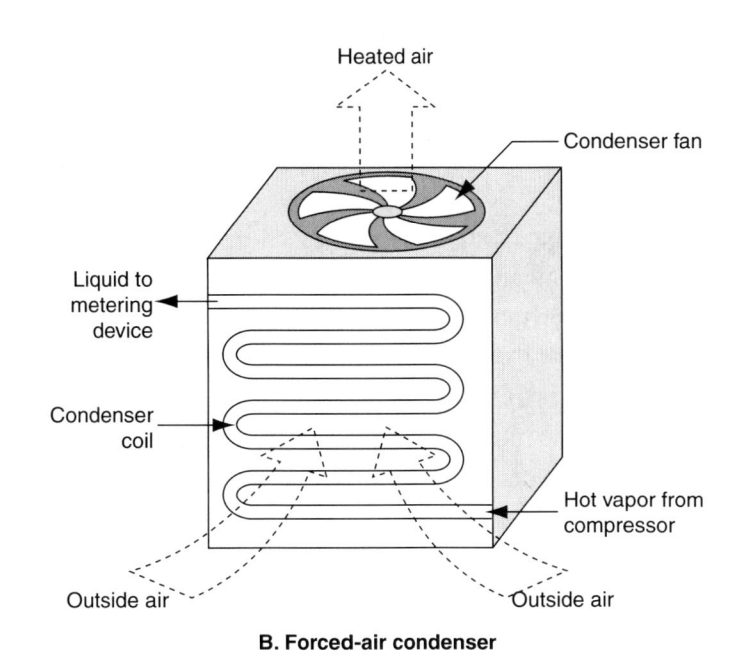

CONDENSER CAPACITY

The capacity of an air-cooled condenser is an important application factor. It is determined by careful calculation. All the criteria of the unit of which it is a part are considered. The system to which it will be applied is also considered.

As an example, assume a 1-hp air-cooled condensing unit operating on an air conditioning load at 40°F suction. The refrigeration effect at the evaporator is 12,000 Btuh and the discharge pressure is 170 psig, using R-134a. Condensing temperature corresponding to 170 psig is 120°F. But the actual temperature of the refrigerant vapor discharged from the compressor is 145°F. The difference between 120°F and 145°F is the *superheat* so often referred to in discussing system operation. Now add 2,546 Btuh (the equivalent of one horsepower) to the 12,000 Btuh. The condenser has to remove 14,546 Btuh. This is about 20% more than the useful refrigerating effect at the evaporator.

FIGURE 6-1. *Air-cooled condensers*

Now assume that the 1-hp compressor is operating at a lower suction temperature—say, –20°F. The refrigerating effect of the system would be much less—approximately 5,000 Btuh. The refrigerant vapor leaving the compressor would be closer to 160°F. The compressor would still be putting the equivalent of 2,546 Btuh into the system, however. So the condenser would be called on to remove about 7,546 Btuh. This is approximately 50% more than the useful refrigerating effect at the evaporator.

101

RAC

Physically, this higher superheat is caused by the higher ratio of compression which occurs with low suction pressures. This is why two-stage systems for low-temperature applications have an interstage desuperheater. It cools hot vapor discharged from the first stage before it enters the suction of the second stage.

Now, assume that the capacity of the condenser in this example was not sufficient. For example, what if the head pressure was 200 psig instead of 170 psig? The ratio of compression would be higher. Less vapor could be moved with the same power input. Compressor discharge temperature would be higher. Power input from the compressor would become a higher percentage of the useful refrigerating effect. Instead of 20% heat of compression, this factor would increase to almost 25%.

This graph shows the Btu per hour that must be removed in a condenser using R-12 for each ton (12000 Btuh) of refrigeration removed by the evaporator at various evaporating and condensing temperatures.

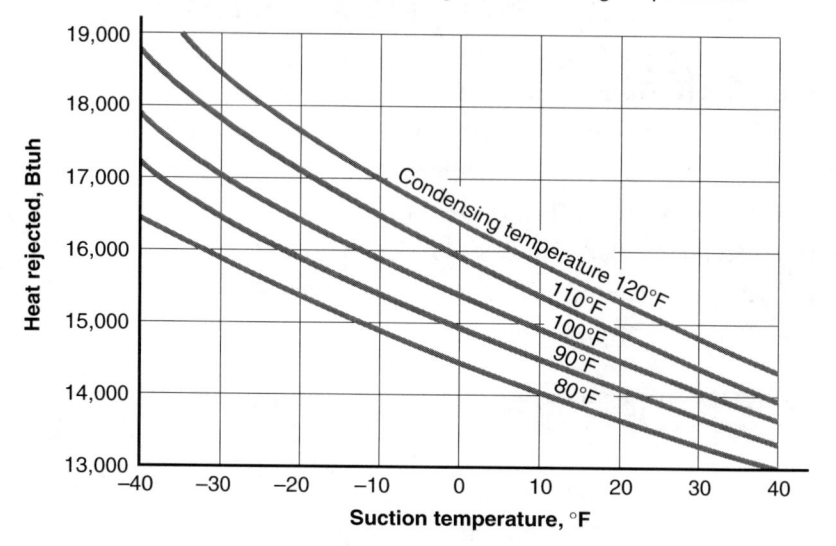

FIGURE 6-2. *Ratio of heat rejection to refrigeration effect*

You can see that the ratio of heat rejection to refrigeration effect is affected by variations of suction and discharge temperature. This is shown in Figure 6-2. Keep the following point in mind. With reduced saturated evaporating temperature, or increased saturated condensing temperature, the compressor does more work. The ratio of rejected heat to useful refrigeration effect is increased. This is because more effort is put into raising the vapor pressure through a wider pressure difference.

Figure 6-3 shows the temperature variation in a refrigerant as it passes through an air-cooled condenser. Hot, superheated vapor enters at point A. From point A to B, the superheat is removed. The vapor is saturated at point B. Condensing then starts, and the saturated vapor is converted into liquid. At point C, the refrigerant is 100% saturated liquid. The third step, from point C to D, is to subcool the liquid refrigerant by reducing its temperature.

An air-cooled condenser needs the surface area and capacity to produce 5 to 10° subcooling of the liquid refrigerant. This occurs from the time the refrigerant is condensed until it leaves the condenser. The refrigerant must be in liquid form when it reaches the expansion valve. Subcooling is needed in order to

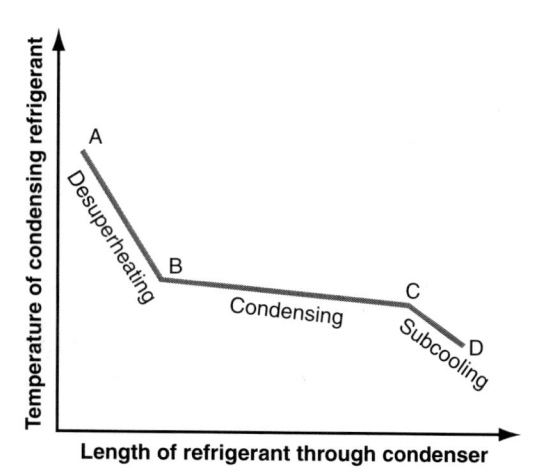

FIGURE 6-3. *Three stages of heat removal in an air-cooled condenser*

prevent the liquid from vaporizing prematurely. Without subcooling, a small pressure drop in the liquid line downstream from the condenser could affect the performance of the expansion valve and the system by producing *flash gas*.

Figure 6-3 shows the three steps of heat removal from the refrigerant—cooling the vapor but not condensing it, condensing the vapor, and subcooling the liquid. They all take place at a relatively constant pressure, because well-designed condensers have a minimal pressure drop. An air-cooled condenser may have a slightly greater pressure drop than water-cooled condensers of the shell-and-tube or evaporative type. However, it will rarely exceed 10 psi. An air-cooled condenser with a greater pressure drop will either have a restriction or be undersized for the application.

NON-CONDENSABLE GASES

Non-condensable gases are usually air and combinations of nitrogen, hydrogen, oxygen, chlorine, oil vapors, water vapor, etc. in the refrigeration system. These gases will not condense with the refrigerant. They will collect—usually in the condenser or receiver. Non-condensables will raise the condensing (head) pressure. Dalton's Law states that *if several gases exist in the same closed vessel, the total pressure will be the sum of the individual pressures that each gas would exert if it were alone in the vessel*. This higher pressure due to non-condensables has several effects:

- It increases the work of compression.

- It raises the power consumption.

- It reduces the useful refrigerating effect of the system.

In addition, the higher discharge temperatures promote oxidation of the oil, especially at the compressor discharge valves.

In most systems, the presence of non-condensable gases can be confirmed by a simple test. Clip a thermometer to the outlet of an air-cooled condenser, then turn off the compressor. Wait until the thermometer reading is the same as that of a nearby thermometer that is monitoring the surrounding air. Now read the head pressure on a gauge connected to the discharge port tapping of the compressor. If the head pressure is higher than the vapor pressure for the system refrigerant corresponding to the ambient temperature, it indicates the presence of non-condensable gases. Proper purging will eliminate most non-condensable gases from a system. With air-cooled condensers, it is a good practice to locate a purge valve at the highest point in the discharge line before it enters the condenser.

TYPES OF AIR-COOLED CONDENSERS

There are several types of air-cooled condensers. One is the *base-mounted* condenser. When a compressor uses a base-mounted condenser, the combination of compressor, condenser, receiver, controls, and base is called a *condensing unit*. Condensing units with base-mounted condensers are limited to no more than 7½ horsepower. *Remote-type* air-cooled condensers are built in much larger sizes. Physical problems create this 7½-hp limit. It is difficult to mount a condenser with enough capacity to function with a 10 or 15-hp compressor, and supply it with enough cooling air. An alternative type had to be produced, as the two most important factors in air-cooled condenser performance are square feet of cooling surface and cubic feet per minute of cooling air.

Current base-mounted condensers are usually made of steel or copper tubing, with steel or aluminum fins. Tubing diameters are generally ⅜ to ½ in. OD on 1 to 1¼-in. centers. Originally, the standard method of fin-to-tube bonding was solder-dipping. The oven type of copper braze is now used more frequently. However, you may find some condensers that use a mechanical grip for the required thermal bond.

Fins are spaced so that there are from 6 to 10 per inch of tube length. The closer the fin spacing, the more often the condenser should be checked for cleanliness. This is very important. Dust and dirt will clog the cooling surface and reduce condensing capacity.

Steel condensers are usually paint-dipped for corrosion resistance. Still, it is preferable to install a condensing unit indoors. If an outdoor location is necessary, provide the best possible type of weatherproof shelter.

Conventional air-cooled condensers may be used with various types of compressors. When the condenser is combined with an *open-type* compressor, which has a V-belt drive, the cooling fan is mounted on the compressor motor shaft. Thus, it revolves at full motor speed. The spokes of the compressor flywheel are pitched to assist in moving air over the condenser. Air is usually drawn through the condenser. This distributes the air more evenly over the entire face area of the condenser. Also, the compressor located downstream can be cooled by the air leaving the condenser.

Figure 6-4 shows another typical condensing unit with an air-cooled condenser. This one uses a *hermetic* compressor. It needs a separate motor to drive the cooling fan. There is an advantage to this arrangement. The fan may be run at slower speed, thus reducing noise level. To reduce overall unit height, this type of unit may use two fan motors and fans.

AIR-COOLED CONDENSER LOCATIONS (BASE-MOUNTED)

If located indoors, an air-cooled condensing unit should be far enough from walls or other obstructions to ensure free air flow into the condenser.

Unfortunately, base-mounted air-cooled condensers are generally not rated at a standard head pressure. The manufacturer tests the entire assembly, but is most concerned with total Btuh capacity value. Standard test conditions include 90°F air temperature. But head pressure under standard conditions can be at higher levels. A unit tested at 90°F air temperature may be subjected to higher entering air temperatures. The resulting high head pressure could cause a variety of problems, including:

- loss of capacity
- continuous operation
- failure to maintain the desired temperature
- compressor motor overloading.

FIGURE 6-4. *Hermetic condensing unit with air-cooled condenser and separate fan motor*

For this reason, locate an air-cooled unit with extreme care. Ensure adequate ventilation to remove condenser heat. This is particularly needed if multiple condensers (condensing units) are installed in close proximity.

SURFACE AREA AND AIR VOLUME REQUIREMENT CALCULATION

The surface area and air volume requirements of a typical base-mounted condenser application can be calculated with reasonable accuracy. Use the following values:

- The surface area should be at least 90 square feet (ft^2) per ton of refrigeration capacity.

- The air volume through the condenser should be a minimum of 1,000 cubic feet per minute (cfm) per ton of refrigeration capacity.

Smaller types of hermetic systems may use *static-type* condensers. These are often found on domestic refrigerators and freezers. This type of condenser has no fan to move the air. It is generally made of ¼-in. OD tubing and mounted vertically on the back of the refrigerator or freezer. Air circulation comes from a thermal draft. The exchange of heat from refrigerant to air causes the air to flow upward. Obviously, these condensers must be kept clean, and air access must remain unrestricted. Also, take care to ensure adequate compressor ventilation. Otherwise, it may overheat even though head pressure is not excessive.

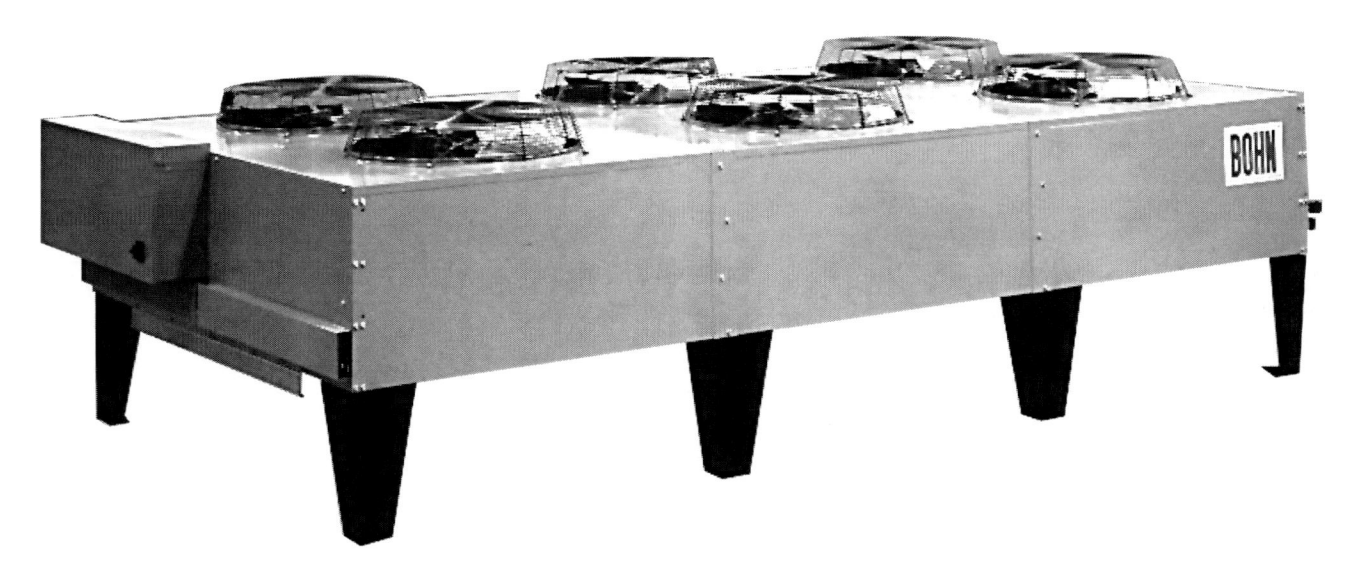

REMOTE AIR-COOLED CONDENSERS

Remote air-cooled condensers are becoming more popular. They offer distinct advantages in many locations. In this type of unit, the condenser is mounted separately from the compressor. Each can be at an ideal location. The condenser can be outdoors where there is a good supply of cooling air at the lowest possible temperature.

The remote-type condenser has its own fan and motor. The required cfm of air is supplied without taking power from the compressor motor. A remote air-cooled condenser also needs about 1,000 cfm of air per ton of refrigeration capacity. Applications are generally in systems of 7½ horsepower and larger. Thus, air quantity is high. This requires particular attention to noise level. The lowest noise level is achieved with low-speed, belt-driven fans of the wide-blade propeller type.

There are also remote-type air-cooled condensers for indoor locations. Such locations may be more convenient, or even necessary. These units use centrifugal

FIGURE 6-5. *Remote air-cooled condenser*

LESSON 6

blowers to handle the external static pressure caused by ductwork. If ductwork is minimal and air velocities low, propeller fan remote air-cooled condensers can be mounted indoors. However, external static pressure must be extremely low for the propeller-fan unit to be efficient.

Remote air-cooled condensers pose less of a dirt problem than base-mounted condensers. They can be raised off the floor or outside mounting surface. In outdoor locations, they are usually mounted off the ground or roof on legs and/or mounting brackets, as shown in Figure 6-5. A remote air-cooled condenser may be supplied with a direct-drive fan or a belt-driven fan. Figure 6-6 shows a direct-drive model.

FIGURE 6-6. *Direct-drive remote air-cooled condenser*

HEATCRAFT REFRIGERATION PRODUCTS

Remote-type condensers are rated by tons of refrigeration handled in a stated ambient at a stated condensing temperature. Manufacturers usually give complete data. With such data, you can make an intelligent selection of a condenser for any desired conditions. Base ratings are usually given in tons or Btuh of refrigeration effect with 90°F ambient (entering) air temperature, and 120°F condensing temperature. That is, there is a temperature difference of 30°F between entering air and condensing temperature. This gives a condensing pressure (head pressure) of 170 psig for R-134a, or 260 psig for R-22. These are pressures corresponding to those refrigerants at a condensing temperature of 120°F.

To simplify correction for variations in conditions, manufacturers provide conversion factors. Table 6-1 on the next page is an example. It gives correction factors for ambient temperatures above or below 90°F. It also gives factors should conditions warrant a higher or lower condensing temperature than the standard 120°F.

Consider the following example of the value of conversion factors such as those shown in Table 6-1. In a northern city, the design temperature (ambient) may be 80°F, not 90°F. Still, it is preferable to keep the condensing temperature at 120°F to retain the same head pressure and capacity of the condensing unit. This makes a temperature difference of 40°F instead of 30°F.

Now refer to Table 6-1. The factor corresponding to 80°F ambient (entering dry bulb temperature) and 120°F condensing temperature is 1.33. This is opposed to 1.00 for 90°F ambient and 120°F condensing temperature. In other words, the capacity of an air-cooled condenser is one ton at 90°F ambient, 120°F condensing. It increases to 1.33 tons at 80°F ambient, 120°F condensing temperature. Obviously, the capacity of an air-cooled condenser varies as the difference between entering air temperature and condensing temperature changes. There is, however, a difference between the capacity of the evaporator and that of the condenser. The capacity of the condenser must include the heat absorbed by the evaporator plus the heat of compression. (Heat of compression is the work done in compressing the refrigerant.)

Dry-bulb temperature of entering air, °F	\multicolumn{7}{c}{Condensing temperature, °F}
	100	105	110	115	120	125	130
70	1.00	1.17	1.33	1.50	1.67	1.83	2.00
80	0.665	0.834	1.00	1.17	1.33	1.50	1.67
90	0.333	0.50	0.665	0.834	1.00	1.17	1.33
100			0.333	0.50	0.665	0.834	1.00

TABLE 6-1. *Conversion factors for temperature differences other than 30°F (condensing temperature minus entering air temperature)*

Heat of compression increases as evaporator temperature decreases. This is because the ratio of compression becomes greater. More work needs to be done on the vapor to compress it. This additional heat requires greater condenser capacity. At low evaporator temperatures, condenser capacity must be greater to achieve the same refrigeration effect in the evaporator. If published capacities of air-cooled condensers are based on 40°F evaporator temperature, they will have to be reduced when a condenser is used on a system that operates with lower temperatures, everything else being equal.

Table 6-2 shows the multiplication factors to use with published capacities of condensers for use with evaporators at the temperatures given. Note that if the evaporator temperature is 0°F instead of 40°F, the condenser capacity will be only 89% of its capacity when used with a 40°F evaporator. This assumes that the ambient air and condensing temperatures are the same.

Suction temperature 0°F	−30	−20	−10	0	10	20	30	40
Conversion factor	0.76	0.81	0.85	0.89	0.92	0.95	0.98	1.00

TABLE 6-2. *Conversion factors for suction temperatures below 40°F*

LESSON 6

Assume that a remote air-cooled condenser is selected for 120°F condensing temperature. The resulting head pressure will be 170 psig with R-134a. This is higher than the usual head pressure associated with water-cooled condensers. It is simple, however, to select an air-cooled condenser large enough to give any reasonable head pressure, using available selection tables.

Prevailing temperatures influence condenser selection. Table 6-3 on pages 112 and 113 gives the recommendations of one manufacturer in this respect. Differences between condensing and ambient temperatures are tabulated. An air-cooled condenser selected accordingly will give condensing pressures that approximate the performance of water-cooled condensers in that same area. This is based on the temperature of available cooling water in that area, and the normal temperature difference between inlet and outlet water. You can see that warmer areas require larger air-cooled condensers than the standard sizes based on a 30° TD—that is, if you are to maintain a condensing pressure comparable to that of a water-cooled condenser.

REFRIGERANT PIPING FOR A REMOTE AIR-COOLED CONDENSER

Piping for a remote air-cooled condenser should follow good refrigeration equipment installation practices. All manufacturer's recommendations should be followed. While some physical aspects will vary, a typical installation is shown in Figure 6-7 on the next page. Remote air-cooled condensers are usually mounted at a higher level than the compressors. Therefore, it is a good practice to provide an oil loop (vertical) at the compressor discharge. It will collect oil and liquid refrigerant that drain back from the discharge line during the "OFF" cycle. This protects the compressor from starting against a liquid column. The height of the loop should be 6 in. for every 10 ft of vertical discharge line. If the height of the vertical discharge line makes this loop impractical, use a check valve instead. Note the location of a purge valve at the highest point in the discharge line, as shown in Figure 6-7.

Pipe size is very important in condenser installation. This is particularly true for remote air-cooled condensers. Table 6-4 on pages 114 and 115 is a pipe size guide. It lists standard practice sizes for piping in various areas of a refrigeration system according to Btuh refrigeration load.

Vertical discharge risers should be small enough to give enough refrigerant velocity to carry oil with the refrigerant vapor. Discharge line sizes tabulated in Table 6-4 for a 20-ft length of run will provide a refrigerant velocity of about 1,500 ft/min. This will suffice for vertical risers. A remote-type condenser installed indoors offers another potential benefit. You can use the rejected heat for room heating in the wintertime. This can be done through the use of ductwork and a damper, as shown in Figure 6-8. Ductwork must be minimal to keep static pressure at a minimum, unless the cooling fan is of the centrifugal type.

Face an outdoor remote-type condenser so that prevailing winds assist air movement through the fan. It may be likely that strong winds will blow into the discharge and against the fan. If so, provide a wind scoop to deflect the wind downward and prevent overloading the fan motor.

When connected to a long discharge line, remote-type condensers may experience discharge-line pulsations, especially with high-speed compressors. The long column of vapor in the discharge pipe acts like a flexible spring. The frequency of the compressor strokes may coincide with the natural frequency of the discharge-line column. If so, a resonant pulsation will build up. This can cause objectionable noise and vibration. A muffler in the discharge line, as pictured in Figure 6-7, will help to absorb the pulsations and eliminate the vibrations.

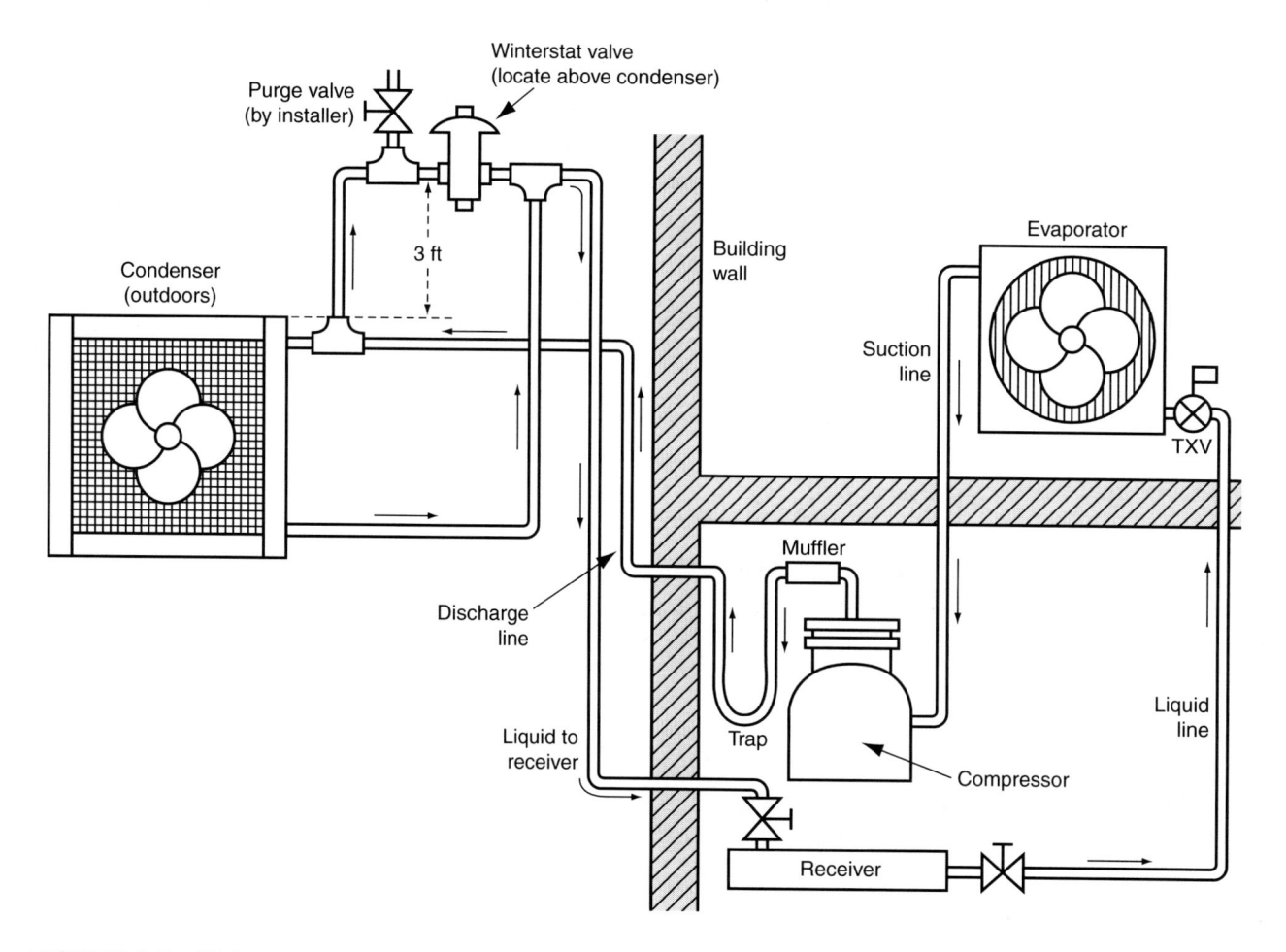

FIGURE 6-7. *Piping diagram for a typical installation, using a remote air-cooled condenser located outdoors*

A remote air-cooled condenser needs special attention if the system is to operate during the winter in a low-temperature area. Cold weather will cause head pressure to drop. It may go below the point at which the required refrigerant flow can be maintained. If this happens, suction pressure will drop, resulting in loss of refrigerating effect. Cycling the condenser fan in response to the action of a head-pressure switch can help. But this often results in extreme variations in head pressure, which is undesirable. Frequent starting and stopping also invites reduced fan motor or switch life. There is a simpler, safer, and more effective means of maintaining consistent head pressure during periods of cold weather—simply place a modulating valve in a bypass line around the condenser, as shown in Figure 6-7. These modulating valves may be supplied with a condenser package. If not, they are available from any supply house.

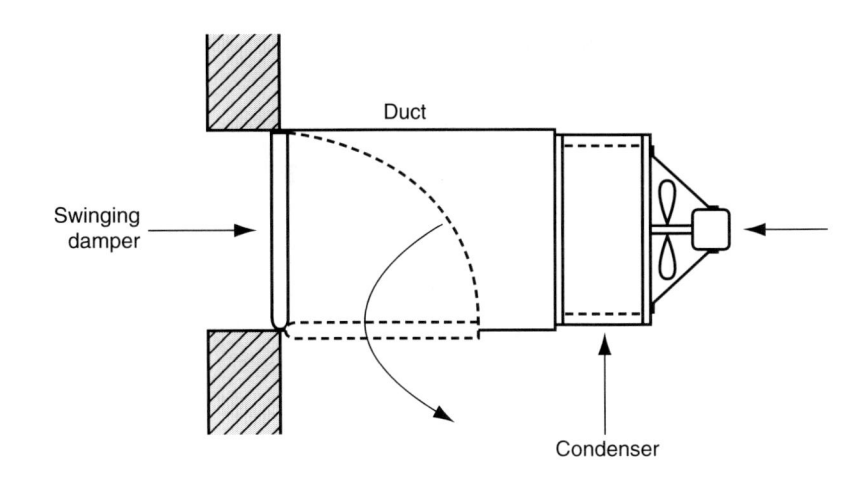

FIGURE 6-8. *Indoor mounting, with duct connection and damper to supply heat to the building in winter*

The winterizing valve in Figure 6-7 is labeled with the Winterstat® trade name, but it is typical of many brands available. The one shown is a spring-loaded valve of the constant downstream-pressure type. It acts to maintain a constant outlet pressure. Valves are usually set at about 115 psig for R-134a and 180 psig for R-22. If head pressure drops below the valve setting, the valve starts to open. Discharge vapor enters the condenser through both inlet and outlet. This restricts drainage of liquid refrigerant from the condenser, causing the condenser to flood sufficiently to maintain condenser (and receiver) pressure at the valve setting.

This valve is actuated by a pressure difference between its inlet and outlet. A loop in the liquid line at the condenser outlet will provide this pressure difference. During hot weather periods (summer), the valve will remain in the closed position. The loop will have no effect on head pressure. The pressure drop in the loop riser is canceled by the siphoning effect of the loop down-swing. The extra refrigerant required to flood the condenser must be drawn from the receiver. If system pump-down is a desired feature, the receiver must hold the normal refrigerant charge plus the condenser charge with the bypass valve operating—that is, partially open or intermittently opening and closing.

An air-cooled remote condenser may have more than one refrigerant circuit built into the same coil. This makes it possible for one condenser to serve a number of different compressors. Each circuit must have its refrigerant lines sized properly.

RAC

(And each must use a winterizing valve for cold weather operation if the condenser is located outdoors.)

A condenser may serve only three or four compressors. If so, the fan motor can be wired to run only when one or more of the compressors is operating. It would be de-energized when all of the compressors are idle. There is an obvious saving on electrical costs. When one condenser serves a greater number of compressors, it is generally more practical to wire the fan motor for continuous operation.

APPLICATION LIMITATIONS

Economy is an important factor in selecting an air-cooled condenser of any type. It is usually easier to evaluate relative economics in larger systems than in small ones. Maintenance becomes an important factor because of the value of the equipment. Cost of maintenance, in fact, is becoming increasingly important.

In the 100-hp and up range, air-cooled condenser installations are not common. However, the few installations made confirm that their use in large sizes has merit. They retain many advantages. These include dry operation, no bad water problems, no winter freezing problems, and little maintenance.

Other factors, both economic and practical, may give priority to other types of condensers. These will be covered in subsequent Lessons. The pros and cons of each will be thoroughly examined. With the information and knowledge gained here, you will be able to list controlling factors as well as make an economic study in the selection of a condenser type. This can be in greater detail for large applications, and rougher for small systems. The simple process of setting down on paper all the costs and other factors involved often clarifies the selection. Keep an open mind and consider all factors in light of actual application conditions. The best selection will be readily made.

State	City	TD	State	City	TD	State	City	TD
Alabama	Birmingham	20	California	Bakersfield	15	Colorado	Denver	20
	Mobile	20		Eureka	25		Durango	20
	Montgomery	20		Fresno	15		Pueblo	20
				Los Angeles	25			
Arizona	Flagstaff	25		Oakland	25	Connecticut	Hartford	22
	Phoenix	15		Sacramento	15		New Haven	20
	Tucson	15		San Diego	25			
	Winslow	15		San Francisco	25	District of	Washington	20
				San Jose	24	Columbia		
Arkansas	Ft. Smith	20						
	Little Rock	20						

TABLE 6-3. *Recommended temperature difference (TD) for selecting remote-type condensers (TD = condensing temperature minus entering air temperature)*

State	City	TD	State	City	TD	State	City	TD
Florida	Jacksonville	20	Montana	Billings	25	Pennsylvania	Erie	22
	Key West	17		Havre	20		Harrisburg	20
	Miami	22					Philadelphia	20
	Pensacola	20	Missouri	Columbia	15		Pittsburgh	20
	Tampa	20		Kansas City	15		Reading	20
				St. Louis	20		Scranton	20
Georgia	Atlanta	20						
	Augusta	17	Nebraska	Lincoln	20	Rhode Island	Block Island	20
	Savannah	20		Omaha	20		Providence	22
				Valentine	20			
Idaho	Boise	20				South Carolina	Charleston	20
	Lewiston	20	Nevada	Reno	20		Columbia	20
				Winnemucca	20			
Illinois	Chicago	20				South Dakota	Huron	20
	Peoria	19	New Hampshire	Concord	25		Rapid City	20
	Springfield	17						
			New Jersey	Atlantic City	20	Tennessee	Chattanooga	20
Indiana	Evansville	20		Newark	20		Knoxville	20
	Ft. Wayne	20		Trenton	20		Memphis	20
	Indianapolis	20					Nashville	20
	Terre Haute	20	New Mexico	Albuquerque	20			
				Roswell	20	Texas	Abilene	15
Iowa	Davenport	20					Amarillo	15
	Des Moines	20	New York	Albany	22		Austin	15
	Dubuque	20		Binghampton	20		Corpus Christi	20
	Sioux City	20		Buffalo	22		Dallas	15
				New York	20		El Paso	15
Kansas	Dodge City	20		Rochester	20		Galveston	20
	Topeka	15		Syracuse	22		Houston	20
	Wichita	15					San Antonio	15
			North Carolina	Asheville	22			
Kentucky	Louisville	20		Charlotte	20	Utah	Modena	20
				Greensboro	20		Salt Lake City	20
Louisiana	New Orleans	20		Raleigh	20			
	Shreveport	15				Vermont	Burlington	25
			North Dakota	Bismarck	20			
Maine	Eastport	25		Devils Lake	20	Virginia	Cape Henry	20
	Portland	25		Fargo	20		Norfolk	20
				Williston	20		Richmond	20
Maryland	Baltimore	20					Roanoke	20
			Ohio	Akron	20			
Massachusetts	Boston	23		Cincinnati	20	Washington	Seattle	30
	Nantucket	20		Cleveland	20		Spokane	20
				Columbus	20		Tacoma	30
Michigan	Detroit	20		Dayton	20		Yakima	20
	Lansing	20		Toledo	20			
						West Virginia	Parkersburg	20
Minnesota	Duluth	22	Oklahoma	Okla. City	15			
	Minneapolis	20		Tulsa	15	Wisconsin	Green Bay	20
	St. Paul	20					La Crosse	20
			Oregon	Baker	25		Madison	20
Mississippi	Meridian	20		Medford	20		Milwaukee	20
	Vicksburg	20		Portland	25			
						Wyoming	Cheyenne	20
							Lander	20

TABLE 6-3 (continued). *Recommended temperature difference (TD) for selecting remote-type condensers (TD = condensing temperature minus entering air temperature)*

| Btuh capacity | Total equivalent length | R-12, R-134a, R-401A ||||| R-22 |||||
| | | Liquid line || Suction line ||| Hot gas and discharge line | Liquid line || Suction line ||| Hot gas and discharge line |
		Condenser to receiver	Receiver to expansion valve	−30°F 5.4 in.	−10°F 4.5 psi	+20°F 21 psi		Condenser to receiver	Receiver to expansion valve	−30°F 5 psi	−10°F 16.6 psi	+20°F 43.3 psi	
1,000	20	1/4	1/4	1/2	3/8	3/8	3/8	1/4	1/4	1/2	3/8	3/8	1/4
	50	1/4	1/4	5/8	1/2	3/8	3/8	1/4	1/4	1/2	3/8	3/8	1/4
	100	3/8	1/4	5/8	1/2	1/2	3/8	1/4	1/4	5/8	1/2	3/8	1/4
1,500	20	1/4	1/4	5/8	1/2	3/8	3/8	1/4	1/4	1/2	3/8	3/8	1/4
	50	3/8	1/4	7/8	1/2	1/2	3/8	1/4	1/4	5/8	1/2	3/8	3/8
	100	3/8	1/4	7/8	5/8	1/2	3/8	3/8	1/4	5/8	1/2	3/8	3/8
2,000	20	3/8	1/4	5/8	1/2	3/8	3/8	1/4	1/4	1/2	1/2	3/8	1/4
	50	3/8	1/4	7/8	5/8	1/2	3/8	3/8	1/4	5/8	1/2	3/8	3/8
	100	3/8	1/4	7/8	5/8	1/2	1/2	3/8	1/4	5/8	1/2	1/2	3/8
3,000	20	3/8	1/4	7/8	5/8	1/2	3/8	3/8	1/4	5/8	1/2	3/8	3/8
	50	3/8	1/4	7/8	5/8	1/2	1/2	3/8	1/4	7/8	5/8	1/2	3/8
	100	1/2	1/4	1 1/8	7/8	5/8	1/2	3/8	1/4	7/8	5/8	1/2	3/8
4,000	20	3/8	1/4	7/8	5/8	1/2	3/8	3/8	1/4	5/8	5/8	1/2	3/8
	50	3/8	1/4	1 1/8	7/8	5/8	1/2	3/8	1/4	7/8	5/8	1/2	3/8
	100	1/2	1/4	1 1/8	7/8	5/8	1/2	1/2	1/4	7/8	5/8	5/8	1/2
5,000	20	3/8	1/4	7/8	7/8	5/8	1/2	3/8	1/4	7/8	5/8	1/2	3/8
	50	1/2	1/4	1 1/8	7/8	5/8	1/2	3/8	1/4	7/8	5/8	1/2	3/8
	100	1/2	3/8	1 1/8	7/8	7/8	5/8	1/2	1/4	1 1/8	7/2	5/8	1/2
6,000	20	3/8	1/4	1 1/8	7/8	5/8	1/2	3/8	1/4	7/8	5/8	1/2	3/8
	50	1/2	1/4	1 1/8	7/8	7/8	5/8	1/2	1/4	1 1/8	7/8	5/8	1/2
	100	1/2	3/8	1 3/8	1 1/8	7/8	5/8	1/2	1/4	1 1/8	7/8	5/8	1/2
8,000	20	1/2	1/4	1 1/8	7/8	5/8	1/2	3/8	1/4	7/8	5/8	1/2	3/8
	50	1/2	3/8	1 3/8	1 1/8	7/8	5/8	1/2	1/4	1 1/8	7/8	5/8	1/2
	100	5/8	3/8	1 3/8	1 1/8	7/8	7/8	1/2	3/8	1 1/8	7/8	7/8	5/8
12,000	20	1/2	3/8	1 3/8	1 1/8	7/8	5/8	1/2	1/4	1 1/8	7/8	5/8	1/2
	50	5/8	3/8	1 3/8	1 1/8	7/8	7/8	1/2	3/8	1 1/8	1 1/8	7/8	5/8
	100	5/8	3/8	1 5/8	1 3/8	1 1/8	7/8	1/2	3/8	1 3/8	1 1/8	7/8	5/8
	200	7/8	1/2	2 1/8	1 3/8	1 1/8	7/8	5/8	3/8	1 5/8	1 1/8	1 1/8	7/8
15,000	20	1/2	3/8	1 3/8	1 1/8	7/8	5/8	1/2	3/8	1 1/8	7/8	5/8	1/2
	50	5/8	3/8	1 5/8	1 3/8	1 1/8	7/8	1/2	3/8	1 3/8	1 1/8	7/8	5/8
	100	7/8	3/8	1 5/8	1 3/8	1 1/8	7/8	5/8	3/8	1 3/8	1 1/8	7/8	7/8
	200	7/8	1/2	2 1/8	1 5/8	1 3/8	1 1/8	5/8	1/2	1 5/8	1 3/8	1 1/8	7/8
18,000	20	5/8	3/8	1 3/8	1 1/8	7/8	7/8	1/2	3/8	1 1/8	1 1/8	7/8	1/2
	50	7/8	3/8	1 5/8	1 3/8	1 1/8	7/8	5/8	3/8	1 3/8	1 1/8	7/8	5/8
	100	7/8	1/2	2 1/8	1 5/8	1 1/8	7/8	5/8	3/8	1 5/8	1 3/8	1 1/8	7/8
	200	7/8	1/2	2 1/8	1 5/8	1 3/8	1 1/8	7/8	1/2	1 5/8	1 3/8	1 1/8	7/8
21,000	20	5/8	3/8	1 3/8	1 1/8	1 1/8	7/8	1/2	3/8	1 1/8	1 1/8	7/8	5/8
	50	7/8	3/8	1 5/8	1 3/8	1 1/8	7/8	5/8	3/8	1 3/8	1 1/8	7/8	5/8
	100	7/8	1/2	2 1/8	1 5/8	1 3/8	1 1/8	5/8	1/2	1 5/8	1 3/8	1 1/8	7/8
	200	7/8	1/2	2 1/8	2 1/8	1 3/8	1 1/8	7/8	1/2	2 1/8	1 3/8	1 1/8	7/8
24,000	20	5/8	3/8	1 5/8	1 3/8	1 1/8	7/8	1/2	3/8	1 3/8	1 1/8	7/8	5/8
	50	7/8	1/2	2 1/8	1 3/8	1 1/8	7/8	5/8	3/8	1 3/8	1 1/8	1 1/8	7/8
	100	7/8	1/2	2 1/8	1 5/8	1 3/8	1 1/8	7/8	1/2	1 5/8	1 3/8	1 1/8	7/8
	200	7/8	5/8	2 5/8	2 1/8	1 5/8	1 1/8	7/8	1/2	2 1/8	1 5/8	1 1/8	1 1/8
28,000	20	5/8	3/8	1 5/8	1 3/8	1 1/8	7/8	1/2	3/8	1 3/8	1 1/2	7/8	5/8
	50	7/8	1/2	2 1/8	1 5/8	1 3/8	7/8	5/8	3/8	1 5/8	1 3/8	1 1/8	7/8
	100	7/8	1/2	2 1/8	1 5/8	1 3/8	1 1/8	7/8	1/2	2 1/8	1 3/8	1 1/8	7/8
	200	1 1/8	5/8	2 5/8	2 1/8	1 5/8	1 3/8	7/8	1/2	2 1/8	1 5/8	1 3/8	1 1/8
36,000	20	7/8	1/2	2 1/8	1 3/8	1 1/8	7/8	5/8	3/8	1 3/8	1 1/8	1 1/8	7/8
	50	7/8	1/2	2 1/8	1 5/8	1 3/8	1 1/8	7/8	1/2	1 5/8	1 3/8	1 1/8	7/8
	100	1 1/8	5/8	2 5/8	2 1/8	1 5/8	1 1/8	7/8	1/2	2 1/8	1 5/8	1 3/8	1 1/8
	200	1 1/8	5/8	2 5/8	2 1/8	1 5/8	1 3/8	1 1/8	1/2	2 1/8	2 1/8	1 3/8	1 1/8

TABLE 6-4. *Recommended refrigerant line sizes*

| | | R-12, R-134a, R-401A ||||||| R-22 |||||
| | | Liquid line || Suction line ||| Hot gas and discharge line | Liquid line || Suction line ||| Hot gas and discharge line |
Btuh capacity	Total equivalent length	Condenser to receiver	Receiver to expansion valve	−30°F 5.4 in.	−10°F 4.5 psi	+20°F 21 psi		Condenser to receiver	Receiver to expansion valve	−30°F 5 psi	−10°F 16.6 psi	+20°F 43.3 psi	
42,000	20	7/8	1/2	2 1/8	1 5/8	1 1/8	7/8	5/8	3/8	1 5/8	1 3/8	1 1/8	7/8
	50	7/8	1/2	2 1/8	2 1/8	1 3/8	1 1/8	7/8	1/2	2 1/8	1 3/8	1 1/8	7/8
	100	1 1/8	5/8	2 5/8	2 1/8	1 5/8	1 3/8	7/8	1/2	2 1/8	1 5/8	1 3/8	1 1/8
	200	1 1/8	5/8	3 1/8	2 5/8	2 1/8	1 3/8	1 1/8	1/2	2 5/8	2 1/8	1 3/8	1 1/8
48,000	20	7/8	1/2	2 1/8	1 5/8	1 3/8	1 1/8	5/8	3/8	1 5/8	1 3/8	1 1/8	7/8
	50	7/8	1/2	2 5/8	2 1/8	1 3/8	1 1/8	7/8	1/2	2 1/8	1 5/8	1 3/8	7/8
	100	1 1/8	5/8	2 5/8	2 1/8	1 5/8	1 3/8	7/8	1/2	2 1/8	1 5/8	1 3/8	1 1/8
	200	1 1/8	7/8	3 1/8	2 5/8	2 1/8	1 3/8	1 1/8	5/8	2 5/8	2 1/8	1 5/8	1 1/8
60,000	20	7/8	1/2	2 1/8	1 5/8	1 3/8	1 1/8	7/8	1/2	2 1/8	1 3/8	1 1/8	7/8
	50	1 1/8	5/8	2 5/8	2 1/8	1 5/8	1 1/8	7/8	1/2	2 1/8	1 5/8	1 3/8	1 1/8
	100	1 1/8	5/8	3 1/8	2 5/8	2 1/8	1 3/8	1 1/8	1/2	2 5/8	2 1/8	1 3/8	1 1/8
	200	1 3/8	7/8	3 5/8	2 5/8	2 1/8	1 5/8	1 1/8	5/8	2 5/8	2 1/8	1 5/8	1 3/8
72,000	20	7/8	1/2	2 5/8	2 1/8	1 3/8	1 1/8	7/8	1/2	2 1/8	1 5/8	1 3/8	7/8
	50	1 1/8	5/8	2 5/8	2 1/8	1 5/8	1 3/8	7/8	1/2	2 1/8	2 1/8	1 3/8	1 1/8
	100	1 3/8	7/8	3 1/8	2 5/8	2 1/8	1 5/8	1 1/8	5/8	2 5/8	2 1/8	1 5/8	1 3/8
	200	1 3/8	7/8	3 5/8	2 5/8	2 5/8	1 5/8	1 3/8	5/8	3 1/8	2 5/8	2 1/8	1 3/8
90,000	20	1 1/8	5/8	2 5/8	2 1/8	1 5/8	1 1/8	7/8	1/2	2 1/8	1 5/8	1 3/8	1 1/8
	50	1 1/8	5/8	3 1/8	2 5/8	2 1/8	1 3/8	1 1/8	1/2	2 5/8	2 1/8	1 5/8	1 1/8
	100	1 3/8	7/8	3 5/8	2 5/8	2 1/8	1 5/8	1 1/8	5/8	2 5/8	2 1/8	1 5/8	1 3/8
	200	1 5/8	7/8	4 1/8	3 1/8	2 5/8	2 1/8	1 3/8	7/8	3 1/8	2 5/8	2 1/8	1 3/8
120,000	20	1 1/8	5/8	3 1/8	2 1/8	2 1/8	1 3/8	7/8	1/2	2 1/8	2 1/8	1 3/8	1 1/8
	50	1 3/8	7/8	3 5/8	2 5/8	2 1/8	1 5/8	1 1/8	5/8	2 5/8	2 1/8	1 5/8	1 3/8
	100	1 3/8	7/8	3 5/8	3 1/8	2 5/8	2 1/8	1 3/8	5/8	3 1/8	2 5/8	2 1/8	1 3/8
	200	1 5/8	1 1/8	4 1/8	3 5/8	2 5/8	2 1/8	1 5/8	7/8	3 5/8	2 5/8	2 1/8	1 5/8
150,000	20	1 1/8	7/8	3 1/8	2 5/8	2 1/8	1 3/8	1 1/8	5/8	2 5/8	2 1/8	1 5/8	1 1/8
	50	1 3/8	7/8	3 5/8	3 1/8	2 5/8	1 5/8	1 3/8	5/8	3 1/8	2 5/8	2 1/8	1 3/8
	100	1 5/8	7/8	4 1/8	3 1/8	2 5/8	2 1/8	1 3/8	7/8	3 5/8	2 5/8	2 1/8	1 5/8
	200	2 1/8	1 1/8	5 1/8	3 5/8	3 1/8	2 1/8	1 5/8	7/8	3 5/8	3 1/8	2 5/8	2 1/8
180,000	20	1 1/8	7/8	3 5/8	2 5/8	2 1/8	1 5/8	1 1/8	5/8	2 5/8	2 1/8	1 5/8	1 3/8
	50	1 3/8	7/8	4 1/8	3 1/8	2 5/8	2 1/8	1 3/8	7/8	3 1/8	2 5/8	2 1/8	1 3/8
	100	1 5/8	1 1/8	5 1/8	3 5/8	2 5/8	2 1/8	1 5/8	7/8	3 5/8	3 1/8	2 1/8	1 5/8
	200	2 1/8	1 1/8	5 1/8	4 1/8	3 1/8	2 5/8	1 5/8	1 1/8	4 1/8	3 1/8	2 5/8	2 1/8
240,000	20	1 3/8	7/8	3 5/8	3 1/8	2 5/8	1 5/8	1 3/8	5/8	3 1/8	2 5/8	2 1/8	1 3/8
	50	1 5/8	7/8	4 1/8	3 5/8	2 5/8	2 1/8	1 3/8	7/8	3 5/8	3 1/8	2 1/8	1 5/8
	100	2 1/8	1 1/8	5 1/8	4 1/8	3 1/8	2 1/8	1 5/8	7/8	4 1/8	3 1/8	2 5/8	2 1/8
	200	2 1/8	1 3/8	6 1/8	5 1/8	3 5/8	2 5/8	2 1/8	1 1/8	5 1/8	3 5/8	2 5/8	2 1/8
300,000	20	1 3/8	7/8	4 1/8	3 1/8	2 5/8	2 1/8	1 3/8	7/8	3 1/8	2 5/8	2 1/8	1 5/8
	50	1 5/8	1 1/8	5 1/8	3 5/8	3 1/8	2 1/8	1 5/8	7/8	4 1/8	3 1/8	2 5/8	2 1/8
	100	2 1/8	1 1/8	6 1/8	4 1/8	3 5/8	2 5/8	2 1/8	1 1/8	4 1/8	3 5/8	2 5/8	2 1/8
	200	2 1/8	1 3/8	6 1/8	5 1/8	3 5/8	3 1/8	2 1/8	1 1/8	5 1/8	4 1/8	3 1/8	2 5/8
360,000	20	1 5/8	7/8	4 1/8	3 5/8	2 5/8	2 1/8	1 3/8	7/8	3 5/8	2 5/8	2 1/8	1 5/8
	50	2 1/8	1 1/8	5 1/8	4 1/8	3 1/8	2 5/8	1 5/8	7/8	4 1/8	3 1/8	2 5/8	2 1/8
	100	2 1/8	1 1/8	6 1/8	5 1/8	3 5/8	2 5/8	2 1/8	7/8	5 1/8	3 5/8	3 1/8	2 1/8
	200	2 5/8	1 3/8	6 1/8	5 1/8	4 1/8	3 1/8	2 1/8	1 1/8	5 1/8	4 1/8	3 1/8	2 5/8
480,000	20	1 5/8	1 1/8	5 1/8	3 5/8	3 1/8	2 1/8	1 5/8	7/8	4 1/8	3 1/8	2 5/8	2 1/8
	50	2 1/8	1 1/8	6 1/8	5 1/8	3 5/8	2 5/8	2 1/8	1 1/8	5 1/8	3 5/8	3 1/8	2 1/8
	100	2 5/8	1 3/8	6 1/8	5 1/8	4 1/8	3 1/8	2 1/8	1 1/8	5 1/8	4 1/8	3 1/8	2 5/8
	200	2 5/8	1 5/8		6 1/8	5 1/8	3 5/8	2 5/8	1 3/8	6 1/8	5 1/8	3 5/8	2 5/8
600,000	20	2 1/8	1 1/8	5 1/8	4 1/8	3 1/8	2 5/8	1 5/8	1 1/8	4 1/8	3 5/8	2 5/8	2 1/8
	50	2 1/8	1 3/8	6 1/8	5 1/8	3 5/8	2 5/8	2 1/8	1 1/8	5 1/8	4 1/8	3 1/8	2 5/8
	100	2 5/8	1 5/8		6 1/8	4 1/8	3 1/8	2 5/8	1 3/8	6 1/8	4 1/8	3 5/8	2 5/8
	200	3 1/8	1 5/8		6 1/8	5 1/8	3 5/8	2 5/8	1 5/8	6 1/8	5 1/8	4 1/8	3 1/8

TABLE 6-4 (continued). *Recommended refrigerant line sizes*

REVIEW QUESTIONS

1. How many sources of heat have to be rejected from the vapor in the condenser?

2. What possible temperature can be anticipated at the compressor discharge valve?

3. Name the three stages in which refrigerant in the condenser is cooled.

4. What purpose do the fins attached to the condenser tubes serve?

5. How many Btu of heat are added to the system by the work of the compressor?

6. On a system that has a 12,000 Btu load with the heat of compression added, what amount of additional capacity is required in the condenser?

7. What is the purpose of subcooling?

8. The pressure drop through an air-cooled condenser will rarely exceed _____ psi.

9. If condensing pressure is higher than the corresponding condensing temperature, what is normally the cause?

10. What instrument can be used to detect the presence of non-condensables?

11. What term is used to describe a combination of compressor, condenser, receiver, and controls mounted on a base?

REVIEW QUESTIONS

12. If the fins on a condenser are closely spaced, what must be checked frequently?

13. Surface area and air volume are usually calculated at what values?

14. What type of air-moving device is needed for a remote air-cooled condenser that is being used for an indoor application?

15. The ratings for base-mounted condensers are usually calculated at an ambient temperature of _____.

16. If an air-cooled condenser rated at 1 ton at 90°F ambient is used at 80°F ambient, what would the rating be? Consider a condensing temperature of 120°F.

17. Why does the heat of compression increase as the evaporator temperature decreases?

18. What is the purpose of providing a loop in the discharge line when a remote air-cooled condenser is located higher than the compressor?

19. Discharge lines are normally figured for a velocity of _____ ft/min for vertical risers.

20. Which direction should a remote air-cooled condenser located outdoors face?

21. The winterizing valve is actuated by a pressure difference between its inlet and outlet. How is this accomplished?

LESSON 7

Water-Cooled Condensers

THE WATER-COOLED CONDENSER

The second of the three types of condensers covered in this book is the *water-cooled* condenser. It uses perhaps the simplest method of condensing. Given the right conditions, it is a good, practical method. Such conditions include a supply of cool, inexpensive water and adequate drainage facilities. The cost of water is less important than having plenty of it.

In a water-cooled condenser, water generally circulates through the inside of a tube. Refrigerant circulates either through a larger tube that surrounds the water tube, or in a shell in which the water tubes are suspended. *Shell-and-coil* water-cooled condensers are widely used. They are most common in smaller systems with capacities up to 10 tons of refrigeration effect. A shell-and-coil condenser has several advantages, including its compact size and its ability to serve the dual function of both condenser and receiver.

In a typical shell-and-coil condenser, the water coil is formed into a cluster within the shell. Both inlet and outlet headers are at one end of the shell. The vertical type is shown in Figure 7-1 on the next page, but a horizontal model is also available. In the condenser shown in Figure 7-1, the water coil is wound up in the shell. Refrigerant vapor condenses on the outside of the water coils and collects in the bottom of the shell. Liquid refrigerant leaves the shell through a bottom outlet or a dip tube.

RAC

A water-cooled condenser with its dip tube missing can be a puzzling experience. The problem can be difficult to find. All signs will point to a shortage of refrigerant. This will be the case even after relatively large amounts have been added. The overcharge will show up suddenly as excessively high head pressure.

A well-designed water-cooled condenser will have water coils arranged so that there is free draining. It is important to drain the coil when a system is idle for any length of time. It helps avoid damage due to freeze-up. Some condensers have external fins on the water coil tubing for better heat transfer. This works particularly well if the tubes are horizontal and the fins are mostly vertical. It permits condensing refrigerant to drain easily from between the fins. For these two reasons, horizontal condensers usually have horizontal tubes or trombone-type coils. Upright (vertical) condensers can have tubes coiled in spirals about a central axis with vertical fins and still be free-draining.

Fins are an advantage because water in the tubes is a better heat transfer medium than the refrigerant outside the tubes. Water is about four times as effective as fluorocarbon refrigerants. Thus, fin area is usually three or four times that of the inside tube area.

FIGURE 7-1. *Vertical shell-and-coil water-cooled condenser*

Water tubing size in *shell-and-tube* condensers is generally restricted to a ¾-in. diameter or less. This means having two or more water flow circuits in parallel in systems above 3 horsepower. This prevents excessive water pressure drop. With two or more circuits in parallel, header joints should be outside the shell. In this way, leaks at header joints will not cause water to enter the refrigeration system.

Tubing within the shell should have about 10% of its surface submerged below the normal liquid refrigerant level. This is usually enough to give the subcooling needed for a solid column of liquid refrigerant in the liquid line. The subcooling portion of the condensing process is shown in Figure 7-2. In shell-and-tube type condensers, the *length of pass* is minimal. It is still necessary, however, to go through the steps of desuperheating, condensing, and subcooling. Desuperheating is done very quickly in the upper portion of the shell. In the major portion of the shell, the vapor is turned to liquid. The condensed liquid drips to the lower portion. The liquid refrigerant collects in the bottom of the shell. There it is subcooled by the submerged portion of the water tubing.

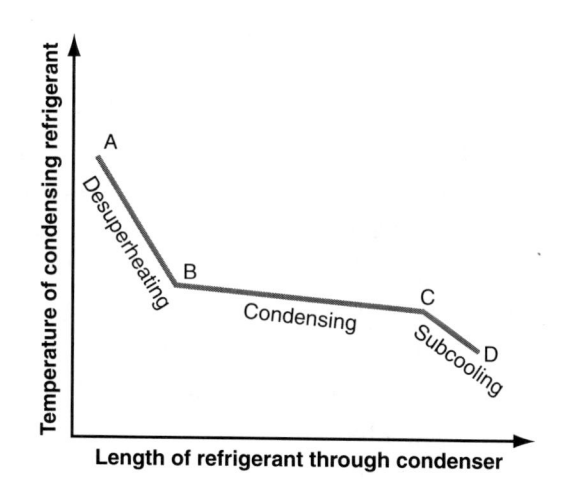

FIGURE 7-2. *Three stages of heat removal in the condenser*

120

As stated in the general definition of a condenser, the condensing refrigerant loses heat and the water gains heat. The water must leave at a higher temperature than when it entered. Under standard water-cooled condenser design conditions, water enters at 75°F and leaves at 95°F with refrigerant condensing at 102°F.

The refrigerant vapor will actually enter superheated. The temperature may be about 130°F for a medium-temperature R-12 system. It could be over 300°F for a low-temperature R-22 system. The superheat is quickly removed, and condensing takes place at 102°F. At least 5°F of subcooling is desirable, so the liquid must leave the condenser at 97°F or lower. The incoming water at 75°F is cold enough to do the subcooling. The water first passes through the bottom tubes, where the heat transfer relationship is best. The warmer water leaving at 95°F can still desuperheat the hot incoming vapor because of the vapor's higher temperature. Passing the water and refrigerant in directions opposite to each other is called *counterflow*. Counterflow is more efficiently done in the tube-in-tube condenser. It is discussed later in this Lesson.

This graph shows the Btu per hour that must be removed in a condenser using R-12, for each ton (12,000 Btuh) of refrigeration removed by the evaporator, at various evaporating and condensing temperatures.

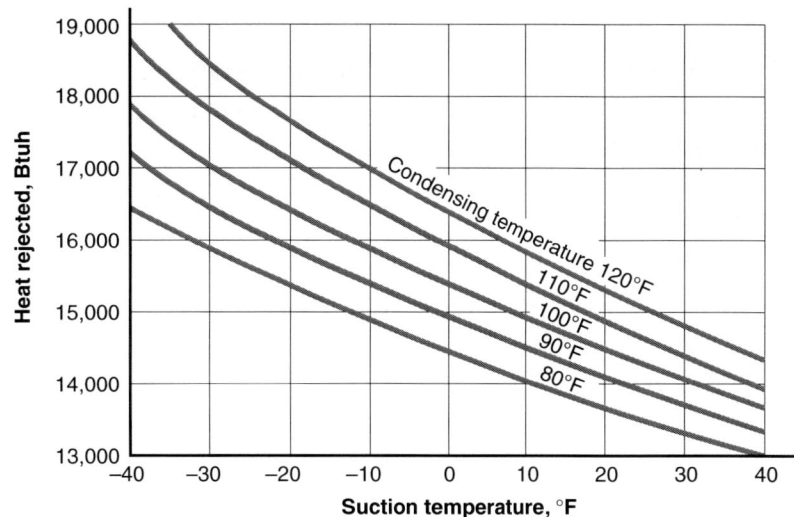

FIGURE 7-3. *Ratio of heat rejection to refrigeration effect*

CALCULATING CONDENSER CAPACITY

The purpose of the cooling water is to condense refrigerant vapor. In doing so, it rises in temperature through a 20°F range (75 to 95°F). From this, you can pre-determine the volume of water flow needed for each ton of refrigeration effect at the evaporator. Look at Figure 7-3 and assume, for example, that 15,000 Btuh is the average condenser heat to be removed for each ton of refrigeration. The volume of water in gallons per minute per ton of refrigeration can be calculated as follows:

$$\frac{15{,}000 \text{ Btuh / ton}}{20°F \times 8.33 \text{ lb water / gallon} \times 60 \text{ min / hr}} = 1.5 \text{ gallons per minute per ton}$$

As an application guide, use 1½ gallons per minute per ton of refrigeration. It is the average water consumption for condensers cooled by city water.

By comparison, a water-cooled condenser connected to a cooling tower system needs a much greater volume of cooling water. Cooling towers will be discussed in another Lesson. They usually cannot cool water to lower than within 7 or 8°F of the existing wet-bulb temperature. The prevailing wet-bulb temperature throughout most of the United States and Canada is 75 to 78°F. Therefore, it is relatively standard to rate cooling towers for a leaving water temperature of 85°F. It would not be practical to allow the water in the condenser to warm up as much as 20°F, to 105°F. The condensing temperature would then have to be 5 to 10°F above 105°F, that is 110 or 115°F. This could result in excessive head pressure. Such an installation, therefore, should provide 85°F water to the condenser from the tower, and 95°F water back to the tower from the condenser. This would keep a standard condensing temperature of about 105°F.

Since the water can warm up only 10°F in the condenser, much more water must be circulated through the condenser to maintain the condensing pressure. The required flow rate per minute per ton of refrigeration is found by using the following calculation:

$$\frac{15{,}000 \text{ Btuh / ton}}{10°F \times 8.33 \text{ lb water / gallon} \times 60 \text{ min / hr}} = 3 \text{ gallons per minute per ton}$$

You can see that twice as much water must circulate through a water-cooled condenser connected to a cooling tower system than through a condenser connected to a city water supply.

It is a characteristic of water flow that if it is doubled, pressure drop increases four times. Obviously, water pressure drop through a condenser connected to a cooling tower system must be given careful consideration. Adequate flow must be maintained, but with the circulating pump motor horsepower kept at a reasonable level. These problems are usually resolved in one of two ways:

- The condenser installed is one designed for a low water pressure drop with the full 3 gallons per minute per ton flow.

- The condenser installed is built with two parallel water circuits, which are piped in series for city water service and in parallel for cooling tower service.

The first solution has several long-range advantages. There are fewer piping connections, and it is easier to convert from city water to cooling tower operation and vice versa. However, in converting a system from city water to a water supply from a cooling tower, condenser pressure drop should be investigated thoroughly. You must be certain that the required water flow will be attained.

One disadvantage of shell-and-coil water-cooled condensers is that mechanical cleaning is not possible. They can be cleaned only by circulating approved cleaning fluids through the system. Mild acid solutions are generally used. A pump suitable for this type of acid should always be available.

TUBE-IN-TUBE WATER-COOLED CONDENSERS

A *tube-in-tube* condenser is built with one or more water tubes inside a refrigerant tube. In some types, the tubes are wound in the shape of trombone coils. Trombone-shaped condensers are generally limited to units of about 3 horsepower. This is because of the problems of bending larger tubes. Also, mechanical cleaning is not possible with this type. Chemical cleaning is required.

Tube-in-tube cleanable water-cooled condensers are built in a wider range of sizes with straight tubes between headers. A cleanable water-cooled condenser is shown in Figure 7-4. Figures 7-5 and 7-6 show the kinds of brushes that can be used to clean straight tube-in-tube condensers. Removable header plates give access to the inside of the water tubes for mechanical cleaning. Individual banks are combined to provide capacities of up to 25 hp and beyond.

FIGURE 7-4. *Cleanable tube-in-tube water-cooled condenser*

Tube-in-tube condensers offer the additional advantage of *counterflow* between water and refrigerant. In other words, the water and the refrigerant flow in opposite directions. The coiled or *coaxial* type of condenser, which is often used for such applications as water coolers and domestic heat pumps, features a counterflow design. This design, shown in Figure 7-7 on the next page, provides excellent heat transfer efficiency.

FIGURE 7-5. *Multi-diameter brush used for cleaning the bore of condenser tubes*

Tube-in-tube condensers require a separate receiver. It should be located so that the condensed liquid drains freely into it from the condenser. The size of the drain line

FIGURE 7-6. *Shoot-through brush*

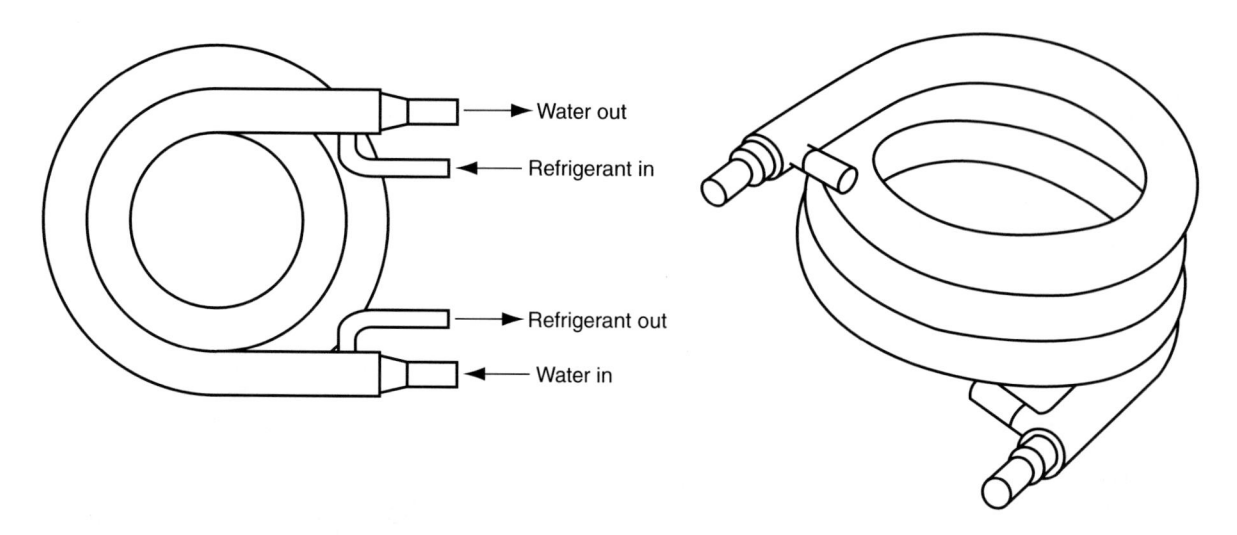

FIGURE 7-7. *Coiled tube-in-tube water-cooled condenser with high-efficiency counterflow design*

from condenser to receiver should be ample. It should always be larger than the liquid line leaving the receiver. Table 6-4 in the previous Lesson gives recommended refrigerant line sizes for systems with capacities ranging from 1,000 to 600,000 Btuh.

A large line size between condenser and receiver serves two purposes:

- It permits free drainage of liquid refrigerant from the condenser to the receiver.

- It permits any flash gas in the receiver to rise to the condenser and be condensed back into a liquid. Gas forming in the receiver could be a problem, particularly if the receiver is in a hot location or in direct sunlight.

SHELL-AND-TUBE WATER-COOLED CONDENSERS

Shell-and-tube condensers are built in sizes ranging from the smallest to the largest capacities. A removable water head is shown on the condenser in Figure 7-8. This makes it possible to clean the (straight) tubes mechanically. Shells larger than 12 in. in diameter often feature bolted cover plates over the water boxes. The plates allow the tubes to be cleaned without disturbing the water connections.

Tubes can be silver-soldered into the tube sheets to make permanent joints. This is common in condensers with shells 10 in. in diameter or less. Larger condensers usually have the tubes rolled into thick tube sheets.

Shell-and-tube condensers usually have finned tubing for more efficient heat transfer. Some manufacturers use tubing with the ends belled out larger than the fin diameter. This makes it possible to replace individual tubes if necessary.

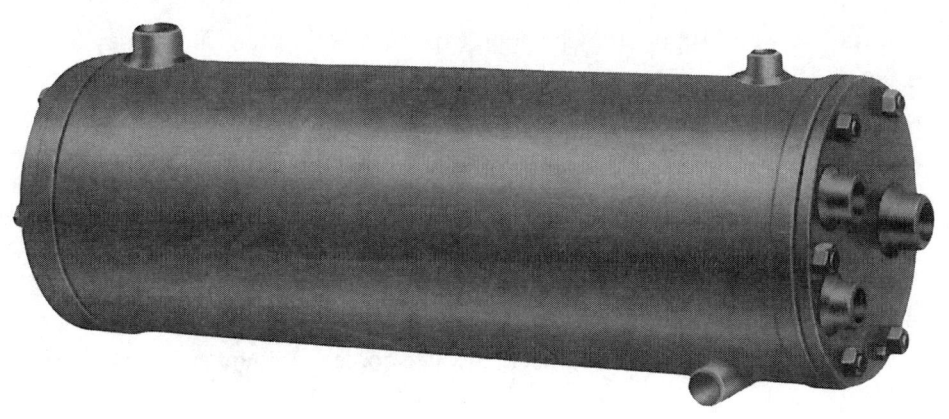

FIGURE 7-8. *Shell-and-tube cleanable condenser*

Generally, shell-and-tube condensers that operate on either city water or cooling tower water with the same connections are not practical. The loss in capacity with the lower city water flow would be uneconomical. For this reason, condensers of this type usually are provided with dual water connections. They are piped so that city water flow is "4 pass" and cooling tower water flow is "2 pass."

PROS AND CONS OF USING WATER-COOLED CONDENSERS

This Lesson has addressed the fundamentals of design, application, installation, and operation of various types of water-cooled condensers. With a good understanding of these basics, you will be able to:

- make the right selection of a water-cooled condenser for a specific application

- make the more important determination of when and where *not* to consider the use of water-cooled condensing.

The right selection is primarily based on product knowledge and capacity requirements. The decision on whether to use water-cooled condensing involves the conditions of each installation or location.

For fractional-horsepower systems, there is little or no choice. Most of these systems are self-contained and have air-cooled condensers. Installations of 1 to 3-hp capacity, however, may use either air-cooled or water-cooled condensing units. One factor to consider is whether the application is a single compressor installation or a multiple installation. A single unit below 3 hp is not a large water consumer. If the water supply is reasonable in price, adequate in quantity, and acceptable in quality, a water-cooled condenser is often the best choice. It will give good operating economy and present no problems in heat transfer.

However, the water supply may be poor, expensive, or scarce. There may be restrictions on its use. The amount of water that may be discharged into the sewer system may be limited. In such cases, the water-cooled condenser on a single unit of less than 3-hp capacity would be impractical.

An installation with a number of small condensing units presents somewhat different conditions than a single unit. Even though each unit is small, total tonnage can be large. The cost of water can become a factor. If the water is good, in good supply, and reasonably priced, a water-cooled condenser is a practical choice.

In the capacity range of 5 to 100 hp, installation conditions are again different. Many installations in this size range are liable to be field-assembled, central station types. If so, the choice of condenser is wide open. There are also package-type systems in this range. These are usually water-cooled, since this method presents the manufacturer with the easiest and most compact choice. When the unit is hermetically sealed, the only field choice is between straight water-cooled and cooling tower operation.

REVIEW QUESTIONS

1. Shell-and-coil condensers are usually limited to a capacity of _____ tons of refrigeration effect.

2. When a large amount of refrigerant is added to a water-cooled system and it still indicates a shortage, what might the problem be?

3. Why is it necessary to have free-draining water coils?

4. Why must parallel circuits be used in shell-and-tube condensers over 3 hp?

5. Why is it necessary for 10% of the tube to be below the normal liquid refrigerant level?

6. Standard water-cooled condenser design is for a water-entering temperature of _____ and a water-leaving temperature of _____.

7. What is the term used to describe water and refrigerant passing in opposite directions?

8. The average water consumption for condensers cooled by city water is _____ gallons per minute per ton of refrigeration.

9. If a cooling tower is used, how great a temperature drop can be expected?

10. How much more water must be circulated in a cooling tower system than in a city water system?

REVIEW QUESTIONS

11. If the water flow through a system is doubled, what happens to the pressure drop?

12. What is one disadvantage of a shell-and-coil condenser?

13. Why is a trombone-shaped condenser limited to about 3 hp?

14. What makes straight tube-in-tube condensers easy to clean?

15. In how many sizes are shell-and-straight-tube condensers built?

16. What feature that permits easy cleaning is often used on shells larger than 12 in. in diameter?

17. Why is it impractical to design shell-and-tube condensers for use on either city water or cooling tower water with the same connections?

18. Systems with _____ capacity are practically never water-cooled.

LESSON 8

Evaporative Condensers and Cooling Towers

INTRODUCTION

There are three types of refrigeration condensers currently in use. They are air-cooled condensers, water-cooled condensers, and evaporative condensers. This Lesson deals with the third type, the *evaporative* condenser. It also discusses the *cooling tower*, a device that conserves water when used with an existing water-cooled condenser.

With any condensing medium, the primary objective is to produce a dependable and uninterrupted refrigeration effect. Sometimes, however, people get so involved in a certain method of condensing, and in analyzing its problems and its costs, that they lose sight of the basic objective. They may also ignore facts and factors that might prove what may seem to be an unusual concept. That concept is that condensing by the most expensive method sometimes can provide the most economical refrigeration.

The air-cooled condenser provides a simple method of condensing. However, high dry-bulb ambient temperatures may make it impractical or too costly. An equally simple method is provided by the straight water-cooled condenser. It is highly practical where cool water is available and drainage facilities adequate.

When facts or factors weigh negatively against either of these methods, there is the third type—the *evaporative* condenser. Evaporative condensers and cooling towers are produced by a number of manufacturers. Each offers a variety of shapes, dimensions, component locations (receivers, pumps, etc.) and air inlet and outlet locations and sizes. Catalogs provide important information on capacity and other specifications. The purpose of this Lesson is to give you information generally not found in such catalogs.

EVAPORATIVE CONDENSERS

The evaporative condenser works on the principle that a pound of water absorbs about 1,000 Btu when it changes from liquid form to vapor form. In an evaporative condenser, water is sprayed downward through a coil while air is drawn upward. Heat from the condensing refrigerant is transferred first into the falling water and then into the rising air and water vapor largely by evaporation. The water is constantly recirculated. The small amount evaporated is replenished by a make-up supply. Air is discharged from the unit in a saturated condition. The air carries with it the heat of the condensed refrigerant. The principal components of a typical evaporative condenser are shown in simplified form in Figure 8-1.

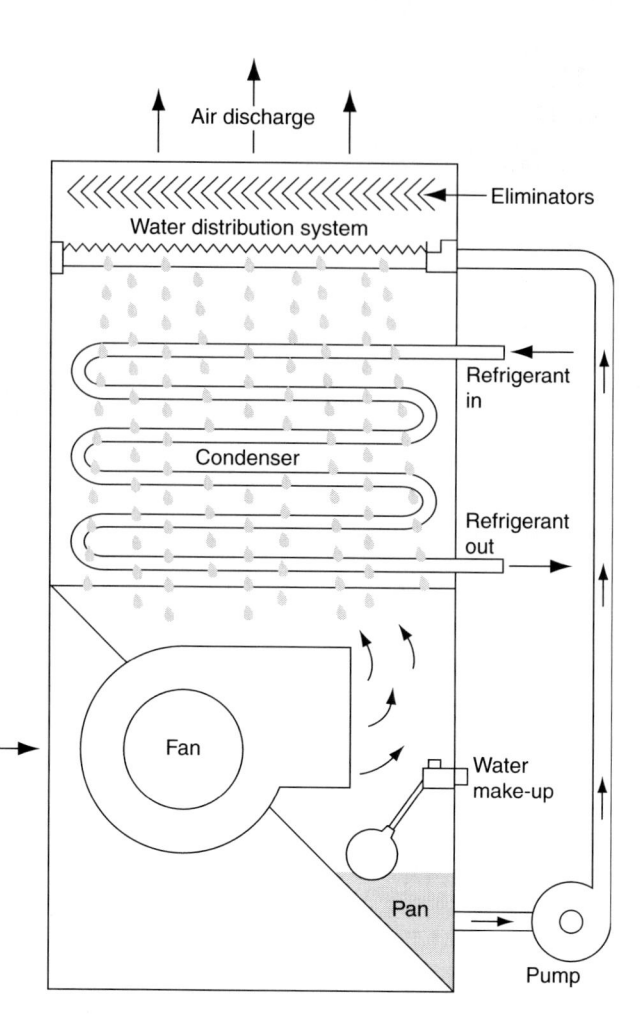

FIGURE 8-1. *Typical evaporative condenser, with conventional arrangement of components*

To select an evaporative condenser, you should understand various areas of application and installation. Many of these are explored in the text that follows. Some of the important selection considerations include:

- available space

- the quality of the air that will be drawn into the condenser

- the surroundings into which the air from the condenser will be discharged.

LOCATING AN EVAPORATIVE CONDENSER

There are evaporative condensers for indoor and outdoor installations. Units installed indoors are protected from the elements, but they take up valuable floor space. To minimize the space used, units may be installed in an out-of-the-way corner or small room. This, however, makes service difficult.

An evaporative condenser requires large quantities of air. In indoor operation, it can exhaust all the heated or cooled air from the building. Also, the air discharge opening must be located where the high-velocity air cannot cause damage. Evaporative condenser discharge air often contains water drift. It may damage adjacent property or the clothing of people passing by. It can even harm polished finishes on automobiles parked near the discharge air outlet.

Consider prevailing wind factors when locating the discharge of an evaporative condenser. Persistent natural drafts between buildings, in alleys, and sometimes on hillsides, can force air back into the duct. This makes it necessary to use a larger motor to drive the condenser fan.

Another important factor is the noise created by the movement of water and air within the condenser. Noise levels will influence your selection of a location for the discharge air outlet. Neighbors may object to the noise accompanying the discharge of air.

Other factors to consider are adequate floor drains close to the condenser, and a plentiful water supply. In the operation of an evaporative condenser, some water will be wasted. It is also necessary to drain and clean the entire unit occasionally. This is no problem if the installation is in a basement with a floor drain nearby. But the condenser may be on a wood floor, or at a level above the basement. If so, there should be a metal or concrete pan-like arrangement under the assembly. This will prevent overflow or cleaning-out operations from damaging anything beneath it. As a safety precaution, confirm the weight-supporting capacity of the floor for the size of condenser that is to be installed.

Roof-mounted evaporative condensers are also common. Again, a primary consideration is the structural strength of the roof. You can get these figures (as well as information about the weight limits of floors) from the architect or engineer who constructed the building.

The weight at either location will be that of the condenser assembly with all of its piping connected, and with the water tank full. When the condenser is roof-mounted, the structural strength factor is much more critical. On many older buildings, the roof might not support the weight of an evaporative condenser *and* the snow and ice that accumulate in winter.

Another consideration for an outdoor evaporative condenser is its aesthetic complement to the surroundings. Most municipalities have ordinances on the placement of evaporative condensers on roofs or in yards. The equipment must not detract from architectural design. It must not be unsightly compared to surrounding buildings, trim, art work, signs, etc. It may be necessary to cover an evaporative condenser with a roof and walls for aesthetic purposes. There should be enough space between the condenser and the walls and roof to allow for proper maintenance and service. This includes the removal and replacement of larger parts.

In roof-top applications, consider the effect of wind on fan operation and spray drift. Pay close attention to wind direction and maximum strength when anchoring and bracing the unit against wind damage.

Take care in locating the inlet side of the condenser. The fan should not pull in smoke from chimneys or air discharged from spray booths, ventilating exhaust fans, etc. This also helps keep out solids such as fly ash, dust, and dirt. An outdoor evaporative condenser also must be placed where overflow or drain-away cannot cause inconvenience or damage to the roof or ceiling beneath it. Roof designs seldom assume a constant wet condition. They depend on periods of drying out between rains, snow, etc. They may leak if not properly drained.

Evaporative condensers should be in an area that is readily accessible. Maintenance technicians and service technicians often have to carry heavy tools and equipment with them.

The cost of running pipes also must be considered. This includes water supply, circulating system, and drain pipes. In areas of freezing weather, the problem of shutting down and draining the condenser must be resolved. When shutdown is necessary, an adequate supply of condensing water from another source may be required. Periods of freezing weather may be of short duration. If so, you can put solenoid valves in the water supply and drain lines. They are energized by one or more thermostatic switches. If the temperature drops below freezing, the water supply will automatically close and the drain line open. The condenser can then operate dry. Experience confirms that air at 32°F or lower drawn through a dry evaporative condenser is adequate for satisfactory refrigeration.

Proper maintenance of an evaporative condenser is essential. Since they are frequently neglected on small condensing units, evaporative condensers are generally not practical in systems of 1 to 5 horsepower. Evaporative condensers are widely accepted for refrigeration systems of 5 to 100 horsepower and more. The exception is those that are hermetically sealed. With these, the choice is between a straight water-cooled condenser and a cooling tower.

In a water-cooled condenser that uses city water, the water picks up about 20 Btu per pound as it passes through the condenser. This results in a 20°F temperature rise. In an evaporative condenser, each pound of water evaporated absorbs about 1,000 Btu.

Theoretically, an evaporative condenser uses only 2% of the water consumed by a water-cooled condenser. However, it is necessary to "waste" some water in the operation of an evaporative condenser, so actual water use will be about 5 to 10% as much as a straight water-cooled condenser.

The waste comes from the *bleed-off* needed to minimize the level of impurities in the recirculated water. All water contains some dissolved or entrained salts and/or solids. But the water that is evaporated is pure—its impurities are left behind in the remaining recirculating water. This requires a continuous bleed-off of a small amount of the recirculating water. Otherwise, it would build up a higher and higher percentage of impurities. These impurities could present real problems, and must be kept to a minimum.

Bleeding off about as much water as is evaporated doubles make-up water flow. This keeps the concentration of impurities in the water in the sump tank and in the water recirculating through the sprays at about double that in the incoming water. If this proves to be too corrosive, it may be necessary to bleed off more water or introduce water treatment.

Because of the constantly circulating water, the plentiful supply of oxygen from the induced air flow, and the warm temperature in an evaporative condenser, operating conditions are conducive to corrosion. Attention to protection from corrosion is needed, from manufacture through maintenance and service.

Easy access to all parts is important for cleaning and inspection. Access doors and removable components simplify the service technician's job. A readily accessible sump section contains a float valve, bleed connection, pump, strainer, and a space for water treatment material. Due to the washing effect of the water, dust and dirt that enter with the air are collected in the sump tank. It must be cleaned periodically. Figure 8-2 on the next page shows typical evaporative condensers.

There are two problems that must be considered if a system is to be operated in cold weather:

- keeping the water from freezing, if periods of extremely cold weather are normal

- maintaining adequate head pressure to ensure refrigerant flow to the evaporator.

If properly sized, an evaporative condenser can be operated dry in the winter to prevent freezing and maintain head pressure. Other options to prevent freeze-ups are shown in Figure 8-3. The problem of maintaining satisfactory head pressure with a condenser can be resolved by means of various control methods. For example, fan operation can be controlled by a switch that is actuated by the temperature of the spray water or the leaving air. Another method makes use of an air bypass assembly, with the by-passed air controlled by a motorized damper that is actuated by the temperature of the spray water or the leaving air. In addition to these control methods, it is possible to use a Winterstat® valve to bypass the refrigerant travel in the condenser, as discussed in Lesson 6 on air-cooled condensers.

Systems operated in a warm ambient may have a separate subcooling coil installed in an evaporative condenser for additional subcooling of the liquid refrigerant. Extra subcooling will improve system operation and increase its refrigerating capacity. As shown in Figure 8-4, liquid from the receiver goes through the subcooling coil before continuing on to the expansion valve.

Circulating water is generally about 7 to 10°F warmer than the ambient wet-bulb temperature. The subcooling coil is suspended in the circulating water. Thus, it is possible to cool the liquid refrigerant from its normal condensing temperature (about 100 to 105°F for R-134a) to a point closer to the wet-bulb temperature. Each pound of R-134a has theoretically picked up about 62 Btu in the evaporator. About 0.35 Btu will be removed from each pound of R-134a for each degree it is cooled in the subcooler. Therefore, each degree of subcooling will provide an increase of about ½% in system capacity. In other words, reducing the temperature of liquid refrigerant by 10° in the subcooling coil gives a 5% gain in overall system capacity. This is often a most welcome increase.

A. Forced-draft (blow-through) type

B. Induced-draft (draw-through) type

FIGURE 8-2. *Evaporative condensers*

A. Evaporative condenser installed indoors

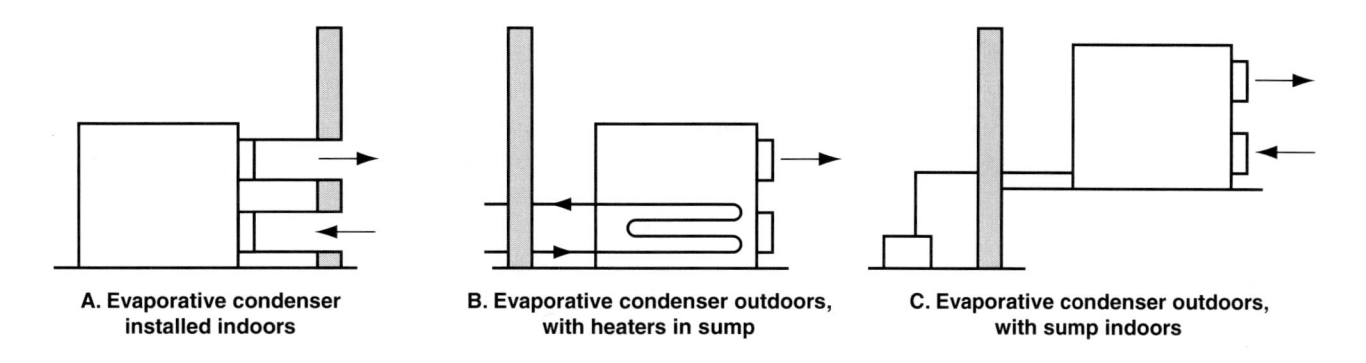

B. Evaporative condenser outdoors, with heaters in sump

C. Evaporative condenser outdoors, with sump indoors

FIGURE 8-3. *Methods of avoiding freeze-up*

EVAPORATIVE CONDENSER INSTALLATION

In an evaporative condenser installation, the route *to* the final location must be checked for structural support. Consider the following example. An evaporative condenser was to be installed on the roof of a building. The roof in the area of installation was checked, and found strong enough to support it. However, the condenser had to be moved to the installation location over another section of the roof. This portion of the roof collapsed, doing considerable damage.

Also, check the route that the condenser must travel to its final installation location for clearance through doors and wall openings. It is possible to dismantle the unit completely and move it in a section at a time, but this is normally a costly procedure.

The need to protect ceilings, walls, and floors directly beneath an evaporative condenser cannot be over-emphasized. Waterproof insulation directly beneath the installed equipment may be necessary.

An evaporative condenser may be installed on a roof, in a yard, or on brackets on the outside of a building. If so, it should be securely tied down so that unusually high winds will not blow it down. This would most likely damage the panels or piping. Always provide sufficient space for maintenance and service on all sides of an evaporative condenser and around its connected components.

Decorative and protective walls and roofs around an evaporative condenser are an

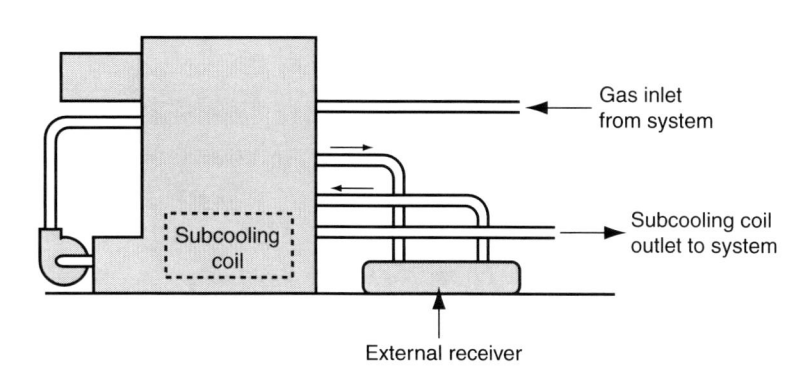

FIGURE 8-4. *Subcooling coil mounted in the spray or sump water cools liquid from the condenser coil or receiver before it goes to the liquid line*

135

asset when you must perform service work during adverse weather conditions. The air inlet must be guarded so that paper, leaves, and other debris cannot be pulled into the fan or against the grill. Many local ordinances require that condenser air discharge outlets be at least 12 ft above street or sidewalk level.

During placement, take basic steps to prevent vibration caused by the evaporative condenser fan and/or fan motor. Generally, new fans and new motors and their component pulleys and belts are well-balanced. They produce little or no vibration in operation. But foreign material collects on fan blades and pulleys. The pulleys and belts wear. The entire unit may begin to vibrate. Study each installation carefully to find the best way to prevent transmitting vibration to surrounding floors and roofs. Sometimes, 2 in. of vibration-absorbing cork under the entire unit or rubber vibration eliminators can be used. It may be necessary to place the unit on steel "I" beams to absorb the vibration. Generally, the problem can be solved by one of these methods. In more difficult situations, look for professional advice before proceeding. Check with the engineering department of a manufacturer of vibration-neutralizing material.

EVAPORATIVE CONDENSER WATER PUMP INSTALLATION

There are two operational characteristics of evaporative condenser water pumps that must be considered *before* the pump is located and installed:

- First, most pumps tend to develop a packing leak at some time. For this reason, they should always be located where a leak will not damage floors, walls, or ceilings. A leak should not cause a wet, slippery floor around the installation.

- Second, noise and vibration are inherent in a centrifugal water pump. Since the pump is usually small, it is easy and inexpensive to install vibration eliminators. It is difficult, however, to isolate pump noise completely.

Pump noise can travel through piping and be amplified in other parts of a building. One way to reduce or eliminate this noise travel is to install sections of flexible, non-metallic material at some point between the pump and the piping. Rubber hose that will withstand high pressures can be used in any length between sections of pipe or copper tubing.

When installing the evaporative condenser water pump, put shut-off valves in both the water inlet supply line and the outlet pipe line. These valves pay for themselves. They allow pump service with a minimum loss of water and service time. Adequate lighting also makes maintenance and/or service easier and faster.

All electric wiring to the pump should be in waterproof piping. This prevents accidents and protects electrical equipment in case of a severe leak around the pump packing or fittings. Fans on evaporative condensers should be controlled by thermostatic switches. The switches will cycle their operation in order to maintain constant condensing temperature during cooler weather. This is especially important in the winter in cold regions when the condenser could be operating dry.

SIZING EVAPORATIVE CONDENSER PIPING

Manufacturers usually provide accurate charts and guides for pipe sizes for the connections between the condenser and other system components. These charts should be used when you install piping. Most of them are proprietary and require extensive computation. This Lesson will not try to use any of them specifically. Instead, a few generally accepted rule-of-thumb formulas that will be of great help in sizing and installing required piping will be presented.

Using correctly sized piping is very important. If water pipes are too small, a larger pump may be needed to supply sufficient water flow. Undersized refrigerant lines can cause a system to fall short of design capacity and operate at excessive cost. The rule-of-thumb method for pipe sizing is to choose a size larger than the existing connection on the condenser. Never reduce the size of the existing condenser connections to use smaller piping at this point.

The connections provided are usually satisfactory when the total length of pipe (refrigerant or water) between them is less than 20 ft. With greater lengths, especially in the case of water piping, flow friction increases considerably. A larger pump or larger pipe will be required to keep enough water flowing at the proper rate. It would be more economical, both in terms of initial cost and maintenance cost, to increase pipe size rather than motor and pump size. Larger pipes also provide long-range benefits. They allow for some scaling and roughness on the inside surface of the pipe.

The connections on the specified water pump may be smaller than the connections on the evaporative condenser. This is especially true if the piping is oversized. However, because of the high velocity of the type of pump used, it will still perform satisfactorily.

WATER PIPING INSTALLATION

The water piping portion of an evaporative condenser installation should show both intelligent design and superior workmanship. Use the following recommendations during the piping installation process. They will significantly reduce the frequency of service, and pipe and fitting service life will be extended considerably.

Unions and disconnecting flanges should be used liberally. Locate them wherever it might be necessary to disconnect piping. They should be on both sides of the water pump, on either side of the condenser, and in about each 30 ft of piping. All ells looking upward should be replaced with tees, as shown in Figure 8-5. The open end of the tee should be closed with a short, capped length of pipe. This method of converting from horizontal to vertical piping provides excellent drain-off connections. It also offers pockets in which foreign material can collect.

When lengths of horizontal pipe are connected together, tees should be used instead of couplings, as shown in Figure 8-5. The side opening of the tee should face downward. This opening should also be closed with a short, capped length of pipe. Long horizontal pipe lines tend to deteriorate at the bottom of the pipe's diameter. This deterioration is caused by the accumulation of acids and other forms of foreign materials. If tees with drop legs are used in the horizontal pipe runs, foreign materials—including sludges and acids—will migrate to the bottom of the drop legs. It is much easier and less costly to replace them than entire lengths of pipe.

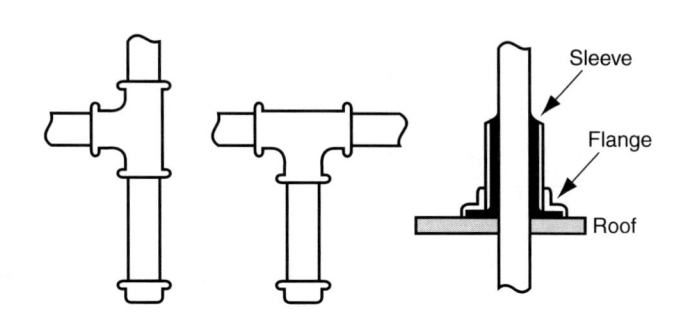

FIGURE 8-5. *Proper piping configurations*

Fewer leakage problems occur when pipes in a roof-mounted condenser pass through a vertical wall horizontally than vertically through a roof. If pipe must run vertically through a roof, place a flange sleeve around the piping. Such a sleeve, also shown in Figure 8-5, should protrude above the roof higher than any snow, ice, or water that might accumulate there. Fill the space between sleeve and pipe with asphalt or other waterproof mastic.

Coat all water pipe threads with a good commercial pipe-thread compound ("dope"). Pipe-thread dope serves three functions:

- It lubricates the threads when they are being joined, which makes it possible to screw pipe into fittings a greater distance with less effort.

- It fills in small defects and rough spots and prevents leakage.

- It coats the exposed threads and protects them from elements that cause rusting and other deterioration.

LESSON 8

Pipe-thread dope is available in two types. One is a permanent type. It sets hard and is very difficult to unseal when taking piping apart. The other is a plastic material that remains "tacky." This allows connections to be taken apart easily after long periods of time. Never use paint or material of uncertain ingredient make-up for pipe compound. They could have harmful effects inside the piping, especially on the seal and bearings of the water pump.

Place oversize strainers in the water system at convenient places in the piping. They will catch any surplus pipe compounds and other foreign materials that can get into the piping. Small, inadequate strainers are usually troublesome. They may adversely affect the entire application.

All piping should be well-braced and strapped to hold it firmly in position. Brace horizontal runs that are exposed near walls so that there is no damage if the piping is stepped on. Support vertical piping every few feet. After installation, paint the piping with a good grade of paint made for water pipe application.

Insulate piping that is subject to extreme temperature changes. Match the type of insulation with the conditions in the room or atmosphere in which it is used. Insulation applied outdoors should be weatherproof. Get advice on selection and use of the best insulation for a specific application.

COOLING TOWERS

Code restrictions and the rising cost of water often affected existing refrigeration systems with water-cooled condensers. Some means of conserving water became necessary. The industry responded with a water conservation device called a *cooling tower*. It cools water by contacting it with air and evaporating a small amount of the water circulated. One type of cooling tower uses wind currents or gravity to circulate the air. Another has fans to force or draw air into contact with water discharged from a water-cooled condenser. The fan is clearly visible in the large cooling tower shown in Figure 8-6 on the next page.

In cooling towers, the surface area of the water is increased by several means. The water can be sprayed from nozzles, for example. Or it can be allowed to splash down from the top of the tower through a series of horizontal baffles. In the latter type of tower, water cascades through slats that act as baffles, and a fan draws air horizontally through the cascading water.

THE HEAT TRANSFER PROCESS

The heat transfer process in a cooling tower moves heat from water to unsaturated air. This heat transfer involves two differentials:

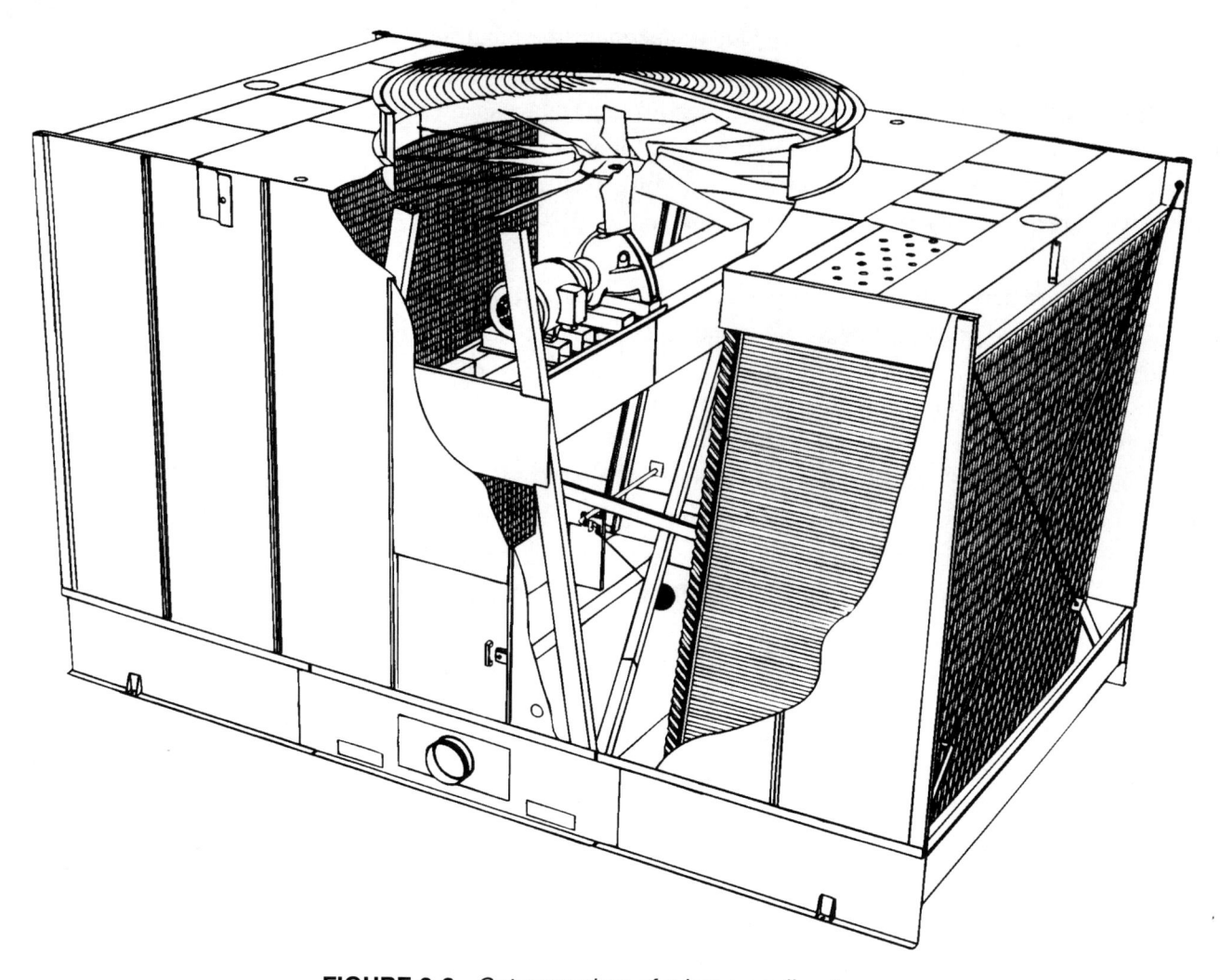

FIGURE 8-6. *Cutaway view of a large cooling tower*

- the difference between the dry-bulb temperatures of the air and the water

- the difference in vapor pressures between the water surface and the moisture in the air contacting it.

Cooling tower efficiency is generally expressed in terms of *range* and *approach*. *Range* is the reduction in temperature of the water passing through the tower. *Approach* is the difference between the wet-bulb temperature of the entering air and the temperature of the leaving water. These two factors are illustrated in Figure 8-7.

One cooling tower design is the *counterflow* type. It is shown in Figure 8-8. Air passes upward through a falling spray of water. The air increases in enthalpy as it rises through the tower. The enthalpy of the saturated film on the drops of water spray decreases as the falling water is cooled.

140

The same principles of heat transfer apply to a *crossflow* tower as well. But the geometrical treatment of the crossflow tower is different. Water enters at the top and falls to the bottom. Air enters from one side and exits on the opposite side.

In a new refrigeration system installation, an air-cooled condenser may not be practical. If not, there is a choice between a cooling tower and an evaporative condenser. A cooling tower has several advantages:

- The system condenser can be an integral part of the condensing unit. This eliminates long refrigerant lines.

- No air ducts are required.

- A cooling tower can be located a long distance from the condenser. Long water lines do not penalize system performance as much as long refrigerant lines.

- It is more adaptable to large-capacity systems. Figure 8-9 on the next page shows a large cooling tower with a hood that provides vertical discharge of the air leaving the tower.

Evaporative condenser and cooling tower operation are similar. But there are several distinct differences:

- The evaporative condenser removes heat directly from the refrigerant vapor. The cooling tower removes heat from water. The heat carried by the water was absorbed from the refrigerant vapor as

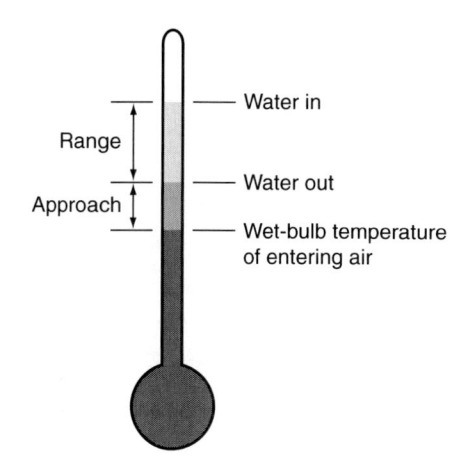

FIGURE 8-7. *Range and approach in a cooling tower*

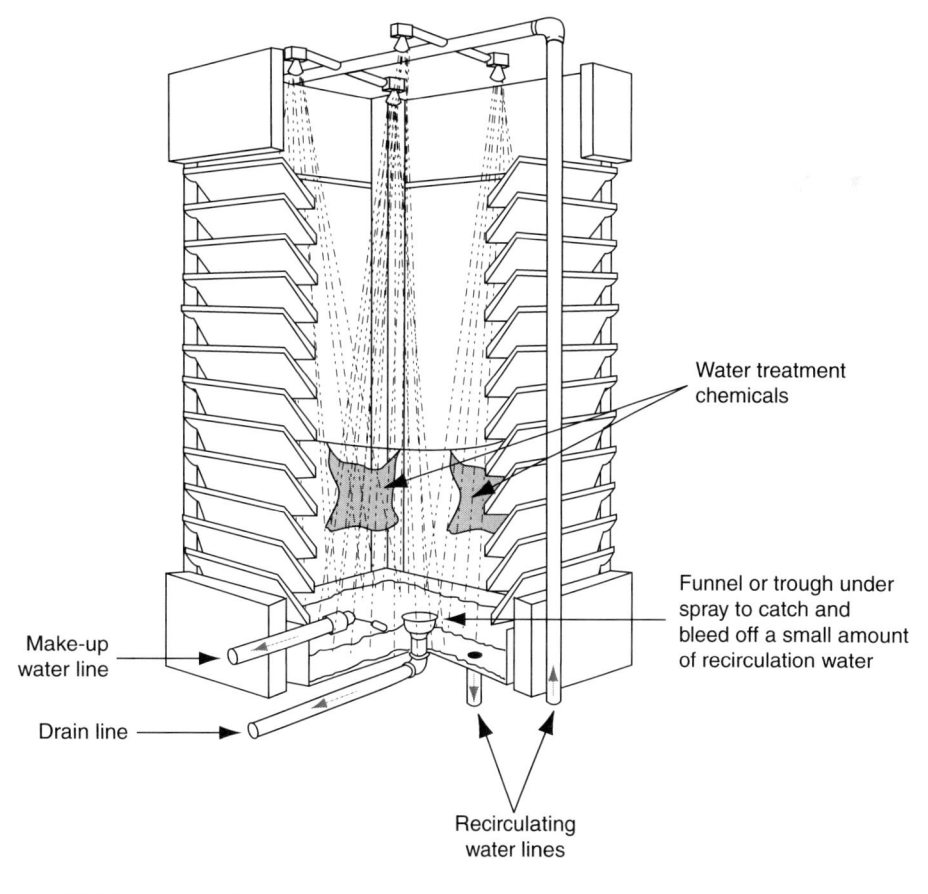

FIGURE 8-8. *Cutaway view of a typical gravity-type counterflow tower*

the water circulated through a water-cooled condenser.

- Both systems use water pumps. In the evaporative condenser, water is simply recirculated from a sump to a spray header. From there, the water returns to the sump. In the cooling tower, the water is first pumped from the sump through the water-cooled condenser. From there it is pumped to the spray header or perforated distributor pan atop the tower.

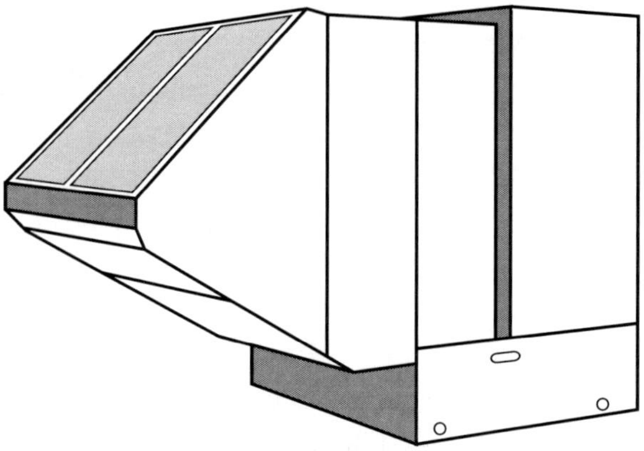

Because of similar operation, the general rules on water-side piping for evaporative condenser installation also apply to cooling tower installation.

FIGURE 8-9. *Cooling tower with a vertical discharge hood*

No evaporative condenser or cooling tower installation is complete without an important final step. Thoroughly brief the equipment owner or owner's representative on system operation. Also, emphasize required maintenance. Some users of refrigerant equipment make no distinction between "maintenance" and "service." *Maintenance* should be defined as the ordinary, simple things done regularly to prevent breakdowns or unsatisfactory operation. They also extend the service life of the equipment. They may be done from day to day, from week to week, and even from month to month. The owner should understand that oiling motors, fans, and pumps, flushing the sump tank, and touching up rust spots are items of maintenance.

Service items should be handled by knowledgeable personnel. Service includes many tasks, including the removal and repair of a motor, fan, or pump, painting equipment, and the thorough cleaning of the sump tank. Owners should understand that a systematic program of preventive maintenance can save considerable money. It also ensures better refrigeration.

REVIEW QUESTIONS

1. Name three types of refrigeration condensers currently in use.

2. What is the primary objective of any type of condensing medium?

3. What effect does a high dry-bulb ambient temperature have on air-cooled condenser selection?

4. What single ingredient is most desirable for the installation of a water-cooled condenser?

5. In an evaporative condenser, approximately how much heat is required for each pound of water evaporated?

6. The air being discharged from an evaporative condenser under full load is in what condition?

7. Name the two general categories of evaporative condensers.

8. What effect can water and air movement through the evaporative condenser have?

9. Why is a convenient floor drain necessary?

10. What is one of the most important factors to be considered in a rooftop installation?

11. How can an evaporative condenser be operated in freezing weather for periods of short duration?

REVIEW QUESTIONS

12. What is the temperature rise across a water-cooled condenser using city (waste) water?

13. In comparison to a city (waste) water-cooled condenser, what percentage of water does an evaporative condenser use?

14. Why is a bleed-off required in an evaporative condenser?

15. Circulating water will generally be at approximately the same temperature as or slightly warmer than the _____ temperature.

16. With R-134a in the system, what will happen to system capacity if the liquid refrigerant is subcooled by 10°F?

17. When you install an evaporative condenser, what precautions can you take to retard sound transmitted through structural supports?

18. What can be done to help maintain constant head pressure?

19. What happens if water piping sizes are too small?

20. Where should unions and/or flanges be located in water piping installations?

21. In a cooling tower, *approach* is the difference between the temperature of the _____ and the temperature of the _____.

22. Name four advantages that cooling towers have over evaporative condensers.

REVIEW QUESTIONS

23. An evaporative condenser removes heat directly from the _____, but a cooling tower removes heat from _____.

LESSON 9

Water Treatment (Part 1)

WHY IS WATER TREATMENT NECESSARY?

Fouling, scale, and corrosion on the water side of refrigerant-condensing equipment can drastically reduce the efficiency of a refrigeration system. Such equipment includes water-cooled condensers, evaporative condensers, and cooling towers. If not dealt with effectively, severe damage can result. Operation of equipment over long periods of time with these conditions present can be far more costly than a sound treatment and preventive maintenance program.

All water, regardless of its source, contains various amounts of minerals. Even rainwater is not absolutely pure. As it falls to earth, rain picks up both gases and solids. These include oxygen, carbon dioxide, industrial gases, dust, and even bacteria.

As far as most municipalities are concerned, water that is sanitary is considered "pure." But this classification means only that the water is free from excessive quantities of bacteria and chemicals and will not cause disease. Mineral salts and other substances that do not affect sanitary conditions may *not* be removed by water treatment plants. Mineral salts, however, *are* objectionable for many other water uses. One such use is in refrigeration system applications. Water that may be fine for human consumption is not always acceptable for use in refrigeration equipment.

Water is used in refrigeration and air conditioning systems primarily to remove heat. Typical applications include:

- once-through condensers

- open recirculating cooling systems that use cooling towers

- evaporative condensers

- chilled water systems

- air washers.

In evaporative condensers, once-through systems, and cooling towers, water absorbs heat from the refrigerant. It is then either wasted or cooled by partial evaporation in air. Knowing about impurities in water used in these systems will help you predict problems and find ways to prevent them.

These problem-causing impurities (fouling, scaling, and corrosion) have at least five sources. One is the earth's atmosphere. Water falling through air, either as rain or in a cooling tower, picks up dust as well as carbon dioxide and oxygen. Similarly, man-made atmospheric gases affect water purity. Decaying plants also are a source of water impurity, producing carbon dioxide. Carbon dioxide is an indirect cause of some refrigerant system water-side problems. Plant decay by-products also provide a nutrient for slime growth.

These three contamination sources make it possible for water to pick up more impurities from a fourth source—minerals. Many minerals make up the earth's subsurface soil. They are made much more soluble by the presence of impurities from the first three sources. Industrial and municipal wastes are a fifth major source of water impurities. Municipal waste affects bacteria count, which is of concern to health officials. This waste also adds to the corrosive nature of water, and indirectly causes a higher-than-normal mineral count.

BASIC CAUSES OF METAL CORROSION

A major source of trouble is corrosion. There are five basic causes of corrosion:

- *Acidity*. The formation of acid can cause general corrosion in many parts of water-side equipment.

- *Oxygen*. Oxygen exists throughout the system, but is less troublesome than acidity.

- *Galvanic action.* Galvanic action takes place when dissimilar metals come in contact with one another.

- *Biological organisms.* Some types of slime living in dark places can eat or digest metal.

- *Impingement.* This refers to the hitting and wearing away of pipe walls by entrained gases, solid particles, or the liquid itself as it travels at high speeds. Curves in pipes and pump impellers are particularly affected by this action.

One of the most universal kinds of trouble is scaling. *Scale* is caused by reduced stability and solubility of mineral impurities. These mineral salts may be divided into three major categories:

- Hardness salts, composed of calcium, magnesium carbonate, and calcium sulfate, produce most common scale.

- Iron compounds also cause scale, often called *rust*. It looks like true rust or corroded iron. Causes and effects of these two compounds are quite different, as you will see later.

- Silica complexes are the third category of mineral scales. Scale composed of silica is very dense, and is a much harder substance than other scales.

Fouling is caused by debris coming from air and water, plant growth, and human negligence. The blanket of sludge that forms allows corrosion by preventing treatment chemicals from reaching and protecting metal surfaces. Silt also collects in condenser tubes. It may completely stop water flow or reduce it so that efficiency is drastically reduced. Foulants can clog suction strainers ahead of circulation pumps and reduce water flow.

Algae and slime come from air or supply water. Algae, a plant that requires sunlight to grow, prefers a temperature between 40 and 80°F. It can be a problem with evaporative condensers and cooling towers located outdoors. Algae feeds on minerals in water and even some treatment chemicals. Live and dead algae can break loose and be carried through the system. It will lodge in some section with reduced flow. This added restriction cuts down on water flow. Dense growths of algae on tower slats may reduce air flow through towers. This reduces the desired cooling effect. Slime results from bacteria. It prefers darkness and thrives in temperatures ranging from 32 to 120°F. Bacteria can grow in condenser tubes, and feed on minerals in water, dead algae, and even metals.

RAC

CORROSION ANALYSIS

At this point, it is important to analyze the causes of corrosion in more detail. *Acidity* is introduced into a system with feed water and water in a tower washing industrial gases out of the air. Acidity causes a generalized eating or dissolving of the metallic components of equipment. But what is acidity?

When some materials are dissolved in water, the molecules retain their identity. Sugar (represented as $C_{12}H_{22}O_{11}$) is an example. Other chemicals, such as common table salt (NaCl) break apart when they dissolve. These smaller parts are called *ions*. In discussions of acidity, two ions are of particular interest. They are hydrogen ions (H+) and hydroxyl ions (OH–). In reality, these ions rarely exist in a pure state. But for analysis purposes, assume that you have a bucket of hydrogen ions and a bucket of hydroxyl ions. Combine the two, and the result is a compound represented by the formula HOH, or H_2O. As you know, this is commonly referred to as water. Although water is composed of two ions, they tend to stay attached once they are united.

Sodium hydroxide (NaOH) combined with an equal amount of hydrogen chloride (HCl) produces water. The hydrogen ion from hydrogen chloride and the hydroxyl ion from sodium hydroxide join to form water. The other two ions, Na+ (sodium) and Cl– (chloride), remain separated. Combine an excess amount of NaOH with HCl and the hydrogen ions will be used up in forming water. Surplus hydroxyl ions continue to retain their identity. This solution now meets the chemist's definition of an *alkaline*, or *basic* material. That is, it contains free hydroxyl ions. If we again combine NaOH and HCl, but use an excess amount of HCl, the solution will contain free hydrogen ions. Now it is known as an *acid* or *acidic* solution.

Defining pH

Chemists define *pH* as the logarithm of the reciprocal of the hydrogen ion concentration. For the purpose of this Lesson, you can think of pH as a measure of excess or deficiency of hydrogen ions. A constant relationship exists between hydrogen ions and hydroxyl ions when their presence is measured in a certain way. The concentration of hydrogen ions plus that of hydroxyl ions always equals 14. A scale or unit of measure of pH—that is, hydrogen ion excess or deficiency—runs from 0 to 14. In the previous bucket example, equal amounts of hydrogen ions and hydroxyl ions were combined. Pure water was formed. No ions were left floating free. In other words, pure water has neither an excess nor a deficiency of hydrogen ions. The pH of pure water should be located midway on the scale of 0 to 14, or at pH 7. In other words, pH 7 indicates *neutral* conditions. At pH 7, there is neither an excess nor a deficiency of hydrogen ions.

LESSON 9

This establishes a very important point. Remember that concentrations of hydrogen ion and hydroxyl ion are related. Their sum is always equal to 14. So, the greater the excess of hydrogen ions—that is, the more acidic the solution—the lower the pH value. Conversely, lower hydrogen ion content increases pH value. A high pH indicates an excess of hydroxyl ions or a deficiency of hydrogen ions. A low pH indicates an excess of hydrogen ions and a deficiency of hydroxyl ions.

The chemist's definition of pH certainly is accurate and valid. But it is also quite complicated. There is really no simple method of showing the hydrogen ion concentration relationship between one pH value and another. As noted previously, the whole scheme is based on logarithms. Therefore, each pH level or value is related to adjacent levels by a factor of 10. For example, look at pH 4 and pH 5. Hydrogen ion concentration at pH 4 is 10 times greater than at pH 5. In the other direction, hydrogen ion concentration at pH 6 is one-tenth of that at pH 5. Hydrogen ion concentration at pH 4 is 100 times greater than at pH 6. This same relationship exists throughout the whole pH scale.

Methods of determining pH

One method of determining pH uses paper strips impregnated with a dye. These paper strips are either red or blue. They are called *litmus paper*. Red litmus will turn blue if dipped into a basic solution—that is, a solution with pH above 7. Blue litmus will turn red in an acid solution—a solution with pH below 7. This method tells you only if a solution is acidic or basic. It does not give any indication of *degree* of acidity or basicity.

A second method also uses paper strips impregnated with different dyes. These strips are called *pH test papers*. They tell you not only if a solution is acidic or basic, but also indicate the specific pH. When the paper is immersed in a solution, it changes color. Comparing it with a color chart indicates the pH of the solution.

A third method also uses a dye. It is the pH indicator chemical method. A small amount of dye solution is added to water, and color change indicates pH. Such solutions are also used to show when pH has been adjusted to a desired level. This is most often used in chemical laboratories in a procedure called *titration*. Dyes are also added to water samples. The color that develops is compared with color standards in a test kit.

The fourth and last method of determining pH is with a meter. It measures pH electrically and without dyes. A glass probe is placed in a solution and pH value is shown on the meter dial.

CORROSIVES

Acids

Aggressive or strong *acids* are found around most industrial areas. They include sulfuric, hydrochloric, and nitric acids. These acids are formed when certain industrial waste gases are washed out of the atmosphere by water in a cooling tower. Any of these acids will cause a drop in circulating water pH. Carbon dioxide dissolved in water forms carbonic acid. It is less aggressive than those noted above. But because it is always present, its corrosive effects can cause serious damage to equipment.

Oxygen

Corrosion by *oxygen* is another widespread problem. Spraying water into air allows it to pick up oxygen and carry it into the system. Oxygen reacts with any parts of equipment containing iron to form iron oxide, a porous material. Flaking or blistering of oxidized metal allows corrosion of the freshly exposed metal to occur. Blistering also restricts water flow and reduces heat transfer—and it is glaring evidence that destructive corrosion has taken place.

Reaction rates between oxygen and iron increase rapidly as temperatures are raised. The most severe corrosion takes place in hot areas of equipment with iron parts. Oxygen also affects copper and zinc, which forms the outer coating of galvanized material. Its damage is much less severe, however. Oxidation of zinc and copper forms an inert metal oxide. It sets up a protective film between metal and attacking oxygen.

Galvanic action

Galvanic action is the third cause of corrosion. Galvanic corrosion is basically a reaction between two different metals in electrical contact. The reaction is both electrical and chemical in nature. Galvanic action requires three conditions:

- two dissimilar metals (metals with different electrochemical properties)

- an *electrolyte* (a solution through which an electric current can flow)

- an electron path to connect the two metals.

Many different metals are used in industry to fabricate air conditioning or refrigeration systems. Copper and iron, for example, are dissimilar metals. Add a solution containing ions, and you have an electrolyte. Until the two metals come into contact, no galvanic action takes place. Add a coupling, and you have brought two dissimilar metals into contact and set up an electron path. This allows electrons to pass from copper to iron. As current leaves the iron and re-enters the solution to return to the copper, corrosion of iron takes place. Copper-to-iron connections are common in cooling systems.

To better understand dissimilar metals, refer to Table 9-1. These metals are arranged in what is known as the *galvanic series*. One end of this series is known as the *anodic* or *corroded* end. The other is referred to as the *cathodic* or *protected* end.

Corrosion tendencies

Greater separation of metals in the galvanic series increases the tendency to corrode. For example, if platinum were joined with magnesium, the platinum would be protected and the magnesium would corrode. Since they are so far apart on the scale, corrosion would be rapid. The relative positions of iron and copper in the series shows that, if joined, the iron would corrode. Corrosion would be to a lesser degree than the magnesium in the previous example, but it would be extensive enough to be very damaging. If copper and silver were joined, it is the copper that would corrode. The degree of corrosion is determined by the relative position of metals in the galvanic series. Improperly grounded electrical equipment or poor insulation can also start or accelerate galvanic action.

Anodic (corroded end)

Magnesium
Magnesium alloys
Zinc
Aluminum
Mild steels
Alloy steels
Wrought iron
Cast iron
Soft solders
Lead
Tin
Brass
Copper
Bronze
Copper-nickel alloys
Nickel
Silver
Gold
Platinum

Cathodic (protected end)

TABLE 9-1. *The galvanic series*

Corrosive organisms

Biological organisms represent another cause of corrosion. These include slime, algae, and fungi. Slimes like to live in dark places. They thrive in complete absence of light. Some slimes cling to pipes and will actually digest iron. This localized attack forms small pits. Over time, they will become holes through pipe walls. Other slimes live on mineral impurities, especially sulfates in water. They give off hydrogen sulfide gas, which forms weak hydrosulfuric acid. (Don't confuse this with strong sulfuric acid.) This acid slowly but steadily deteriorates pipes and other metal parts of the system. Slime and algae release oxygen into water. Small oxygen bubbles form and cling to pipes. This oxygen may act the same as a dissimilar metal and cause corrosion by galvanic action. Such action is commonly called *oxygen cell* corrosion.

Wood deterioration

Destruction is not limited to metal equipment. Wood components of cooling towers can also deteriorate. Wood is composed mainly of cellulose fibers. They are held together by a substance called *lignin*. Wood relies on these materials for strength. Wood fibers are subject to attack and deterioration. Fungi attack the cellulose fibers of wood. The result is either brown or white rot. *Brown* rot, as the name implies, results in darkening and rotting of wood. *White* rot is just as destructive. It results in a shredding action. Towers subject to rotting may actually collapse under their own weight.

Lignin is dissolved not by biological organisms, but by very alkaline water. The effect on the tower is similar to that of fungi. But in this case, the fibers that are left look like shredded rope.

Other corrosive elements

Impingement is also a cause or type of corrosion. It is the effect on the walls of pipes or other metal parts by matter moving at high speeds. A sandblasting-like action causes pipes to be worn or eaten away. High-speed particles can be gas bubbles or solids entrained in a high-velocity fluid stream. In some instances, high-velocity fluid itself may cause a weakening action.

Scale

Scale is the most prevalent problem of all. It is composed of hardness salts, iron compounds, and silica complexes. Scale formations reduce water flow and heat transfer. Scale is primarily calcium and magnesium carbonate, but may also form as calcium sulfate, silica complexes, and ferric oxide. These materials enter systems dissolved in water. Due to certain chemical and physical forces, they become insoluble and fall out of solution. In doing so, scale and/or sludge is formed. Few things in nature are pure, and most scales are a mixture of these chemical compounds.

Mineral insolubility

An experiment with cane sugar and a gallon of water demonstrates how minerals become insoluble. At 90°F, 18.6 lb of cane sugar will dissolve in one gallon of water. If heated to 120°F, 21.6 lb of sugar will dissolve in the same amount of water. A chemist would plot such values at various temperature readings on a graph. A line connecting these points would be a solubility curve for cane sugar.

There are other materials that have an opposite reaction to temperature. With these kinds of material, an increase in temperature *lowers* solubility. This is known as *inverse* solubility. There are still other materials (gravel, for instance) that are considered insoluble. But even gravel is soluble to a slight degree. Most of the materials that form scale have solubilities similar to gravel. With material of this sort, solubilities are very small. It is difficult to use conventional units of

LESSON 9

measure for them. Instead, the industry has adopted much smaller units—namely, *parts per million*.

Units of measure

Parts per million (abbreviated ppm) may at first seem confusing. Actually, it is quite similar to a percentage. It is the number of pounds, ounces, tons, etc., dissolved in one million corresponding weight units of solution. For example, assume that a water sample has a hardness of 38 ppm. This means that the water has 38 parts of hardness for every one million parts of solution. Without the parts per million system, this would be written 0.000038 parts in one part of water. Grains per gallon (abbreviated gpg) is another measure of concentration. In relation to ppm, one grain per gallon equals 17.1 parts per million. There is another handy thing to remember. One pound of material dissolved in 1000 gallons of water makes a solution of 120 ppm. This relationship is useful in making up solutions or calculating chemical feed rates.

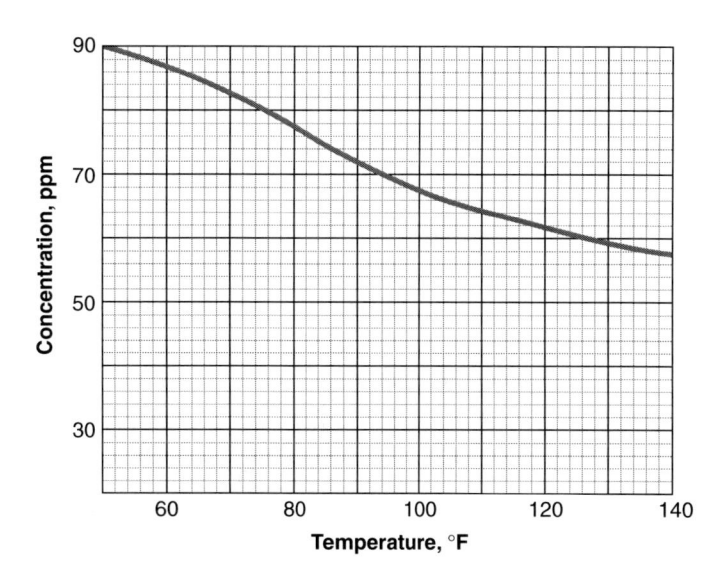

FIGURE 9-1. *Solubility of calcium carbonate in water*

Solubility

The graph in Figure 9-1 shows the solubility of calcium carbonate in water at various temperatures. Note that, at best, calcium carbonate is only slightly soluble. As temperature rises, the amount of material remaining in solution drops off rapidly. Figure 9-2 is a graph that shows the effect of temperature on the solubility of calcium sulfate. Unlike calcium carbonate, it increases in solubility up to about 100°F. But as temperature is increased further, solubility drops off rapidly.

There are several factors that cause this change. First, there is heat. Heat affects the stability of bicarbonates. Increasing temperatures reduce their stability. The resulting breakdown causes formation of carbonates. Because of their low solubility, these become scale. In addition to heat, alkalinity affects the stability of bicarbonates. Alkalinity is a measure of the amount of carbonates, bicarbonates, and/or hydroxides

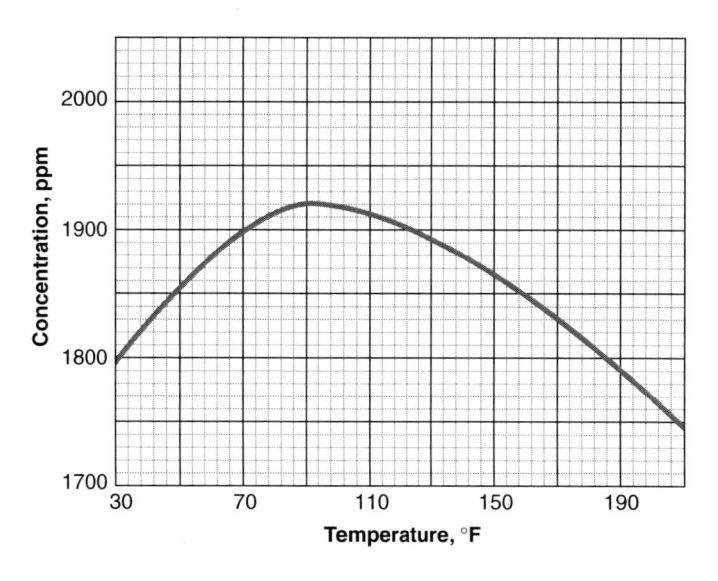

FIGURE 9-2. *Solubility of calcium sulfate in water*

present in water. It is expressed as equivalent parts per million of calcium carbonate. All of these chemicals are alkaline or basic in nature. Calcium bicarbonate reacts with alkaline materials to form less soluble calcium carbonate. Mechanisms differ, but the result of the effects of heat or the reaction between calcium bicarbonate and alkaline material is the same—the formation of calcium carbonate.

What if bicarbonates are converted to carbonates? Consider a typical 50-ton system operating without bleed or treatment. It uses feed water with 275 ppm calcium bicarbonate. Bicarbonate in the presence of heat or alkalinity will break down to form 170 ppm of calcium carbonate. It releases carbon dioxide and water in the process. The solubility curve of calcium carbonate, graphed in Figure 9-1, shows that at 90°F only 70 ppm would stay in solution. What about the remaining 100 ppm? It is forced out of solution and forms scale or sludge. This would amount to about eight ounces of calcium carbonate in the water originally contained in a 50-ton system.

This system is constantly evaporating water into the air and must take on new feed water. Feed water brings with it more bicarbonates. They, in turn, break down to carbonate and deposit as scale or form sludge. In a one-month period, potential scale and/or sludge formed in the system would equal 90 lb of limestone. This is quite a lot of scale. It eventually must be removed chemically or mechanically. When present, it reduces equipment efficiency and increases operating costs.

The pH affects the solubility of carbonates in much the same way as heat does. If pH is lowered (the solution is made more acid), solubility increases. If the solution becomes more basic (pH is increased), solubility is lowered.

Solids

Total dissolved solids also affect solubility. Water can hold many solids in solution. But as more solids are dissolved, the least soluble material will come out of solution and form sludge or scale.

Just as heat and pH affect scale formation, so do dissolved solids. When total dissolved solids content is low, there is room for more carbonates. This means that there is less tendency to form scale. When the total dissolved solids content is high, more carbonates come out of solution. Scale is formed at a faster rate.

Carbonate scale is the most prevalent. Yet it presents the least problem from a chemical cleaning standpoint. Remember, carbonates come into systems as soluble bicarbonates and are converted to carbonates.

Sulfates

Sulfates, on the other hand, enter systems as sulfates. They do not undergo any chemical changes. Solubility of calcium sulfate increases rapidly as temperature is increased. This occurs up to at least 90°F. Then the rate of solubility increase tapers off until about 100°F is reached. At this point, with increasing temperature, calcium sulfate becomes less soluble at a very rapid rate.

The importance of condensing temperature

At this point, you might say, "No problem! Temperatures in my towers average 90°F. Calcium sulfate will remain soluble and won't give me any trouble." But what about temperatures in the condenser unit? Here, hot gas temperatures may reach 180°F or more. Some calcium sulfate will come out of solution as scale. You may think that water is going through so fast it doesn't have a chance to become this hot. This is not the case. Water in condenser tubes moves faster in the middle than it does along the tube wall. The force of friction between water and metal causes this. Intense heat on the refrigerant side of the tube heats the water film next to the tube wall. It reaches a temperature near that of the hot gas. Assume that water entering the condenser is saturated with calcium sulfate at 90°F. The portion of water adjacent to the tube wall is heated to 180°F. In this case, solubility is exceeded by 100 ppm and scale is formed. Total dissolved solids and pH affect the solubility of calcium sulfate in much the same way as they affected the solubility of calcium carbonate.

Another less troublesome element is magnesium sulfate. Like cane sugar, it increases in solubility no matter how high the temperature. For this reason, magnesium sulfate does not pose a scale problem. Chemically speaking, sulfate scale is much less reactive than carbonate. When sulfate scale forms along with carbonate scale, calcium sulfate acts like cement. Even though a scale consists mostly of carbonate, the sulfate makes it more difficult to remove.

SILICA SCALE

Another problem scale is *silica*. Although quite soluble, silicates form an even harder cement when deposited with other scales. The actual mechanics of silica scale formation are not fully understood. It is known that total dissolved solids and pH affect the rate of calcium silicate scale formation, just as they affect the formation of calcium carbonate and sulfate scales. Silica dioxide is the material from which glass is made. Mineral scale with moderate amounts of silica is very hard to dissolve. It is like trying to dissolve glass in water or acid. It takes a very strong acid—like hydrofluoric acid, which is used to etch glass—to remove silica scale.

FERRIC OXIDE

Ferric oxide is the last of the common scales. This potential scale comes into a system in the form of soluble iron compounds. It is changed into iron scale in two ways, depending on its form in feed water. Water-soluble iron most commonly occurs as a bicarbonate. In some areas, other soluble iron compounds are present. Ferrous bicarbonate, like other bicarbonates, breaks down at higher temperatures. It forms ferric oxide, carbon dioxide, and water. Soluble iron compounds other than bicarbonates combine with water and oxygen to form ferric hydroxide. It then breaks down with heat into ferric oxide and water. Another way in which iron becomes ferric oxide is by the action of a microorganism called *Gallionella*. This bacteria usually consumes iron and oxygen and "spits out" ferric oxide. The ferric oxide then deposits as iron scale.

GEOGRAPHICAL LOCATION

Water treatment problems differ from one geographical region to another. Different parts of the world, because of their geological makeup, are subject to different amounts of impurities. There are maps that show average water hardnesses in various areas. From these maps, you might be able to predict the kinds of problems that will occur—but don't count on it. There are other factors that also affect water conditions. These include soil, seasonal variations in rainfall, the presence of industrial acid-forming gases in the air, industrial waste, and so on.

WATER ANALYSIS

The types of scale or corrosion problems to expect from the use of a particular feed water can be estimated. The best data for such estimates are those from individual water analyses. There are three basic ways to get these analyses. When city water is being used, water departments can supply all of the necessary information. Feed water data can be obtained from analyses made with a portable test kit. Or, a sample can be sent to a testing laboratory, such as the ones maintained by Virginia Chemicals in West Norfolk, Virginia, and in St. Louis, Missouri. Remember that surface water is affected by drought or rainy seasons. Periodic checks should be made during these times. In any event, a feed water analysis should be made at least once a year. This is true even with a deep well water source.

FOULANT REMOVAL

Removal of foulants, corrosion products, and scale is essential for full capacity, low-cost equipment operation. Methods for removing these fluid and heat flow restrictions depend on the nature of scale or foulant. Removing foulants prior to chemical cleaning has major benefits. Most foulants can react with or consume scale remover. To hold down chemical costs, remove as much loose material as possible mechanically before undertaking chemical cleaning.

Sludge deposits in condenser tubes can prevent the flow of cleaning solution to scaled areas. Removing this material allows the scale remover to do a complete cleaning job. Also, cleaning time may be shortened because of immediate contact between scale remover and scale. Fouling material is composed of loose or semi-packed sludge and debris. This material may be removed mechanically by flushing, scraping, and dumping the sump. It may also be removed with high-pressure water streams, or by rodding and brushing condenser tubes. It is more economical to remove loose material this way than with chemicals.

Remove large masses of algae or slime before chemical cleaning whenever possible. Scale remover kills these algae and slime colonies. It causes them to break up and be carried through the system by the water flow. These pieces of dead organic material can easily lodge in restricted flow areas such as condenser tubes, valves, or pump suction screens. They then prevent cleaning solution from reaching scaled areas.

SCALE IDENTIFICATION

Scale removal depends on the chemical reaction between scale and cleaning chemical. Scale identification is important. Of the four most common scales, only carbonate is highly reactive with cleaning chemicals generally regarded as safe for use in cooling equipment. The other scales require a pretreatment that makes them more reactive. This pretreatment depends on the type of scale to be removed. Trying to remove a problem scale without proper pretreatment is like throwing money down the drain.

Scale is identified in one of three ways:

- experience

- field tests

- laboratory analysis.

With the exception of iron scale, which is orange, it is very difficult to identify scale by appearance. Experience is gained by cleaning systems in a given area over a long period of time. Pretreatment procedures and the amount of scale remover required for the type of scale most often found becomes common knowledge. Unless radical changes in feed water quality occur, the type of scale remains fairly constant. Experience is further developed by using the other two methods of scale identification.

FIELD TESTING

Field tests are quite simple to perform. They determine the reactivity of scale with the cleaning chemical. Prepare a small sample of cleaning solution. Add one tablespoon of liquid scale remover, or one teaspoon of solid scale remover, to a half pint (one cup) of water. Then drop a small piece of scale into the cleaning solution. The reaction rate usually will determine the type of scale. The reaction between scale remover and carbonate scale is vigorous bubbling. The scale eventually dissolves or disintegrates. If the scale sample is hard or flinty, and there is little or no bubbling in the acid solution, apply heat. Sulfate scale will dissolve at 140°F. The small-scale sample should be consumed in about one hour. If the scale sample has a high percentage of silica, there will be little or no reaction. Iron scale is easily identified by appearance. Testing with a clean solution usually is not required.

This identification procedure is quite elementary, and combinations of all types of scale are often encountered. Obviously, more precise methods may be required. Such methods are most easily carried out in a laboratory. Most manufacturers provide this service to users of their scale removers. Scale samples that cannot be identified in the field may be mailed to these laboratories. Here a complete breakdown and analysis of the problem scale will be performed. Detailed cleaning recommendations will be returned to the sender.

Most scales are predominantly carbonate. However, they also contain varying amounts of sulfate, iron, or silica. Calculate the amount of scale remover required for cleaning specifically for the type of scale present. The presence of sulfate, iron, or silica also affects other procedures that are part of the total cleaning operation. These will be covered later in this Lesson.

CHEMICAL REACTIONS

Chemical reactions take place between compounds in solution. Calcium carbonate is only slightly soluble in water. The presence of hydrogen ions increases solubility of calcium carbonate. This solubility increases substantially as the pH is lowered. For this reason, scale remover that has a low pH is added, but not only to react with scale. It is added also to hold the pH at a fairly low level, where the rate of dissolution of scale is improved.

The total quantity of scale remover required is dependent on two basic factors:

- the water volume of the system to be cleaned

- the weight of the scale to be removed.

The amount of scale remover required to adjust the pH to the desired low level depends on the amount of water in the system. The pH or hydrogen ion concentration is a function of solution volume, so you must compute—or at least accurately estimate—the system's total water capacity.

COMPUTING WATER VOLUME

What is the system's total water volume? It is the volume of the sump and/or holding tank plus the volume of water contained in the pipes and condenser. Sumps and holding tanks come in a variety of sizes and shapes. They generally can be divided into two categories—rectangular and cylindrical.

Water volume in rectangular tanks is calculated as follows:

length × width × height of water × 7½ gallons per cubic foot

If the tank is round:

$\pi \times r^2 \times$ height of water × 7½ gallons per cubic foot

Note: All linear measurements are expressed in feet.

Let's work out a sample problem using this equation. Assume the existence of a sump that is 5 ft long and 4 ft wide, with a water depth of 6 in., or 0.5 ft. Using the equation above for a rectangular tank, the result is:

5 × 4 × 0.5 × 7.5 = 75 gallons

It is important for all of the numbers in this equation to be in feet. It is easy to go astray in determining water depth. If 6 in. had been used in this example, rather than the proper 0.5 ft, the answer would have been 900 gallons rather than the correct 75 gallons.

Similarly, the volume of water in cylindrical tanks is calculated as follows. Measure the diameter of the tank and the depth of water in feet. Use the equation above for a round tank. The answer will give you water volume in gallons. For example, let's say that a hypothetical tank has a diameter of 3 ft and a water depth of 3 ft. You know that a tank with a 3-ft diameter has a 1.5-ft radius. Apply the equation:

$$\pi \times 1.5^2 \times 3 \times 7.5 = 159 \text{ gallons}$$

Here again, it is important for all of the measurements to be in feet or fractions thereof. Cylindrical tanks usually are used as indoor holding tanks. Some installations may require using both of these calculations.

In many installations, water in pipes is a large portion of the total volume in the system. Sump sizes and pipe diameters usually increase with system capacity. A simple method of estimating the volume of water in pipes has been devised, as follows:

- **Step 1.** Estimate the total footage of pipe from tower to condenser and return. (Let's use 200 ft as an example.)

- **Step 2.** Divide this figure by 50. (In our example, 200 ÷ 50 = 4.)

- **Step 3.** Divide the sump volume—including holding tank, if one exists—by 10. (Assume a sump volume of 75 gallons, so 75 ÷ 10 = 7.5.)

- **Step 4.** Multiply the results of Steps 2 and 3 to obtain the total pipe volume. (In our example, 4 × 7.5 = 30.)

The system's total volume, then, equals this figure added to sump value—i.e., 30 gallons plus 75 gallons equals 105 gallons. You may have noticed that the water in the condenser coils has not yet been taken into account. In most cases, the amount of water in the condenser can be overlooked. It is a very small fraction of the system's total water capacity.

Figures obtained from the Trane Corporation indicate that water volume in an absorption system can be estimated very closely by dividing the machine-rated tonnage by 2 and adding 30. The result is the number of gallons of water contained in the two condensers.

Many refrigeration service technicians prefer to estimate the amount of water in a system using the following approximations:

- for evaporative condenser systems—2 to 3 gallons per ton

- for shell-and-tube condenser systems—5 to 10 gallons per ton (cooling towers).

Good judgment based on past experience should be exercised when using this method of determining water volume.

LESSON 9

DETERMINING SCALE REMOVER REQUIREMENTS

Once you know the water volume, you can determine the quantity of scale remover required to adjust the pH to the desired level. This will, of course, depend on the type of scale to be removed. The amount is in addition to the scale remover that will be consumed by the scale. When cleaning a system, add to the water the scale remover needed to adjust the pH to the desired level. As it reacts with scale, hydrogen ions are consumed and the pH slowly rises. Since the best reaction rate occurs at the lower pH, add more scale remover to replace that which has reacted with scale.

pH TESTING

Scale remover solution strength may be checked in several ways, including the use of:

- test papers

- dye indicators

- pH test kits.

Test papers or acid test strips are packed with many types of scale remover. These colored paper strips change color when dipped into acid solutions with a certain pH. The dye in these strips is chosen so that color change occurs at the pH desired for cleaning.

Some scale removers have a dye already mixed with the active ingredients. As the pH rises, the dye in the cleaning solution changes color. This shows a need for more scale remover. These test kits can determine the pH of scale remover solution at any stage of the cleaning operation. Check solution strength repeatedly throughout the cleaning operation to be sure that proper strength is maintained. This makes it possible for scale removal reaction to take place, and also decreases the time required.

REACTION RATES

As previously noted, there is a relationship between reaction rate and scale remover concentration. You might reason that if a low pH improves the reaction rate of scale removal, why not double the amount of scale remover? It might seem that taking such an action would cut cleaning time in half. However, this is not the case. Adding an extra gallon or two actually would be like pouring money down the drain.

However, there is a way to reduce cleaning time with no increase in material cost. The type of chemical reactions that dissolve mineral scales in acid solutions proceed faster with the addition of heat. An increase of 18°F in water temperature will, under ideal conditions, cut reaction time in half.

Note the phrase "under ideal conditions." If the scale is in a very fine powdered form and can be mixed well with scale remover solution, the reaction will be much faster. But the scale remover is able to react only with the surface of the scale. It must dissolve this outer layer before it can get to fresh scale. Because less than ideal conditions exist, it is difficult to double the reaction rate. Still, cleaning time can be reduced. The money saved by buying fewer cleaning chemicals more than pays for the few minutes required to raise the temperature.

You can raise temperature in several different ways, all of which reduce the cooling effect of the tower during cleaning:

- shut off the tower fan

- remove the spray nozzles

- wrap the side or sides of the tower facing the wind with canvas or a plastic sheet to reduce the air flow.

TYPES OF SCALE REMOVERS

Up to this point, scale removers have been referred to in a very general or broad sense. There are many brands and physical forms of scale removers. Basically, though, there are two forms—solid and liquid.

A solid scale remover is primarily composed of sulfamic acid. This type offers several advantages that will be covered in subsequent paragraphs. Two hydrochloric acid formulations are also available in liquid form. They differ only in acid strength. The first, referred to as *regular* formulation, is a scale remover that has been in use for the past several years. After extensive research, a *concentrated* liquid scale remover has been introduced more recently. It provides the same degree of equipment safety as with products using regular formulation. This concentrated material offers an appreciable increase in scale removal capacity.

TYPE SELECTION IS IMPORTANT

To select the proper type of scale remover for a particular need, take a few minutes to examine the products in detail. Consider these points:

- storage space and precautions

- ease of handling

- application preparation

- personnel and equipment safety

- cost.

First, consider storage. In most service establishments and wholesalers' storerooms, storage space is at a premium. The solid scale remover required to remove 50 lb of carbonate scale takes up only 1.5 cubic feet (ft^3). The regular liquid formulation requires 3.7 ft^3. The concentrated material takes up 2.6 ft^3. In this regard, the importance of which may be debatable, solid scale remover wins hands down. However, there is another facet of the storage picture that is worth considering.

Quite often, due to carelessness or just unfortunate circumstances, scale remover packages are punctured or ruptured. With a liquid, this can be critical from a product loss standpoint. With acids, damage to property also can occur. By comparison, if a package containing the solid product is damaged, a small quantity of dry crystalline material may be lost. If there is no moisture present, the powder is easily swept up and no further damage can or will occur.

Handling is another important consideration. "Handling" means getting the scale remover on the truck or to the job. How much weight has to be carried? How many trips will it take? It takes 100 lb of solid scale remover to remove 50 lb of carbonate scale. In the package, this weighs about 108 lb. A husky man might handle this amount in one trip. The liquid regular and concentrated materials require 18 and 13 gallons, respectively. This amounts to 178 or 127 lb, depending on product selection. Packed in 5-gallon containers, a minimum of two trips will be required.

Next, consider application preparation. Solid scale remover must be dissolved before it can be used. The crystals, if allowed to get into the pump, could cause serious damage to shaft seals or packing. Liquids are ready to use and are best applied by pouring into the sump close to pump suction.

BASIC SAFETY PRECAUTIONS

Personnel safety is of the utmost importance. Both liquid formulations are made from hydrochloric acid, which has a tendency to fume. Fumes appear as wisps of white smoke when they first leave the containers. These fumes are irritating to the nose and eyes in high concentrations. Since hydrogen chloride fumes are corrosive, they can cause equipment damage when no ventilation is available. For this reason, both liquid products should be used outdoors. If used inside, there must be adequate ventilation. The use of the solid sulfamic acid type of scale remover for all indoor applications is strongly recommended. This is especially true in areas where the equipment to be cleaned is located in confined spaces, with little or no ventilation. There are no fumes with solid scale remover.

Liquids are easily splashed when being handled. This is a constant risk when you use any liquid scale removers. Solid material can be handled with comparative safety until it is dissolved and ready to use.

Hydrochloric acid should never be used with stainless steel. Chlorides from any source, even common table salt, can cause what is called *chloride stress cracking*. This susceptibility of stainless steel to attack by chlorides is one of its few weaknesses. Sulfamic acid again is recommended. There are no chlorides to prevent its use on stainless steel, no fumes, and, in addition, solid scale remover is safer for use with aluminum.

It is important to pursue the subject of equipment safety further. Liquid scale removers are essentially hydrochloric acid. Solid products are usually sulfamic acid. As far as actual scale removal is concerned, it's the acid component of scale remover that really does the work. Acids, including hydrochloric, are very aggressive chemicals. They cannot "tell the difference" between the scale to be removed and various metal parts of the equipment. Industrial-grade hydrochloric acid, commonly called *muriatic acid*, is very effective as a cleaning chemical. Muriatic acid, however, is just as effective when it attacks metal parts of the system. For this reason, straight uninhibited acids should not be used for system cleaning. Cleaning formulations usually contain inhibitors that are blended with the acids. This results in a powerful but safe cleaning chemical.

Good inhibitors should protect all of these metals:

- copper
- bronze
- brass
- iron
- steel
- zinc
- tin
- lead
- silver
- aluminum.

PRETREATMENT

Carbonate scale is by far the most common scale. It would be logical to start with it as the primary target. As previously indicated, carbonate scale is quite reactive and no pretreatment is necessary.

Sulfate scale, however, is less reactive and does require pretreatment. Sodium carbonate (commonly called *soda ash*) or sodium bicarbonate (baking soda) are pretreatment chemicals for sulfate scale. Either may be used. The amount depends on the total volume of water in the system. One-half pound of soda ash or one pound of baking soda should be added for each gallon of water. Both chemicals are relatively inexpensive. They are available at any industrial chemical supply house. In the case of sodium bicarbonate, it may be found in any grocery store.

This pretreatment solution should be circulated for at least eight to 12 hours. Best results are obtained with a 24-hour pretreatment period. The bleed or blowdown line should be closed during this time to prevent loss of pretreatment chemicals. Normal operating temperatures should be maintained. The system's circulating pump should remain in operation during this entire period. Following pretreatment, drain the entire system, but rinse and flush tower slats and sump only. During the pretreatment period, soda ash or bicarbonate will impregnate the scale. Its presence is essential for good cleaning action. That is why the scaled portion of equipment should not be flushed or rinsed.

Iron scale, although relatively unreactive, will respond to other than normal cleaning conditions. It does not require a pretreatment. Silica scale, or scale mixtures containing a high percentage of silica, are real troublemakers in the scale family. They not only require extreme cleaning conditions, but also a thorough pretreatment. Both soda ash and lye are used as pretreatment chemicals. Soda ash should be added at the rate of one pound per gallon of water in the system. Lye is added at the rate of one pound per 100 gallons of water. Lye must be handled with caution. It can cause severe chemical burns. This pretreatment solution is circulated for 24 to 36 hours at 110°F. The draining and rinsing procedure is the same as that outlined for sulfate scale.

Another treatment procedure does not apply to a true scale. An oil or grease film on scale can seriously deter scale removal reaction. This film may come from kitchen exhausts drawn into the tower by its fan. Oil or grease, if carried through the system, will coat the scale. The film keeps scale remover from reaching scale. Low-foaming laundry detergents in concentrations of 1½ pounds for each 100 gallons of water will remove this barrier. Circulate detergent solution for 15 to 20 minutes at normal operating temperatures to destroy the film and make sure that excessive foaming does not occur. The detergent will not interfere with the cleaning operation. Scale remover may be added without draining and flushing the system. See Table 9-2 for complete pretreatment procedures.

REACTION RESULTS

Before getting into the actual application of scale remover, it's important to examine the scale removal reactions. For example, this is what takes place when a liquid scale remover is applied to calcium carbonate scale:

$$CaCO_3 + 2HCl \rightarrow CaCl_2 + H_2O + CO_2$$

The products formed as a result of the reactions are of some interest. Calcium chloride ($CaCl_2$), as is true of most chlorides, is quite soluble in water. Once calcium chloride is formed, it is no longer potential scale. Water, or H_2O, is of negligible interest, since the volume formed is very small. The carbon dioxide, or CO_2, is of concern. This is a gas and causes the bubbling referred to during scale identification tests. The release of large amounts of this gas should be expected, especially with calcium carbonate scale. This fizzing or bubbling has a tendency to cause foaming.

Type of scale	Pretreatment chemicals	Quantity[1]	Time[2]	Temperature	Special procedures
Carbonate	None required				
Sulfate	Soda ash or sodium bicarbonate	½ lb/gal 1 lb/gal	24 hr (8 to 12 hr minimum)	Normal operating temperature	Following pretreatment period, drain entire system. Flush tower slats and sump only. Refill system and clean.
Iron	None required				
Silica	Soda ash and lye	1 lb/gal 1 lb/100 gal	24 to 36 hr	110°F	Following pretreatment period, drain entire system. Flush tower slats and sump only. Refill system and clean.
Oil film removal (see "Special procedures")	Low-foaming detergent (such as "Dash")	1½ lb/100 gal	15 to 20 min	Normal operating temperature	Oil or grease films present come from kitchen exhausts drawn into the tower. The film keeps scale remover from reaching the scale. Cleaning may be done without flushing the detergent solution.

[1] Based on total water volume in system during cleaning.
[2] The bleed or blowdown line should be closed during the pretreatment period to prevent the loss of chemical strength.

TABLE 9-2. *Pretreatment procedures*

For this reason, small plastic envelopes of anti-foam liquid are packaged with scale remover. There is one packet for each gallon in the package. This liquid is designed to prevent excessive foam formation. It will not effectively break a blanket of foam once it has formed. If properly used, however, it will prevent the formation of excessive foam. It is important that at least half of all the anti-foam received with scale remover be poured into the sump prior to adding scale remover. Additional supplies of anti-foam are available in pint bottles.

THE TWO-FOLD PURPOSE OF SCALE REMOVERS

It has been noted that scale remover is used for two purposes in the chemical cleaning of scaled systems. First, it adjusts the cleaning solution pH to a low level, where the solubility of the scale is increased. This sets the stage for chemical reaction to take place. Second, it reacts with scale as it dissolves and produces material that is not scale-forming. Remember that the quantity of scale remover that adjusts and maintains the required low pH is in addition to that which actually reacts with scale.

Methods used to determine the amount of scale remover required to lower the pH have been covered in detail. Coverage of the reacting portion of the cleaning chemical is also important for a thorough knowledge of scale removal. In comparing the three types of scale removers, you will find that to remove 50 lb of carbonate scale, it takes 100 lb of solid scale remover, 18 gallons of regular liquid, or 13 gallons of liquid concentrate. Obviously, the greater amount of scale present, the greater the amount of scale remover consumed. In other words, you must be able to estimate the weight of scale present before you can know the weight or volume of scale remover needed for the actual cleaning.

DETERMINING THE AMOUNT OF SCALE

To determine the actual weight of scale in a system is very difficult. The figure is affected by many factors. These include system size, operating load, chemical treatment efficiency, time of operation since last cleaning, cooling water properties, and so on. Impossible? No—it can be done!

Laboratory tests coupled with extensive field experience have produced a method of estimating quantity of scale present. This means that you can also know the amount of scale remover required to effect complete removal. The method involves a visual inspection of scaled surfaces. The inspection should be in the area where the cooling water is hottest. At this point, scale-forming minerals will be least soluble and the scale heaviest. In evaporative condensers, give special attention to the lower levels of condenser tubing. In water tube condenser systems, inspect near the water discharge or in the tubes through which water passes just before leaving the condenser. After making these observations, refer to the scale remover requirements shown in Table 9-3. This will assist you in determining quantity of scale remover required.

Up to this point, you have studied the methods of calculating the total amount of scale remover required, and the methods of readying the system for cleaning—including chemical pretreatment. The following paragraphs will discuss the actual application of scale removers and the cleaning conditions recommended for economical scale removal.

APPLICATION BASICS

Again, start with carbonate scale. Either regular liquid or solid scale remover is recommended for this highly reactive scale. To obtain the solution pH required for chemical reaction, use a starting concentration of one gallon of liquid scale remover for each 15 gallons of water in the system. If solid scale remover is used, 5 lb per 10 gallons is required. Since carbonate scale is quite reactive, auxiliary chemicals are not needed.

Unless the system is very heavily scaled, the cleaning operation should require about two hours. Raising the temperature of cleaning solution is helpful, but not necessary, for good results. The fact that a vigorous reaction takes place and

Thickness of scale layer	Pounds of solid scale remover	Gallons of liquid (regular)	Gallons of liquid (concentrate)
Less than 1/16 in.	15	2.5	1.8
1/16 to 1/8 in.	30	5.0	3.5
1/8 to 1/4 in.	60	10.0	7.0
1/4 in. and over	90	15.0	10.0

The quantities of scale remover indicated in this table are estimated requirements for each 10 tons of system capacity.

Evaporative condensers whose bottom rows of tubes are bridged over—that is, the spaces between tubes are completely filled with scale—will require approximately three times the amount of scale remover indicated in the table for systems that have over 1/4 in. of scale.

Visual observation is the most accurate method of estimating scale remover quantities. However, if the compressor is cutting out on high head, it can be assumed that the system is fairly heavily scaled and has at least 1/8 in. of scale on the heat exchange surfaces.

NOTE: These figures relate to one company's products. Other product requirements may vary, and manufacturers' specifications should be followed.

TABLE 9-3. *Estimated scale remover requirements*

large amounts of carbon dioxide are given off makes it quite probable that excessive foaming will occur. This happens unless ample anti-foam is added to the system prior to the addition of scale remover. Because reaction proceeds at a rapid rate, frequent checks of cleaning solution strength should be made. Fresh scale remover should be added when needed.

Use extreme caution when cleaning a corroded system. Leaks may develop as scale remover dissolves rust scale, which is actually corroded parts of the equipment. It is for this reason that solid scale remover is also used for iron scale removal. The cleaning action of this chemical is gentler. If leaks develop in indoor areas, odor and corrosive or toxic fumes are not a problem. Solid scale remover is added at a rate of 10 lb per 10 gallons of water. *This is the strongest solution that is ever recommended for this cleaning chemical.*

Scale containing a high percentage of silica complexes is the last of the problem scales. This type of scale has much in common with glass and is quite unreactive. Silica scale can be removed only through application of very hazardous chemicals, or by mechanical means. A very low pH is needed to start and sustain reaction. A starting concentration of three gallons of liquid scale remover concentrate per 10 gallons of system volume is recommended.

After the initial dosage, allow reaction to slow down somewhat. This initial reaction is the dissolving of any carbonate scale which may be present. Auxiliary cleaning chemical is added at this time. Either 3½ lb of sodium fluoride or 2½ lb of sodium bifluoride is added for each 100 gallons of cleaning solution. It takes from four to six hours to clean the average system. Cleaning temperature should be held as close to 110 to 120°F as possible.

Sodium bifluoride is extremely toxic and should be handled with care. Fumes and vapors from circulating solution should not be inhaled. The solution should not be allowed to contact the skin or splash into the eyes. Goggles must be worn. Sodium bifluoride can be obtained from local chemical supply houses, and sodium fluoride can be found in feed and seed or farm supply stores. This chemical is commonly used as a rat poison. In acid solutions, it is nearly as hazardous as sodium bifluoride and equal care should be exercised in its use. See Table 9-4 on the next page for complete cleaning procedures.

SAFETY IN APPLICATION

Safety is an all-important concern. A review of the cleaning operation with this in mind is most appropriate. All chemicals—especially acids—should be treated with great respect and handled with care. The use of rubber gloves, acid-proof coveralls, and safety goggles should be seriously considered.

Type of scale	Type of scale remover	Starting concentration[1,3]	Auxiliary chemical and concentration	Approximate time[2]	Temperature[4]	Special attention
Carbonate	Liquid regular	1 gal/15 gal of water	None required	2 hr	Normal operation	Reaction is vigorous. Use ample anti-foam to prevent formation of excessive foam.
	or solid	5 lb/10 gal of water				
Sulfate	Liquid concentrate	2 gal/10 gal of water	None required	2 to 4 hr	100 to 110°F	Keep scale remover concentration high.
Iron	Liquid concentrate	2 gal/10 gal of water	None required with liquid scale remover	4 hr minimum	100 to 110°F	If iron rust is due to corrosion, *beware* of leaks that may develop in pipes, etc., as oxides are dissolved by scale remover. See Sulfate "Special attention."
	or solid	10 lb/10 gal of water	Use 2.5 lb salt (sodium chloride) per 10 gallons of water in system		120°F	
Silica	Liquid concentrate	3 gal/10 gal of water	3.5 lb sodium flouride or 2.5 lb sodium bifluoride per 100 gallons, added *after* scale remover	4 to 6 hr	110 to 120°F	Exercise *extreme* caution when using acid solutions containing sodium bifluoride. This is an aggressive acid solution. *Beware*: sodium fluoride and sodium bifluoride are dangerous poisons.

[1] Based on volume of water to which scale remover is added. Additional scale remover will be required as scale removal reactions proceed.

[2] Dependent on amount (thickness) of scale in system. Close attention should be paid to keep scale remover concentration at recommended level as indicated by scale remover test strips. Most scale removal reactions proceed at a faster rate at elevated temperatures.

[3] Keep bleed or blowdown line closed during cleaning to prevent loss of scale remover.

[4] Chemical reactions proceed at a faster rate at elevated temperatures. Operate system during cleaning. Remove spray nozzles, shut off fan, and/or wrap tower to reduce water evaporation and cooling.

NOTE: Information relates to one manufacturer's products. Other product requirements may vary, and manufacturers' specifications should be followed.

TABLE 9-4. *Cleaning procedures*

Cleaning a system through the tower, although easier and faster than some other methods, presents one unique hazard. Wind drift, even with the tower fan shut off, is possible. Wind drift is composed of tiny droplets of acid. They can burn eyes and skin. They can do a great deal of damage to automobile finishes and buildings.

Should cleaning solution come in contact with any part of your person, wash it off immediately with soap and water. If contact is made with the eyes, flush eyes thoroughly with water and then see a doctor. Forethought and reasonable precaution will prevent grief and expense.

OPERATIONAL KNOWLEDGE IS A NECESSITY

All facets of the cleaning operation must be understood. Let's go through a typical cleaning job, step by step.

Pretreatment should be started the day before cleaning is to be done. In the case of silica scale, pretreatment should take about 36 hours, when possible. Cleaning time estimates given in the tables are for scale remover reaction only. Ample time should be allowed for dumping and flushing the system before and after chemical cleaning. Only the tower sump and slats are flushed and rinsed *after* pretreatment. Any water flushing or mechanical cleaning of pipe lines and condensers should be done *prior* to chemical pretreatment. At this time, remove any large masses of algae that may be present in the sump or distribution pans. If they break loose, they could lodge in distribution holes, spray nozzles, or pump suction screens.

During pretreatment, be sure that the system bleed or blowdown line is closed. This prevents loss of chemicals during the 24- or 36-hour period. Do not allow any undissolved chemicals to be sucked into the pump. Do this by predissolving material in an empty drum or using the sump as a dissolving tank. When the sump is used, make sure that the pump is shut off until all material is dissolved.

CLEANING PREPARATION

Following pretreatment, completely drain the system, and rinse and flush the sump and tower. Refill the system for cleaning. Do not overfill the sump. Excess water requires excess cleaning chemical for pH adjustment. Fill the sump so that the pump suction is barely covered and will not suck air when operating. If higher-than-normal cleaning temperatures are required, shut off the tower fan and operate manually when needed. If spray nozzles are present, remove them and place them in a plastic mesh bag in a corner of the sump. Most of the sludge and small chunks of scale that usually collect in and plug nozzles will be removed during the cleaning of the rest of the system. If necessary, shield the tower from the wind. Make sure that the water bleed line is shut off to conserve cleaning chemicals.

CLEANING PROCEDURES

If solid scale remover is used, predissolve as much as possible in the sump prior to starting the circulating pump—or make up a starting solution in an empty drum. Operate the compressor to generate heat during cleaning. Start the pump and, when liquid scale remover is used, add three or four packets of anti-foam for each five gallons of scale remover. Pour liquid scale remover into the sump as close as possible to the pump suction. Add slowly at first until you can evaluate foam development. The quantity of foam depends on both the reactivity of scale and the amount of scale remover in the system. Continue to add scale remover until the calculated starting concentration has been reached.

Test the strength of the solution using test strips. Solid scale remover has a color indicator incorporated in the formulation, and test strips are not always used. If the scale present is reacting quickly, it is possible that the reaction is proceeding faster than scale remover is being added. More than the initially calculated starting dosage will be required to get the pH down to the desired level. During addition of the starting dosage, check the solution strength with test papers. Stop adding as soon as the required pH is reached. Wait for 15 to 20 minutes, and then recheck. If the test strip indicates a weak solution strength, more scale remover should be added. During waiting periods, monitor the cleaning operation by checking return water temperature and compressor performance.

Several factors will tell you when scale has been removed:

- Good heat transfer is indicated by a satisfactory water temperature differential across the tower.

- Head pressures are reduced to normal.

- Test papers fail to indicate a need for additional scale remover for a period of 20 to 30 minutes.

Most systems that are operating properly (with the tower fan running) will show a temperature differential across the tower of 8 to 10°F. If near normal heat transfer is taking place, but the water flow rate is low due to pump action or pipe line restrictions, the temperature increase of the water will be higher than normal. With a near normal flow rate, but scaled heat exchange surfaces, the water temperature increase will be less than normal, and high head pressures will exist.

Several factors will indicate if chemical reaction has ceased, without removal of the problem:

- Head pressure and water temperature continue at other than normal levels.

- Test papers fail to indicate a need for additional scale remover for extended periods (over 30 minutes).

Either there is an obstruction other than scale in the water lines, or a problem scale exists that did not receive proper pretreatment.

POST CLEANING PROCEDURES

Once the system has been cleaned, spent scale remover must be disposed of. Drain the solution to the sewer. Do *not* drain spent scale remover onto lawns or near plants. This could cause plant damage, just as any other strong salt or acid solution would. Do *not* drain into a septic tank. Thoroughly rinse out the system with at least two fillings of fresh water. Use the unused portion of the anti-foam during the first rinse. Refill the sump with fresh water, replace the spray nozzles, turn on the fan, open the bleed line, and resume normal operation. You can eliminate the second or final rinse by adding one pound of soda ash for each five gallons of water in the system and using a higher-than-normal bleed rate for about 24 hours. When the system is being flushed to remove cleaning solution, do not use the test strips that come with the scale remover to judge the success of the flushing operation. These strips change color at a very low pH. Fresh water, after being circulated through the system for 10 to 20 minutes, should have a pH reasonably close to that of the make-up water. A simple, inexpensive pH test kit should be used to determine this.

REVIEW QUESTIONS

1. Name the three types of refrigerant-condensing equipment where fouling scale and corrosion are most detrimental.

2. What kinds of impurities are contained in rainwater?

3. Is water that is acceptable for human consumption satisfactory for use in refrigeration equipment?

4. What are the sources of impurities in water?

5. What are the basic causes of corrosion?

6. What generally is the cause of scaling?

7. What generally is the cause of fouling?

8. What conditions are necessary for algae to grow?

9. What are ideal conditions for slime?

10. What scale measures the acidity of a solution?

11. What is the pH value of pure water?

12. What methods can be used to measure acidity or pH?

REVIEW QUESTIONS

13. What are the strong industrial acids sometimes found in atmospheric gases?

14. Name the causes of corrosion.

15. What causes rot in wooden towers?

16. Impingement corrosion is the result of _____.

17. What are the three basic composites of scale?

18. Which unit of measure is generally used to define the concentration of a solution?

19. Alkalinity is a measure of the presence of _____ in water.

20. How does pH affect the solubility of carbonates in water?

21. What is required to remove silica scale with a solution?

22. In what three basic ways may individual water analysis be obtained?

23. What should be done before chemical treatment is begun?

24. In what three ways can scale best be identified?

REVIEW QUESTIONS

25. How may the content (in gallons) of a rectangular tank be calculated?

26. How can you increase the condenser water temperature while chemically treating a system?

27. Which ten metals should be protected by inhibitors?

LESSON 10

Water Treatment (Part 2)

PREVENTIVE MAINTENANCE

Preventive maintenance is probably the most important step in a program of condenser and cooling tower water treatment. Preventive maintenance prevents the problems requiring cleanup that were discussed in the previous Lesson. The best time to start a preventive treatment program is immediately after a water-side system has been thoroughly cleaned. Preventive treatments cost money, but they are by far the most logical choice. The alternatives are reduced capacity, increased power costs, wear and tear on equipment due to heavier loads, plus the higher cost of cleaning "from scratch."

The control of algae and slime is of the utmost importance in a good preventive treatment program. Algae and slime do their damage in several ways. The most obvious is the sheer bulk and size of colonies that restrict air flow and block water passages.

Slime organisms do not require sunlight. They often grow unseen inside condensers. They tend to collect entrained dirt and debris, increasing their bulk still more. Slime growths insulate and block condenser tubes, and the condenser temperature rises. The system eventually cuts out on high head pressure. In addition, high condenser temperatures increase scaling tendencies. This, in turn, increases the possibility of breakdown.

Slime contributes to corrosion problems. Colonies spread and cover metal surfaces. This prevents the formation of a proper protective film of treatment. Certain bacterial slime will digest iron. Others release corrosive gases. Both algae and slime contribute to corrosion by forming oxygen concentration cells. Deep pits tend to form around them.

SELECTING A CONTROL AGENT

Obviously, an essential part of every preventive maintenance program is to keep a system free of biological growths. There are many effective chemicals available for controlling algae and slime.

A broad range of control agents is required to meet the various conditions that can be found in water-cooled equipment. Product selection depends on several factors:

- the type of biological organism present

- the extent of the infestation

- the resistance of the existing growths to chemical treatment

- the type and specific location of equipment to be treated.

APPLICATION OF AGENTS

There are a wide range of products available for the treatment of slime and algae. Some products give off toxic or irritating fumes. They must be used only outdoors. Take care to keep the fumes from drifting to any area where there are people. Other products may be used indoors or outdoors. Consult the manufacturer's data for instructions and special precautions. Do not use products in applications not recommended by the manufacturer.

There are different opinions in the trade as to how often algaecides should be added. Is *slug feeding* or *continuous feeding* the better method? It is generally agreed that slug feeding is better for several reasons. First, continuous feeding costs more than slug feeding. Second, and most important, algaecides fed on a continuous basis often defeat their intended purposes. They promote the development of extremely resistant, hard-to-kill strains.

Resistant strains are most likely to develop when an algaecide is fed at threshold levels. This means feeding enough to retard growth, but not enough for a complete kill. The frequency of addition depends largely on the frequency of reinfestation. To be on the safe side, add algaecides on a regular weekly or bi-weekly basis. Do so whether or not the system appears to need treatment. In this way, slime and algae growths are stopped before they are able to gain a firm foothold.

Even though a tower appears to be free of algae, slime could be growing in the pipes or condenser. Airborne spores of algae and bacterial slime are continually picked up by the tower. As soon as the algaecide content of the water has dropped below killing level, these spores take root and start new colonies. How quickly this happens varies from one location to the next. In areas along the Gulf Coast, heavy growths will reinfest within a week after previous colonies have been killed. In other areas, new growth may not appear for four to six weeks after treatment.

DOSAGES

Recommended dosages are sufficient for routine control. They give a complete kill of growths of normal resistance and density. Very heavy or resistant colonies usually take three to five times this amount for a complete initial kill. Thereafter, regular normal dosages will prevent future growths. Without a complete kill, algae and slime tend to grow resistant to the algaecide used, even when slug fed. For this reason, it is best to alternate algaecides from time to time. For example, a good treatment program could use an effective algaecide for three weeks in a row. Every fourth week, switch to another type recommended for the control of resistant strains.

Where very heavy or resistant strains are found, another step can be taken. Add the three to five times normal algaecide dosage, but also close the bleed-off valve. The initial high concentration of algaecide will be maintained. It will have maximum contact with the algae or slime. *Note*: Do not leave the bleed line closed for more than 24 hours. Be certain that it is reopened and flowing at the proper rate.

Manufacturers usually recommend using a certain amount of algaecide with a specified amount of water, but you may not know the system's exact water-holding capacity. You can safely assume that there are 10 gallons of water for each rated ton (20 gallons per ton for absorption systems). This figure gives a good safety margin in calculating dosages.

There are four simple guidelines to follow in treating for algae and slime:

- Use enough algaecide for a complete kill. Avoid threshold dosages when dealing with established colonies.

- Keep resistant strains from developing. Alternate between two or more different algaecides.

- Remember that algae treatment is not a one-shot affair. Reinfestation can occur as soon as the algaecide has been used up. Set up a regular weekly or bi-weekly treatment schedule. Kill new growths before they become well established.

- When heavy or resistant strains are found, use three to five times the normal dosage for a complete kill. Then add treatment on a regular schedule.

Remember this final point when treating heavy biological growths. When these organisms die, they break loose and circulate through the system. Large chunks or masses can easily block screens, strainers, and condenser tubes. Make provisions to keep them from blocking internal parts of the system. The best way is to remove thick, heavy growths before adding treatment. Then, the day after completing treatment, drain and flush the system and clean all strainers.

THE PROBLEM OF SCALE IN WATER-COOLED SYSTEMS

Water-cooled systems can be broken down into just two types. The first involves "once-through" operation. The water picks up heat and is then discarded or wasted. This, in effect, is 100% or total bleed. Little, if any, mineral concentration occurs. Scale that forms does so because heat causes bicarbonates to break down and form carbonates, which are less soluble at high temperatures. There are two courses of action for once-through systems. One is simply to accept the scale that forms. The other is to take steps to prevent the formation of scale.

The other type of system removes heat from water by partial evaporation, and the water then recirculates. Water lost by evaporation is replaced. This type of system is more economical from a water use standpoint. However, it leads to a concentration of dissolved minerals. If not controlled and chemically treated, this condition results in heavy scale formation.

There are three approaches to the operation of water-cooled systems. One method of operating evaporative recirculating systems involves 100% evaporation of the water with no bleed. This causes excessive mineral concentration. Without a bleed on the system, water conditions soon exceed the capability of any treatment chemical. A second method uses a high bleed rate without chemical treatment. Scale will form and water is wasted. The third method is the reuse of water, with a bleed to control concentration of scale-forming minerals. By adding minimal amounts of chemical treatment, good water economy is achieved. This approach is by far the most logical and least expensive.

SCALE PREVENTION

There are three ways of preventing scale. The first is to eliminate or reduce hardness minerals from feed water, and control the factors that cause hardness salts to become less soluble, to the degree that scaling no longer is a problem. This is the function of a water softener.

Softeners actually exchange sodium ions for calcium and magnesium ions. The treated water is referred to as being "soft." (Water softeners sometimes are called ion exchangers.) Through use of ion exchange resins, the hardness minerals content is greatly reduced. The scale-forming tendency, or potential, of feed water is minimized. This method, although expensive, is used where high-quality water is a must, or where hardness content is so great that adding chemicals for scale prevention is not economical.

The second method of preventing scale is to control water conditions that affect the solubility of scale-forming minerals. There are five factors that affect the rate of scale formation:

- temperature

- TDS (total dissolved solids)

- hardness

- alkalinity

- pH.

These factors can, to some extent, be regulated by proper design and operation of water-cooled equipment. Proper temperature levels are maintained through a good water flow rate and adequate cooling in the tower. Water flow in recirculating systems should be about three gallons per minute per ton. Lower flows allow the water to contact the hot surfaces of the condenser for a longer time and pick up more heat. The temperature drop across a tower should be 8 to 10° for a compression refrigeration system, and 18 to 20° in most absorption systems. This cooling effect, due to evaporation, depends on tower characteristics and atmospheric conditions.

The amount of evaporation depends on air flow through a tower and the degree of water breakup. Since evaporation uses heat energy, the amount of water changed to vapor and lost from the system determines the amount of heat dissipated. One pound of water, at cooling tower temperatures, takes 1,050 Btu to convert from liquid to vapor. Therefore, the greater the weight of water evaporated, the greater the cooling effect or temperature drop across the tower.

Total dissolved solids, hardness, and alkalinity are affected by three inter-related factors. These are evaporation, make-up, and bleed or blowdown rates. Water, when it evaporates, leaves the system in a pure state. It leaves behind all dissolved matter. Water volume in evaporative cooling systems is held at a relatively constant figure by using float valves.

The third method of preventing scale is to improve the solubility characteristics of scale-forming minerals. Modern methods of scale control include many sophisticated chemicals. Some are liquids that require pumps or other metering devices.

CHELATION

Scale and corrosion inhibitor crystals are controlled-solubility, glassy polyphosphates. This type of chemical is sometimes referred to as a *sequestering* agent. Years of field and lab testing have shown it to be a very effective chemical for the control and prevention of scale in cooling systems. These chemicals are known by other names that include *complexing* or *chelating* agents. Probably *chelating* is the most appropriate word. "Chela" is a Greek word for the claws found on crabs or lobsters. Think of chelating agents as having claws or bonding positions. These "claws" pick up or wrap around materials such as iron, calcium, or magnesium and hold them in solution. In true chelation, the chemical reacts with hardness minerals, calcium, or magnesium in solution on a one-to-one molecular ratio. That is, one molecule of chelating agent will hold onto one of calcium or magnesium ion. Since a molecule of chelating agent weighs about 15 times more than a hardness ion, it takes 15 times more weight of chelating chemical to keep the hardness in solution. For example, for true chelation, 300 ppm hardness requires 300 times 15, or 4,500 ppm of chelating agent. If this held true with a scale inhibitor, controlling scale by phosphate chelation would be very expensive.

There is a similar but slightly different mechanism to achieve sequestration or chelation. It is the *threshold treatment* for scale control, that uses polyphosphates. For true chelation, a polyphosphate concentration of about 1,300 ppm is required with raw water that has a hardness of 85 ppm. This is a 15-to-1 ratio. Experiments have found, however, that encrustation or scale build-up was greatly reduced with lesser phosphate treatments in the range of 0.5 to 17 ppm. The rate of scale build-up increases rapidly if phosphate concentration drops below or rises above this level. In this range, a negligible scale build-up takes place. The preferred treatment concentration range is about 2 to 10 ppm.

A new generation of phosphorus-containing compounds has been developed. When formulated with dispersants and stabilizers, they are better for some applications than the old reliable polyphosphates. The new material is in liquid form. It can readily be metered by various volumetric feeding devices in common usage.

THE "BLEED-OFF"

Fresh make-up water brings with it dissolved material. It is added to the material left behind by water that has evaporated. In theory, assuming that all the water leaves the system by evaporation and that the system volume stays constant, the concentration of dissolved material will continue to increase indefinitely. Dissolved solids, it would seem, are on a one-way street into a system with no way out. This is why a "bleed" or "blowdown" is used. There is a limit to the amount of any material that can be dissolved in water. When this limit is reached, added material will cause either sludge or scale to form. By controlling the rate at which dissolved material is removed, the degree to which this material is concentrated in circulating water is controlled.

For example, assume that liquid R-12 passes through the expansion valve in a one-ton system every hour, and picks up 12,000 Btu at the evaporator. The temperature is raised from 0 to 40°F. The vapor leaves the cooler and returns to the compressor. On the way, it is further superheated to about 65°F. This heat pick-up equals 814 Btu. The heat of compression—2,845 Btu—is then added. In one hour, the refrigerant has collected a total of 15,659 Btu. This heat is picked up by the water. It must be removed from the system by evaporation. Each pound of water will consume about 1,050 Btu, so 14.9 lb of water must evaporate each hour to keep the system running. The 14.9 lb of water is equivalent to 1.8 gallons. This is an important and useful figure to remember: *In a one-ton system, 1.8 gallons of water will evaporate for every hour of full-load operation.*

CYCLES OF CONCENTRATION

Now consider a 50-ton R-12 cooling system with a total water capacity of 270 gallons. In one hour, this system will evaporate 1.8 times 50, or 90 gallons.

In three hours, it will evaporate 270 gallons. If no make-up water were added, the system would be bone dry. Only material that had been dissolved in the water would remain. Since the float valve was operating, however, the volume of water is the same, but the dissolved minerals are double in quantity. The water now holds the original minerals plus all those brought in with the make-up water. In six hours, the volume of water held by the system would have been evaporated and replaced again. Now mineral content is three times the original. These evaporation and replacement *cycles* occur at the same time. Therefore, the process of *concentrating* the minerals proceeds unnoticed.

This process is referred to as *cycles of concentration.* If allowed to proceed unchecked, this process will cause scale-forming minerals to approach and possibly exceed their solubility limits. When these limits are reached, scale forms. To prevent this, the concentrated solution of minerals is withdrawn from the system to make room for fresh water with a lower mineral content. By adjusting the bleed rate, the dissolved mineral content can be held at any desired level. The higher the bleed rate, the lower the concentrating effect of evaporation. In other words, a higher bleed rate lowers the cycles of concentration.

Cycles of concentration can be calculated from the data collected in water analysis. An ion found in most water supplies is the chloride ion. This ion is readily detected and the amount present can be measured easily. Most water-testing kits can test for chlorides. Assume that testing shows the feed or make-up water in an evaporative cooling system to have 5 ppm chlorides, and the recirculating water 15 ppm. It is easy to see that the chlorides have been concentrated three times.

Sump water chloride content divided by feed water chloride content equals cycles of concentration. If chlorides have been concentrated three times, then so have all other dissolved minerals. At least they should have been. If, however, hardness solubility is exceeded before the three-cycle level is reached, these minerals have begun to form scale. They would not show the three-to-one relationship in sump and feed water analyses.

It was stated previously that all dissolved minerals would be concentrated. This is true. However, pH in itself is a measure of the excess or deficiency of hydrogen ions, and each unit represents a concentration change of 10. As alkalinity is concentrated, the amount of alkaline or basic material increases. The deficiency of hydrogen ion becomes greater. Since basic solutions have high pH volumes, you would expect the pH to rise, and this is the case. The concentration of hydroxyl ions may triple. But it takes a tenfold change to cause one pH value change. By controlling bleed, the factors that cause hard minerals to become less soluble are also controlled.

LESSON 10

TREATMENT FACTORS

Two factors that dictate water treatment requirements are *hardness* and *alkalinity*. These factors are closely related, since hardness minerals usually are alkaline in nature. Similarly, high-alkaline waters are generally hard. Both hardness and alkalinity contribute directly to the formation of scale. Hardness minerals form scale, and alkalinity increases the rate at which it is formed. As either or both increase, the rate of scale formation also increases. The most severe scale-forming waters are those that have both high hardness and high alkalinity.

Polyphosphate treatment can keep about 500 to 600 ppm hardness in solution in the recirculating water, without significant scale formation. This requires alkalinity to be kept below about 300 ppm, and temperature below 100°F. The liquid scale inhibitor is quite effective at 800 to 1,000 ppm hardness, and up to about 450 ppm alkalinity. The degree of effectiveness would decline at higher hardness or alkalinity values. Bleed is an absolute necessity. It should be an integral part of any scale prevention program.

In Table 10-1 below, you can find the number of cycles of concentration allowed before exceeding the capability of the polyphosphate. You must know the feed water quality in order to be able to use the table. Determine the cycles by entering the hardness, alkalinity, and total dissolved solids. The smallest number of cycles for any of these three factors is the maximum concentration allowed. For example, assume that hardness is 100, alkalinity 50, and total dissolved solids 350. The maximum cycles allowed is three. In this example, the total dissolved solids is the controlling factor. It shows the smallest number of cycles allowed. After finding the cycles of concentration level to be used, refer to the bleed rate, as shown in Table 10-2 on the next page. This shows the desired bleed rate in gallons per hour per ton.

Total hardness (ppm)	M.O. alkalinity (ppm)	Total dissolved solids (ppm)	Maximum cycles of concentration
0 to 60	0 to 60	0 to 200	5.5
60 to 120	60 to 90	200 to 300	4.0
120 to 200	90 to 130	300 to 400	3.0
200 to 300	130 to 200	400 to 600	2.0
300 up	200 up	600 up	1.5

TABLE 10-1. *Maximum cycles of concentration*

METHODS OF TREATMENT

There are three acceptable ways to apply crystals. The easiest but least desirable way is to suspend them in the tower in a plastic mesh bag so that water flows through them. Feed rates vary widely because trash and algae accumulate in the mesh and keep crystals from dissolving. Bags should be cleaned often to prevent accumulation of trash and slime or algae growth.

The second method is to build a basket of ¼-in. galvanized wire mesh. Such a basket is shown in Figure 10-1. Construct the basket so that crystals will not be stacked more than 3 in. deep. Build one or more of these baskets, depending on the amount of treatment required. Place them in the tower basin in an area of strong water circulation. Never place them flat on the bottom of the sump or in an area of poor circulation. Dirt and debris may cover the crystals and prevent them from dissolving. They should be supported off the sump bottom, high enough so that the top of the crystals is just beneath the water surface.

The third and best method of treatment is to install a feeder in the make-up water line. For large systems, needing a starting dosage of 30 lb or more, use a closed feeder installed in a bypass on the make-up line. These feeders are easily installed. They have no moving parts to wear out, and are made of glass-lined steel. This type of feeder is often installed in the recirculating line on the discharge side of the condenser. Water temperature at this location gives the most uniform dissolving rate over a 30-day period. Although this method gives the best results, you can usually achieve good solubility by allowing all of the make-up water to pass over the crystals. Several feeders have been fabricated in the field or are offered for sale. Most will give satisfactory results.

Number of cycles	Bleed rate (gallon/hour/ton)
1.5	3.6
2.0	1.8
2.5	1.2
3.0	0.9
3.5	0.72
4.0	0.6
4.5	0.52
5.0	0.45
5.5	0.4

TABLE 10-2. *Bleed rate*

WATER TEMPERATURE

Although there is no direct control over water temperature, there are three distinctly different temperatures available:

- feed water—the lowest temperature

- water flowing to the tower from the condenser—the highest

- water returning to the condenser from the tower—intermediate temperature.

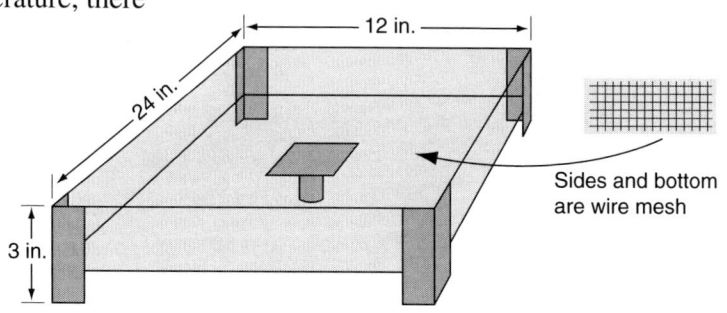

FIGURE 10-1. *Water treatment basket*

LESSON 10

The higher the water temperature is, the higher the rate of solubility will be. The amount of exposed surface area and the water flow rate go hand in hand. Both of these factors can be regulated. As either increases, so does the rate of solubility.

FEED REGULATION

Exposed surface area is adjusted by adding more or fewer crystals to the feeding device. Flow rate is controlled by the placement of the treatment charge, or by using a valve to adjust flow through the feeder. With proper flow, controlled solubility, which is built into some scale and corrosion inhibitor crystals, allows 20 to 25% of the original weight of crystals to dissolve in one month. For example, assume 100 lb is placed in the feeder. Between 75 and 80 lb will remain after one month of operation. Treatment is lost from the system only through bleed. Thus, the bleed rate will determine the amount of treatment that must be fed to the system in a given time period.

As previously mentioned, phosphates are effective at concentrations ranging from 2 to 10 ppm. In calculations, assume a treatment concentration of 8 ppm to be optimum. Start with the fact that 1 lb dissolved in 1,000 gallons yields a concentration of 120 ppm. From this, you can calculate that ¼ lb of inhibitor must dissolve in one month for every five gallons per hour of bleed to produce the desired 8 ppm. This dissolving rate gives a polyphosphate concentration of 8 ppm.

This ¼ lb is about 25% of the original charge. Therefore, the weight of crystals added initially should equal 1 lb for every five gallons per hour of bleed obtained from previous tables. For example, using the bleed rate data provided in Table 10-2, you will find that for three cycles of concentration, a bleed of 0.9 gallons per hour per ton is required. A 100-ton system would require a 90-gal/hr bleed. Dividing 90 by the basic 5 gal/hr, you find that 18 lb should be added as the initial charge. Since ¼ of this amount will dissolve each 30 days, the initial charge will be divided by 4 (4½ lb). These calculations are not necessary for every job. The figures in Table 10-3 on the next page, however, were derived in just this manner.

The amount of initial treatment is directly related to water bleed. When water evaporates, only pure water leaves the system. All dissolved material remains behind. The bleed, however, removes dissolved minerals and treatment. Make-up water that replaces bleed loss must be treated. It is known from research data that polyphosphates dissolve at the rate of 1% per day. That is, after each day, 99% of the amount present at the beginning of that day will be left. This may be expressed mathematically as follows:

(reference) 0.99^{dx}

where d = the number of days

x = the weight of the starting charge.

Unit size (tons)	Table 1 Feed water hardness 100 to 199 ppm (6 to 11 grains/gal) Water treatment (lb)	Table 1 Water bleed (gal/hr)	Table 2 Feed water hardness 200 to 299 ppm[1] (12 to 17 grains/gal) Water treatment (lb)	Table 2 Water bleed (gal/hr)	Table 3 Feed water hardness 300 to 400 ppm[2] (18 to 24 grains/gal) Water treatment (lb)	Table 3 Water bleed (gal/hr)	Table 4 For any water hardness Water treatment (lb)	Table 4 Water bleed (gal/hr)	Unit size (tons)
10	2	9	4	18	8	36	5	4	10
20	4	18	8	36	16	72	10	8	20
30	6	27	12	54	24	108	15	12	30
40	8	36	16	72	32	114	20	16	40
50	10	45	20	90	40	180	25	20	50
60	12	54	24	108	48	216	30	24	60
70	14	63	28	126	56	252	35	28	70
80	16	72	32	144	64	288	40	32	80
90	18	81	36	162	72	324	45	36	90
100	20	90	40	180	80	360	50	40	100
150	30	135	60	270	120	540	75	60	150
200	40	1`80	80	360	160	720	100	80	200
250	50	225	100	450	200	900	125	100	250
300	60	270	120	540	240	1080	150	120	300
350	70	315	140	630	280	1260	175	140	350
400	80	360	160	720	320	1440	200	160	400
450	90	405	180	810	360	1620	225	180	450
500[3]	100	450	200	900	400	1800	250	500	500

Note: After each month of operation, replenish the crystals remaining with an amount equal to one-fifth of the original charge.
Hardness conversion factor: 17.1 ppm = 1 grain per gallon.
[1]For waters over 200 ppm, use water treatment scale and corrosion inhibitor "H."
[2]Over 400 ppm, contact manufacturer for a special recommendation.
[3]Contact manufacturer for special recommendations on units over 500 tons.

TABLE 10-3. *Scale control and corrosion prevention tables*

LESSON 10

With this formula you can calculate that at the end of 30 days, 75% of the starting charge remains—or 25% has been dissolved.

Regardless of the method of feeding, it is important to keep a good flow through the crystal bed. If the system is shut down for long periods of time (five days or more), remove the crystals from the water, or drain the feeder and remove the top. Otherwise, separate crystals may fuse together and form a solid mass. When this occurs, the feeder may be unusable until this mass is chipped or broken out. A word of caution: the crystals, when they have been in water for a few days, develop extremely sharp and jagged edges. They can easily cut hands or fingers. Wear gloves if you have to handle used crystals.

A new liquid scale inhibitor was mentioned earlier. This product contains organic and inorganic dispersants and stabilizers. It effectively prevents scale deposition over wide ranges of pH and temperature. Since this allows no protective film to form, corrosion inhibitor may be required if ferrous metals are present. To start a treatment program, determine the bleed-off requirements in accordance with the make-up water hardness and alkalinity values listed in Table 10-4. The highest rate indicated for specific conditions should be used. Use the following problem as an example for these calculations.

With a hardness of 250 ppm and an alkalinity of 110 ppm, the highest bleed-off rate (90 gal/hr) is selected. Scale inhibitor (liquid) must be fed continuously in proportion to the bleed-off rate to obtain optimum results. With a 90-gal/hr bleed-off per 100 tons, the average load will be only 30 tons. The required bleed will be only 27 gal/hr:

    pH below 8.0 ....maintain 20 to 30 ppm
    pH above 8.0.........maintain 30 to 40 ppm

The pH condition of the system water will determine the concentration requirements. High pH conditions require the highest treatment concentration. To maintain the required concentration, scale inhibitor (liquid) must be fed in proportion to the average continuous bleed-off rate, shown in Table 10-5 on the next page. It was found that 1.75 pints of treatment is required each month for every 10 gal/hr continuous bleed. It was also found that a 27-gal/hr bleed is required under the conditions selected. Therefore, it is easily calculated that 4.7 pints per month will be required to treat the 30 tons.

Make-up water		Bleed-off rate
Total hardness (ppm)	Total alkalinity (ppm)	Gallons per hour per 100 tons of average load
Below 100	Below 60	30
101 to 140	60 to 85	45
141 to 180	86 to 110	60
181 to 215	111 to 130	75
216 to 250	131 to 150	90
251 to 290	151 to 175	120
291 to 330	176 to 200	150
331 to 400	201 to 240	180
401 to 450	241 to 270	240
451 to 500	271 to 300	300
Above 500	Above 300	360

TABLE 10-4. *Bleed-off requirements*

Scaling is by far the most common problem encountered on the water side of air conditioning and refrigeration equipment. But corrosion, where it exists, is far more serious. Corrosion reduces water flow and heat transfer. If allowed to proceed unchecked, it also results in the destruction of costly equipment.

There are basically five types of corrosion:

- corrosion from acidity in the circulating water
- oxygen corrosion
- galvanic corrosion
- corrosion caused by the presence of algae and bacterial slime
- impingement corrosion.

Scale inhibitor (liquid) required, parts per million	Pints per month for each 10 gal/hr of continuous bleed-off
20	1.00
25	1.25
30	1.50
35	1.75
40	2.00

TABLE 10-5. *Average continuous bleed-off rates*

There are two approaches to corrosion control—either eliminate the cause or provide chemical protection. The possibility of biological corrosion is greatly reduced by an effective biological growth control program. Such a program does not combat the effect, but rather eliminates the cause.

Neither galvanic nor impingement corrosion can be effectively controlled with chemical treatment alone. Both are essentially the result of poor equipment design or installation. Galvanic corrosion results from electrochemical reaction between two dissimilar metals in electrical contact. While this situation exists, some corrosion will take place no matter what type of chemical treatment is used. Impingement corrosion usually results from high-speed material impacting on portions of piping, causing erosion. Larger pipe diameters, which allow the same volume flow at a lower speed, will help reduce or eliminate this type of corrosion. Entrained solids, such as sand in well water, produce a sandblasting effect. Settling tanks or strainers can trap or filter out these particles to eliminate this cause.

The remaining two types—oxygen corrosion and acid corrosion—are by far most common. They can be controlled effectively by properly selected and applied chemical treatment. Corrosion by oxygen occurs to some degree in nearly all evaporative cooling systems. Although oxidation can be markedly reduced, it is almost impossible to eliminate completely, since oxygen is being continually washed from the air and into the system by water showering through the cooling tower. At its outset, oxidation is generalized throughout the system.

It forms a film that protects the metal. Various physical, mechanical, and chemical factors work to break down this film in spots. Wherever this break occurs, the attack is concentrated. Localized corrosion proceeds at an accelerated rate. It forms deep pits that eventually penetrate the metal.

Acid corrosion is due either to naturally acidic feed water or to the collection of acid gases from the atmosphere. The most common corrosive gases are carbon dioxide, sulfur dioxide, sulfur trioxide, hydrogen chloride, and hydrogen sulfide.

Where simple acid corrosion is the problem, neutralization of part or all of the acid is an effective preventive maintenance approach. When the pH of recirculating water drops below 6.5, acid corrosion is very likely. The lower the pH, the greater the possible corrosion rate. Under acid conditions, the rate of attack from other types of corrosion may also be accelerated. Acid dissolves the oxide film that ordinarily tends to shield and protect metal. If conditions exist for acid corrosion, one or more blocks or other inhibitors should be added to raise the pH to a level between 7.0 and 8.0, but never above 8.5. If a water system checks out with a pH slightly above 8.0, consider a 35-ppm treatment concentration as 1.75 pints per month for each 10 gal/hr of continuous bleed-off.

The foregoing has covered methods of controlling scale, slime, algae, and corrosion in refrigeration water-side systems by using treatment agents at threshold levels coupled with bleed control. References to volumes, percentages, the make-up of compounds, etc., have intentionally been of a general nature, without reference to the specific recommendations of the various manufacturers of water treatment materials. The instructions prepared by the producer of the treatment material selected should be followed to the letter. This will ensure a successful water treatment program.

The success or failure of any initial cleaning program, and of any subsequent preventive maintenance water treatment program, can be directly related to two factors:

- the quality of the products used

- the efforts of the people involved in applying the products strictly in accordance with the instructions of the manufacturer.

REVIEW QUESTIONS

1. In a water treatment program, what is the most important step?

2. How are algaecides generally used?

3. How often should algaecides be introduced?

4. List four guidelines in treating for algae and slime.

5. What must generally be done after treating for biological growths?

6. List three ways of operating the water side of evaporative recirculating systems.

7. List three ways of preventing scale in a system.

8. In a one-ton system, about how much water will evaporate in every hour of full-load operation?

9. In a 50-ton R-12 system, how much water will evaporate in three hours?

10. What two factors dictate water treatment requirements?

11. Which three acceptable ways are used to apply water treatment crystals in a system?

12. Where are three different temperatures of water available?

REVIEW QUESTIONS

13. What should be done with chemical feeding materials and/or equipment when a system is shut down for five days or more?

14. List five types of corrosion resulting from acidity.

15. Which types of corrosion cannot be controlled with chemical treatment?

16. Which types of corrosion can be controlled effectively with chemical treatment?

17. What level of pH is desirable in the water side of the system?

18. What is the single most important factor in proper water treatment and control?

LESSON 11

Closed-Circuit Water Coolers

INTRODUCTION

The introduction of the evaporative condenser and cooling tower was a major step forward in conserving water used to cool and condense the refrigerant in refrigeration systems. The advantages of using water to cool refrigeration condensers are well known. As the size of refrigeration systems increased, they required larger and larger amounts of water. Supply and disposal problems caused more communities to adopt conservation measures. Evaporative condensers and cooling towers satisfy these measures.

Evaporative condensers and cooling towers require maintenance to control scale deposits. These deposits result from the increasing hardness of the circulating water. This problem needs close attention, particularly in cooling towers. In cooling towers, the cooled water is circulated through the water-cooled condenser. This is different from the evaporative condenser, in which the water circulates around the outside of tubes to absorb heat from the refrigerant that circulates inside these tubes.

Fouling of the outside surfaces of tubes in evaporative condensers will not affect system capacity as much as the same deposit on the inside of tubes in a shell-and-tube condenser. There is a large and immediate reduced capacity as condenser tubes become fouled internally. Figure 11-1 on the next page, drawn from ASHRAE data, shows how impurities affect shell-and-tube condensers. The "K" value, at 300-ft/min water velocity with clean tube surfaces, is about 440 Btuh. The "K" value dropped to less than 400 Btuh after the system operated for only 16 hours. Installations in many areas were researched and tested to find the *probable condition of practice*. When an example was found, it resulted in a "K" value of slightly more than 200 Btuh at 300-ft/min water velocity. This was less than 50% of the capacity built into the condenser.

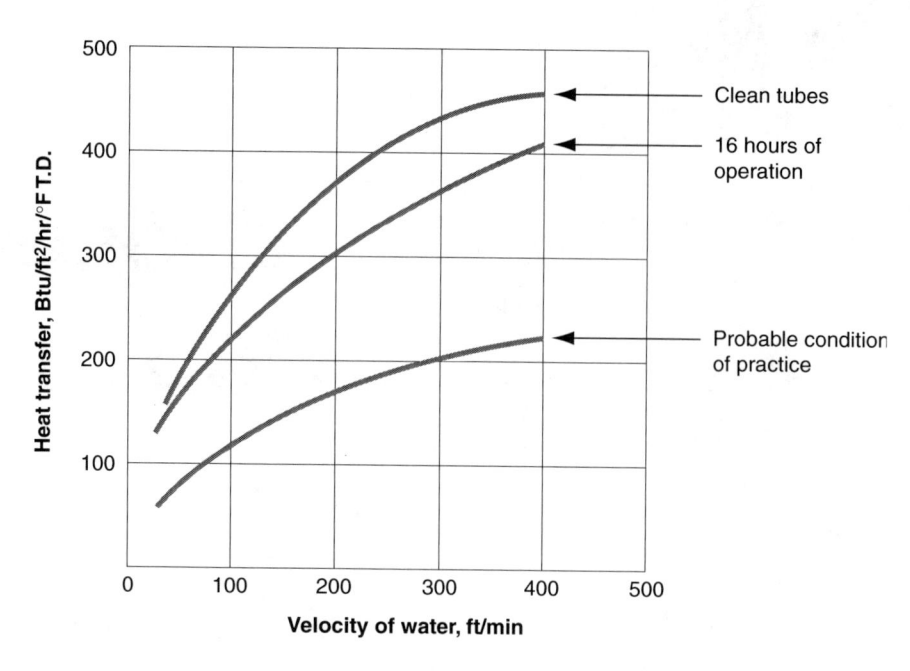

FIGURE 11-1. *"K" value of tube surface in a shell-and-tube condenser*

The evaporative water cooler is a way to use water, with its many advantages, without losing the effectiveness of condenser surfaces. The water is sealed in the circulating system and an economical method of removing condenser heat is provided. The water can be reused indefinitely. Any impurities or abrasives in the initial water charge are quickly caught in screens, or they precipitate out so that abrasive action or scale formation cannot continue.

The evaporative water cooler consists of all the components of an evaporative condenser. The difference is that the condenser water, not refrigerant, circulates through the tube bundle. This water then circulates through a water spray to cool it. Even though the same components are used in both an evaporative condenser and an evaporative water cooler, there is some modification of the condenser-oriented tube bundle. This is needed to have the required heat exchange while circulating large amounts of water with minimum pressure drop. Tube bundles should be constructed so that tubes can be completely drained.

The final disposition of condenser heat is to the evaporating spray water, as shown in Figure 11-2. In an evaporative water cooler, spray water requires make-up, as do cooling towers and evaporative condensers.

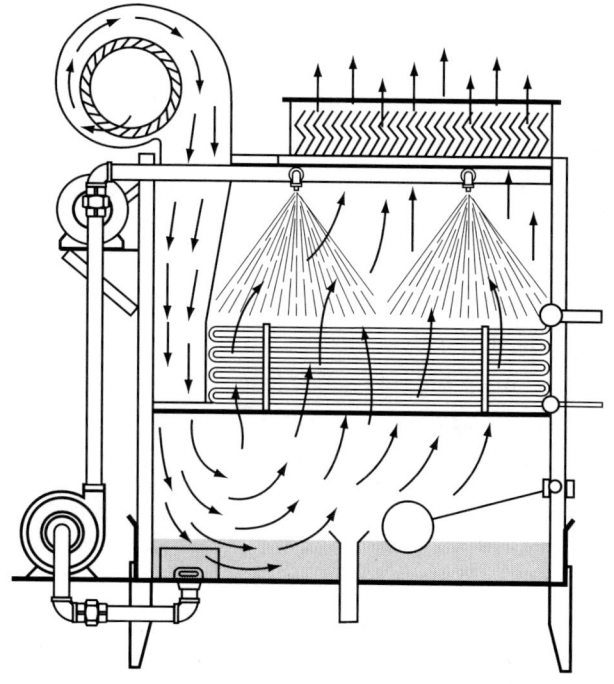

FIGURE 11-2. *Air stream and water spray in relation to tube bundle*

LESSON 11

SELECTION CRITERIA

The selection of an evaporative water cooler can be relatively simple. This is true whether you are dealing with a single system or with many systems, such as a supermarket application. Several fundamentals must be considered:

- cooling range
- the wet-bulb temperature
- the leaving water temperature
- approach
- temperature differences.

Cooling range is the temperature reduction of the circulating water needed to remove the heat gained from the condensing refrigerant. Since the water does not change state, the cooling range always equals the temperature rise in the water-cooled condenser. An effective heat transfer, either warming or cooling, is 500 Btuh per gallon per minute per degree Fahrenheit change. You can find this value with one of the following equations:

$$R\ (°\text{F change}) = \frac{\text{Btuh}}{500 \times \text{gpm}}$$

or

$$\text{gpm} = \frac{\text{Btuh}}{500 \times R}$$

or

$$\text{Btuh} = 500 \times R \times \text{gpm}$$

The *wet-bulb temperature* is the temperature of the air passing through the spray. It determines the amount of water that will evaporate. This, in turn, determines the amount of heat released from the water circulating through the tube bundle.

Assume that water enters the tube bundle in an evaporative water cooler at a temperature of 95°F. It has gained 8°F passing through a water-cooled condenser. Now it must be cooled 8°F, to 87°F (95 minus 8). This is the *leaving water temperature*.

RAC

Approach is the difference between the wet-bulb temperature and the leaving water temperature. Little can be done to alter the wet-bulb temperature. However, the leaving water temperature will vary in proportion to the cooling range required. This will directly affect *approach*. Figure 11-3 shows that as approach increases, cooler capacity increases rapidly.

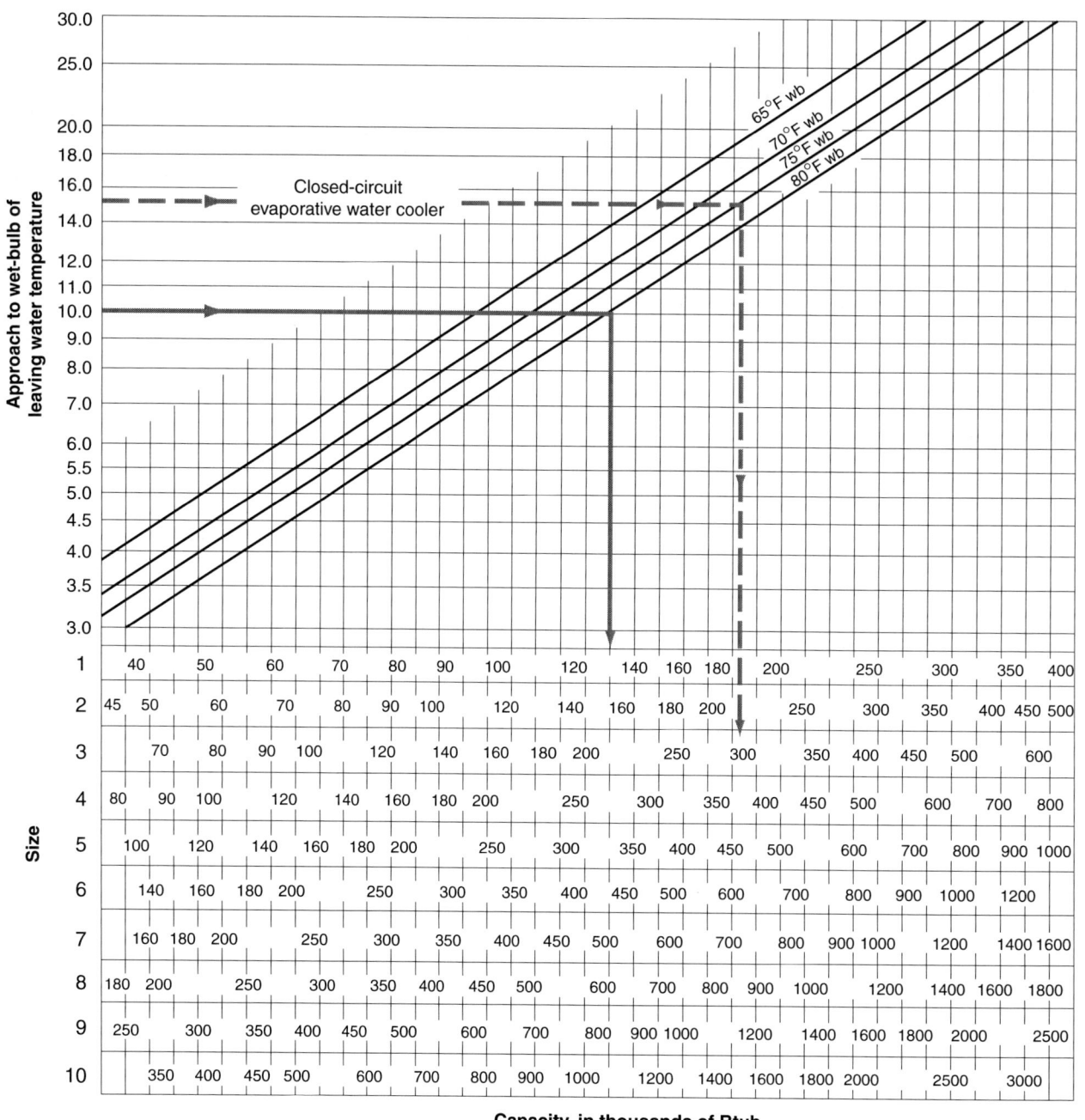

FIGURE 11-3. *Performance of evaporative water coolers*

Temperature difference is a term used widely in the refrigeration industry. Regarding evaporative water coolers, it is the difference in temperature between water leaving the water-cooled condenser and the condensing refrigerant. For example, with water circulating through a shell-and-tube condenser at a rate that results in a 16-ft head loss (a 7-psi drop), the terminal temperature difference will equal *range*. This flow rate would generally represent peak condenser performance.

When mounted on the chassis of a water-cooled condensing unit, shell-and-tube condensers are usually the same size for a given compressor horsepower regardless of design suction temperature. For example, a 5-hp condensing unit usually has a condenser that circulates 15 gpm with a satisfactory head loss. At maximum compressor capacity (high suction temperature), a 5-hp condenser may dissipate 75,000 Btuh.

The same compressor operating at –30°F will put a load on the condenser of about 21,000 Btuh. At high suction temperature condenser load (75,000 Btuh), water circulating at 15 gpm would gain 10°F. A terminal temperature difference of 10°F (equal to range) from 105°F condensing results in water leaving the condenser at 95°F. To cool this water 10°F (range), the water leaving the evaporative cooler must be 85°F.

Now, assume that this same 5-hp compressor at low suction temperature operation imposes a condenser load of only 21,000 Btuh, instead of 75,000 Btuh. Water circulating at 15 gpm would gain about 3°F. If water enters the condenser at 85°F and leaves at 88°F (a 3°F gain), and the terminal temperature difference is 3°F, 91°F condensing would result.

Multiple condensers may be cooled by one evaporative water cooler. The water mixes and enters the cooler with an average gain that requires an average cooling range. It is possible to take advantage of the lower condensing load on low-temperature circuits. This is done by regulating the flow rate through individual condensers. High-temperature, high-load circuits are adjusted to condense at temperatures of 100, 105, or 110°F. Uniform condensing can be maintained on all circuits, if desired. This is done with manual or automatic flow control valves. They will be discussed later in this Lesson.

The total capacity of an evaporative water cooler, and the temperature of the water leaving the cooler, can be regulated. Modulating dampers are installed in the air supply and controlled by sump pan water temperature.

With water-cooled motor jackets, the volume of water circulating through the jackets is minor compared to that circulating through the condenser. This results in a minimal pressure drop through the jackets. Water intended for the condenser can be kept from going through the motor jackets. This is done by installing balancing cocks and piping jacket circuits in parallel with condensers. It is not advisable to pipe a condenser and motor jacket in series. The amount of water required for a condenser would cause an excessive pressure drop if it had to pass through a motor jacket.

In a multiple-circuit application, all the heat from all condensers is carried by a common conveyor to a common heat rejection device. In this case, it is the evaporative water cooler. Any idle or partially loaded compressor/condenser circuits reduce the load on the device. When many compressors are involved, a *multiple compressor factor* can be applied to the total load. Table 11-1 shows factors that have been found to be conservative and reliable.

Multiple compressor factors

Number of compressors	Belt-driven	Hermetic (includes some motor heat)
1 to 3	1.00	1.08
4 to 9	0.80	0.86
10 to 16	0.70	0.75
17 and up	0.65	0.70

TABLE 11-1. *Factors to apply in multiple-circuit applications*

There are several advantages to this method of heat rejection:

1. Reduced operating costs result from lower condensing pressures during hot weather.

2. Reduced noise:
   a. Less equipment room air is required than for chassis-mounted air-cooled units.
   b. Reduced wall louver area keeps more compressor noise inside. (Consequently, there is less neighborhood aggravation.)

3. Fewer space limitations:
   a. Installations can be in inside rooms or basements, where ducts for chassis-mounted air-cooled units would be too large.
   b. Odd-shaped equipment rooms can be used. Units do not have to be lined up against an outside wall.

4. Closer compressor balance:
   a. Compressors need not be oversized to carry hot weather load.
   b. Constant head pressure control allows closer balance of compressor and coil where high humidity conditions are important (meat and produce boxes).

5. Constant condensing can be maintained without winter controls.

6. A longer compressor life is possible, due to constant and relatively cooler condensing temperatures.

7. Water returns to the cooler at approximately 95°F. Scaling on the tube bundle is almost nil, and is easily removed.

8. Circulating water does not foul condenser tubes. The original "K" value is maintained.

INSTALLATION IN EQUIPMENT ROOMS

There are several important factors to consider when you make an installation in an equipment room:

1. Air intake:
   a. Provide an air intake to the equipment room. Size it to allow 2 ft² of free area for each 1,000 cfm of air required. Find the cfm required in the cooler manufacturer's catalog.
   b. For mild climates (winter design above +10°F), locate air inlet louvers so that air will ventilate the room.
   c. For cold climates (winter design +10°F or lower), locate air inlet louvers as close to the evaporative cooler air intake as possible. Provide an exhaust fan in the ceiling or roof at the furthest possible distance from the air inlet. Size the exhaust fan for 50 cfm per hp of compressor.

2. Air discharge:
   a. The air exhaust duct must be at least as large as the outlet or discharge stack of the evaporative water cooler.
   b. All seams and joints in the exhaust duct should be water-tight.
   c. In winter ambient of 0°F or lower, use a gooseneck to keep cold air from dropping into the unit if fans cycle off. *Do not use back draft dampers near the duct outlet.*

3. Cold weather controls and precautions:
   a. Use modulating dampers in the cooler intake. These are supplied on order by the cooler manufacturer. Control the dampers through a modulating motor. It should respond to a potentiometer-type thermostat that senses the temperature of the pan water or main spray-line.
   b. Use a damper or motor with an end switch. Adjust it to stop the blower *after* the dampers are tightly closed, and start it as the dampers start to open.

c. In areas of 0°F winter design (or lower), add antifreeze to the closed water system. Any non-corrosive antifreeze (methyl alcohol or propylene glycol) can be used. The amount required is in proportion to the amount of water in the system and the lowest temperature expected. See Tables 11-2 and 11-3.

d. If antifreeze is put into a system, attach a prominent sign to the expansion tank. It should read: "This system contains ____% (type of antifreeze). If water is added for any reason, replace with same proportions."

4. For water loop sizing for a 10-ft head loss (50 ft of loop with average valves and fittings), see Table 11-4.

Pipe ID, in.	ft/gal
½	82.0
⅝	55.0
¾	40.0
1	23.0
1¼	15.0
1½	11.0
2	6.0
2½	4.0
3	3.0
4	1.6
6	0.7

Totaling system elements

____ Gallons in cooler (from manufacturer)
+ ____ Gallons in piping (from table at left)
+ ____ Gallons in condensers (from manufacturer)
= ____ Gallons subtotal (total of 3 elements above)
+ ____ Gallons in expansion tank (5% of subtotal)
= ____ Total gallons in system

TABLE 11-2. *Calculating gallons in a system*

SELECTION OF CLOSED-CIRCUIT COOLERS

Assume that all units are operating at the same condensing temperature. Then:

1. Determine the total Btuh to be rejected:
   a. Group compressors that will operate at same suction temperature.
   b. Determine the total fixture load for each group.

Total gallons in system	Gallons of glycol at 0°F	−20°F	−40°F
60	18	24	30
80	24	32	40
100	30	40	50
120	36	48	60
140	42	56	70
160	48	64	80

TABLE 11-3. *Amount of antifreeze required for different temperatures*

Maximum gpm/50 ft	
Pipe ID, in.	Maximum gpm
1½	35
2	80
2½	140
3	200
4	400

TABLE 11-4. *Water loop sizing (10-ft head loss/50 ft)*

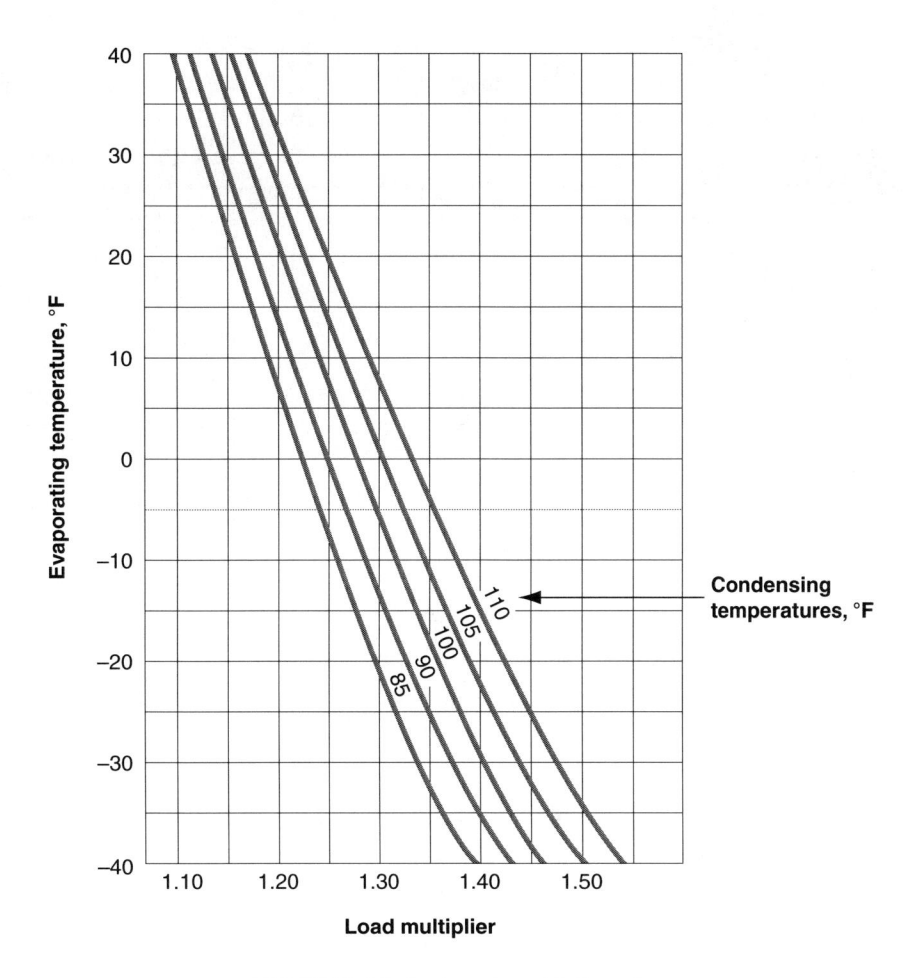

FIGURE 11-4. *Load multiplier chart*

c. Establish the desired condensing temperature.
   Note: Economical sizing can result if:
   95°F condensing is used in 65°F wb areas.
   100°F condensing is used in 72°F wb areas.
   105°F condensing is used in 78°F wb areas.
   110°F condensing is used in 80°F wb areas.
d. Multiply each group total by the appropriate load multiplier, as shown in Figure 11-4.
e. Add the total rejection load. This is the *total Btuh*, shown in Table 11-5 on the next page.

2. Apply the *multiple compressor factor* for selection load, shown in Table 11-1 on page 202, and add the total.

3. Next is the selection of *range* and the determination of gpm:
   a. *Close* range results in a *smaller* cooler with a larger circulating pump.

Number of compressors	Suction temperature, °F	Condensing temperature, °F	Load multiplier	Fixture load, Btuh	Rejection load, Btuh
1	+35	100	1.15	47,500	54,750
1	+25	100	1.19	18,300	21,800
7	+20	100	1.20	177,000	212,000
1	+10	100	1.24	16,500	20,500
2	−15	100	1.34	31,900	42,700
1	−20	100	1.36	13,000	17,700
5	−25	100	1.41	94,500	133,000
18				Total rejection load (Btuh) =	502,450

TABLE 11-5. *Calculating total Btuh*

b. *Wide* range results in a *larger* cooler with a smaller circulating pump.
c. Many larger installations (a typical supermarket is a good example) that have 10 or more compressors can use an average range of 5 to 8°F.
d. Range is related to gpm per 15,000 Btu rejected, as shown in Table 11-6.

4. For the selection of an evaporative cooler, assume a 75°F wet-bulb temperature. The total Btuh (502,450 Btuh, from Table 11-5) × 0.70 (18 hermetic compressors, from Table 11-1 on page 202) = 352,000 Btuh selection load.

Example 1:
For 100°F condensing, 6°F range:

$$\frac{502,450}{6 \times 500} = 170 \text{ gpm}$$

Condensing	100°F
Terminal TD	− 6°F
Water to cooler	94°F
Range	− 6°F
Water off cooler	88°F
Wet bulb	− 75°F
Approach	13°F

Rejection, gpm/15,000 Btuh	Range, °F
3.0	10
3.75	8
5.0	6
6.0	5

TABLE 11-6. *Relation of range and gpm rejected*

Select cooler No. 5 from Figure 11-3 on page 200: 400,000 Btuh (48,000 Btuh spare capacity).

Example 2:

For 100°F condensing, 10°F range.

$$\frac{502,450}{10 \times 500} = 100 \text{ gpm}$$

Condensing	100°F
Terminal TD	−10°F
Water to cooler	90°F
Range	−10°F
Water off cooler	80°F
Wet bulb	−75°F
Approach	5°F

Select cooler No. 9 from Figure 11-3 on page 200: 385,000 Btuh (33,000 Btuh spare capacity).

Example 3:

For 105°F condensing, 6°F range.

$$\frac{502,450}{6 \times 500} = 170 \text{ gpm}$$

Condensing	105°F
Terminal TD	−6°F
Water to cooler	99°F
Range	−6°F
Water off cooler	93°F
Wet bulb	−75°F
Approach	18°F

Select cooler No. 3 from Figure 11-3 on page 200: 352,000 Btuh (no spare capacity), or cooler No. 4: 450,000 Btuh (98,000 Btuh spare capacity).

Chassis-mounted water-cooled condensers may be involved. They will usually pass 3 gpm per compressor hp with a pressure drop of about 7 psi. The pressure drop through a water-cooled condenser should not exceed 8½ psi. It is economically sound to circulate this amount of water as long as the flow rate does not cause an excessive head loss through the evaporative water cooler. Check head losses in the cooler manufacturer's catalog.

5. When condensers and compressors are selected separately, condensers should be selected according to the suction temperature at the compressor with the greater water flow through low-temperature units. Condensers with gpm flow as shown in Table 11-7, with pressure losses not to exceed 8½ psi (20 ft), should be chosen.

6. Balancing flow control valves:
   a. Hand-adjustable valves should have packed valve stems to avoid leakage.
   b. Automatic valves (responding to head pressure) should be sized as shown in Table 11-8.

Piping and purging arrangements for a typical application are shown in Figure 11-5. The purging procedure for the system pictured below is as follows:

Suction, °F		Rejection, gpm/15,000 Btuh
−40	−25	6
−24	0	5
1	25	4½
26	45	3½

TABLE 11-7. *Condenser selection*

Maximum flow, gpm	Minimum valve size, in.
3	⅜
4½	½
7½	¾
15	1
22½	1½

TABLE 11-8. *Sizing automatic water valves*

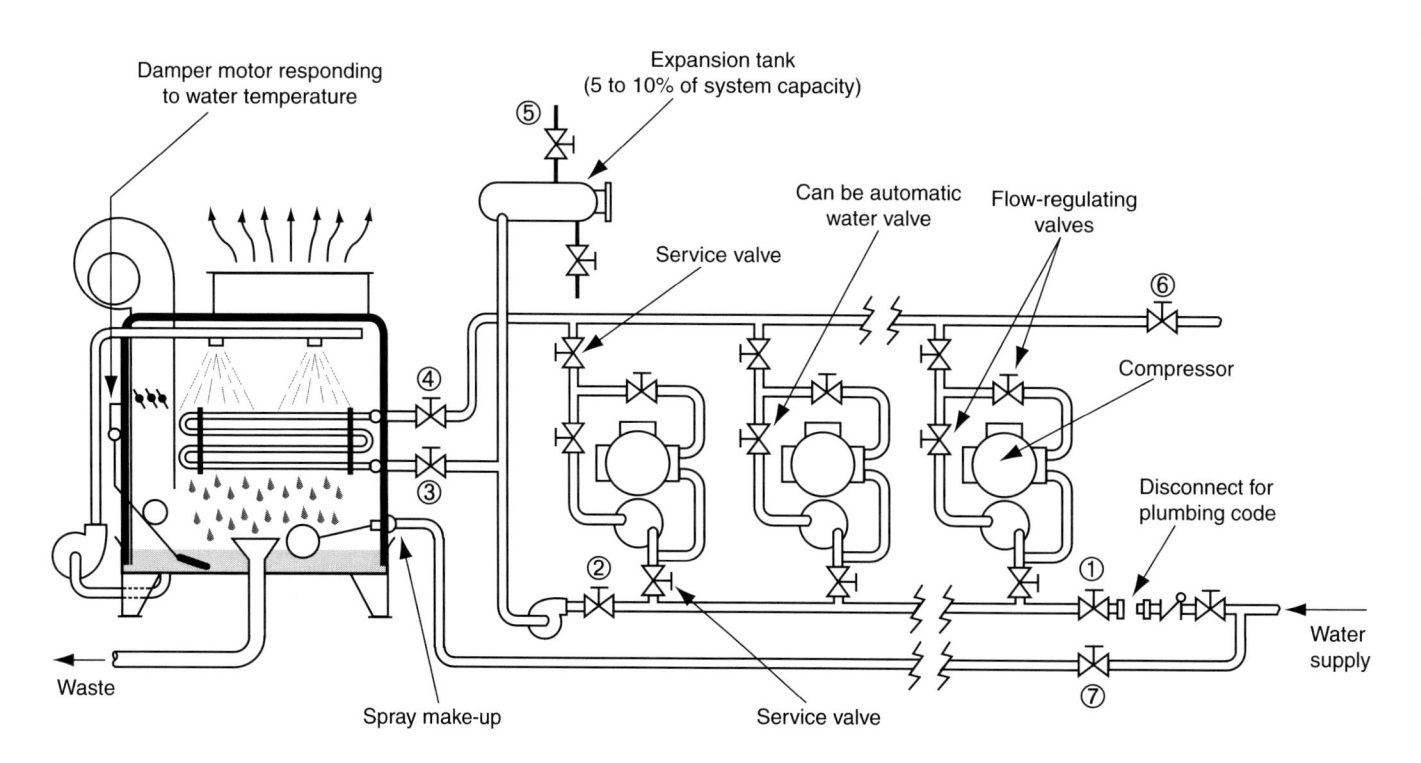

FIGURE 11-5. *Schematic of piping and purging arrangement for a typical closed-circuit evaporative water cooler with multiple condensing units*

LESSON 11

1. Close all service valves ① through ⑥.

2. Open valves ① and ⑥.

3. Purge through each unit, one at a time, to valve ⑥.
   Note: If pressure-responsive water valves are used, the compressor must run during the purge operation in order to open the valves.

4. Purge the tube bundle, then open valves ②, ③, and ④ with the pump idle.

5. Close valve ⑥.

6. Open purge valve ⑤ until the expansion tank is half full. Close valve ⑤.

7. Open all operating valves.

8. Open the water supply ⑦ to the spray system.

9. Start the compressors.

10. For the first several hours of operation, crack valve ⑤ (valves ① and ⑥ remain closed). If the water level in the expansion tank fall, replenish by opening valve ①. When the water level remains constant, close valves ① and ⑤.

REVIEW QUESTIONS

1. What is the difference between a closed-circuit (evaporative) water cooler and an evaporative condenser?

2. Will fouling of the outside surfaces of tubes in evaporative condensers affect system capacity as adversely as the same amount of deposit in shell-and-tube condensers?

3. What is the "K" value, at 300-ft/min water velocity, of clean water-cooled condenser tubes?

4. Does spray water in a closed-circuit (evaporative) water cooler require make-up, as do cooling towers and evaporative condensers?

5. Name three of the five fundamentals that must be considered in selecting a closed-circuit (evaporative) water cooler.

6. Define *cooling range*.

7. What determines the amount of water that will evaporate in a closed-circuit cooler?

8. What is *approach*?

9. Will a shell-and-tube condenser usually be the same size for a given compressor horsepower, regardless of whether the unit is designed for high-temperature or low-temperature operation?

10. How can total capacity—as well as the temperature of water leaving a closed-circuit water cooler—be regulated?

REVIEW QUESTIONS

11. Why is it not advisable to pipe a condenser and motor water jacket in series?

12. In a multiple-circuit application, what effect will idle or partially loaded compressor/condenser circuits have on a closed-circuit water cooler?

13. What will allow a closer balancing of the compressor and the evaporator coil in applications where high humidity conditions are important (meat and produce boxes)?

14. When a closed-circuit water cooler is installed in an equipment room in a cold-climate application, where should the air inlet louvers be located?

15. How large must the ducting for air exhaust be in a room that houses a closed-circuit water cooler?

16. In areas where temperatures of 0°F and lower may be experienced during the winter, what should be added to a closed-circuit water cooler?

17. What is the maximum pressure drop that should exist in a water-cooled condenser?

18. When condenser and compressor are selected separately, what should be the basis for condenser selection?

LESSON 12

Air-Cooled Condensing Unit Room Requirements

CONDENSING UNIT ROOM DESIGN

Approximately 75% of the condensing units installed in food stores and supermarkets in this country over the last decade have been of the air-cooled type. The reasons for this popularity are two-fold. One has to do with the restrictions on water consumption and waste discharge levied by many communities. The other is lower cost. Air-cooled units virtually eliminate the preventive maintenance required by water-cooled condensers, evaporative condensers, and cooling towers.

Efficiency, appearance, environment, and the value of sales areas preclude scattering individual condensing units throughout a building. Air-cooled condensing units should be housed in one or more rooms designed for this purpose.

Satisfactory room design will vary, depending on building design and the severity of winter in the area. In southern sections of North America—such as Florida—condensing units can simply be put outdoors under a roof to protect them from rain. The farther north the location, the more elaborate the unit room must be. The emphasis is on protecting the equipment from sub-freezing temperatures in winter.

RAC

This Lesson will provide you with the basic factors to be considered in practical condensing unit room design. There are several objectives in condensing unit room design:

- adequate ventilation of all condensing units

- protection of all units from rain, snow, and low temperatures

- provision of an automatic control system to maintain year-round condensing temperatures as close to optimum as possible.

These objectives are illustrated in the examples of typical store installations discussed in this Lesson.

In a typical above-ground condensing unit room, the intake louvers can extend the full length of the outer wall. This simplifies the problem of evenly distributing intake air to all units. Unit rooms may be below ground level, or may not have an outside wall. In such cases, it is both expensive and difficult, from a practical standpoint, to get proper inlet air to all condensing units. Condensing unit rooms on the ground floor, or above the main floor on a balcony, are more practical. Balcony installations are widely used. They allow more profitable use of the valuable area below.

FACTORS IN UNIT ROOM PLANNING

Air inlet size

Figure 12-1 shows the cross section of a well-designed air-cooled condensing unit room. It has the proper arrangement of baffles, exhaust fans, and other components. A sufficient supply of outside air is the most important factor to consider. As shown in Figure 12-1, the wall opening for intake air must be adequate vertically and horizontally. It should extend the full length of the condensing unit line-up. You can calculate the total area of wall opening needed for intake air on the basis of 2½ ft² for each condensing unit horsepower. For example, condensing units that total 40 hp require 100 ft² of intake air opening.

Condensing unit location

Condensing units should be located side by side, facing the wall, with the air openings at a distance of 24 to 36 in. from the wall. This ensures that all units get a sufficient supply of outside air. There should be clearance of 3 to 6 ft in back of the units. This is for work space, and for locating ceiling exhaust fans.

LESSON 12

Condensing unit room size

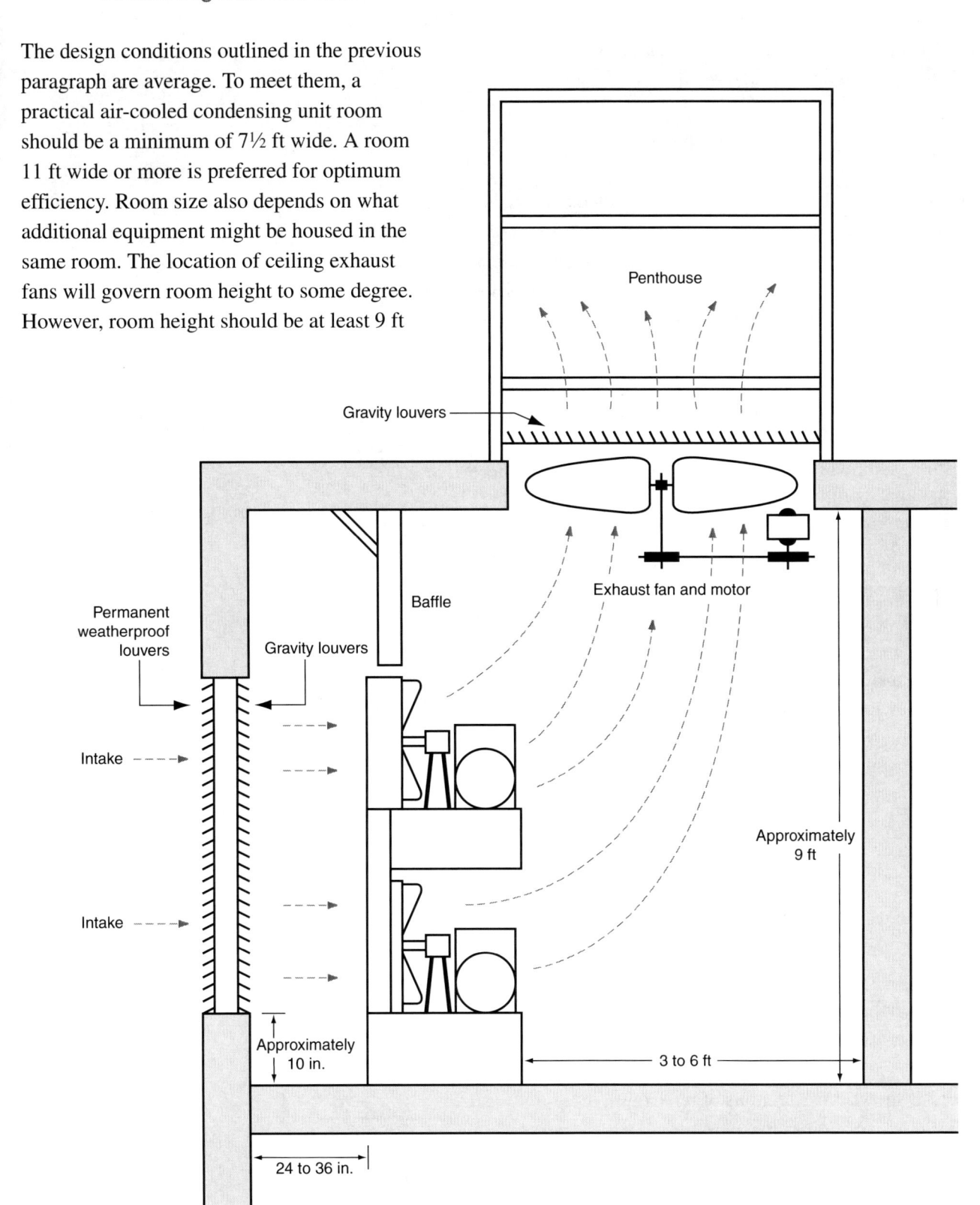

The design conditions outlined in the previous paragraph are average. To meet them, a practical air-cooled condensing unit room should be a minimum of 7½ ft wide. A room 11 ft wide or more is preferred for optimum efficiency. Room size also depends on what additional equipment might be housed in the same room. The location of ceiling exhaust fans will govern room height to some degree. However, room height should be at least 9 ft

FIGURE 12-1. *Cross section of a typical well-designed air-cooled condensing unit room*

to ensure even air distribution throughout the condensing unit line-up. While it provides no condensing benefit, good construction practice will provide a floor drain in the unit room. The preferred location is between the wall housing the intake air louvers and the condenser side of the units.

Exhaust fan criteria

Exhaust fans should be spaced so that all installed condensing units benefit from optimum exhaust conditions. They should be a maximum of 16 ft apart on centers. The preferred distance is 10 to 12 ft. Fans should be sized according to summer temperatures. If it is frequently above 90°F, fans should provide at least 1,000 cubic feet per minute (cfm) air exhaust per condensing unit horsepower. If it is seldom 90°F or above, exhaust fans may be sized at 750 cfm per unit horsepower. For applications in most of the northern United States and Canada, exhaust fans could be sized for 750 cfm per horsepower. In the midwestern, southwestern, and southern United States, better design practice would use 1,000 cfm per horsepower.

As for the type of exhaust fan selected, direct-drive exhaust fans are noisier and less efficient than the slower belt-driven fans. When noise is a factor, belt-driven fans should be used.

With an exhaust rate of 1,000 cfm per unit horsepower and 2½ ft² of inlet air louver per unit horsepower, the inlet air velocity averages less than 500 ft/min. This is a comparatively low velocity. It permits the condensing units to get the amount of cooling air they need from the slow-moving inlet air stream.

Louver design

The exterior of an intake air louver has the main function of keeping rain or snow out of the unit room. It consists of a stationary weatherproof louver. It might incorporate burglary bars, and a screen to keep birds out of the room.

Figure 12-2 shows cross sections of typical weatherproof louvers. Stationary, adjustable, stormproof, weatherproof, and automatic varieties are illustrated. Each is designed for a specific application. In selecting or designing the intake louver, make sure that the net opening is as large as possible. A well-designed louver will have a minimum net opening of

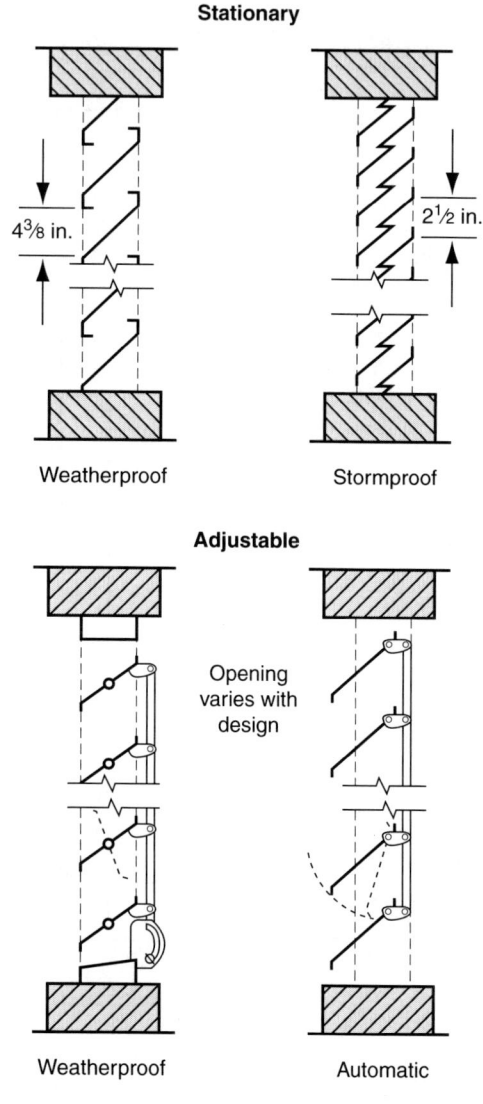

FIGURE 12-2. *Cross-sectional views of different types of outside louvers*

75%. Figure 12-2 shows stormproof louvers for identification purposes. However, they are not recommended unless absolutely necessary. They present excessive resistance to entering air.

The inner portion of an intake louver in areas with winter temperatures below 25°F should be the adjustable motorized damper type. They provide tight closing of the dampers even under the force of winter winds. Controls and electric wiring of motorized dampers will be covered later in this Lesson.

In areas with low temperatures above 25°F, gravity-type adjustable dampers are usually adequate. No inner dampers are generally required if the lowest temperatures are above 40°F.

CHECKING AIR FLOW

You can check an installation to be sure that it is getting the 750 or 1,000 cfm air flow per unit horsepower. Measure the "free" or net opening of each intake louver. Multiply by the number of such openings. From this, you can calculate the square footage of actual intake opening.

Now, measure the inlet air velocity through a louver at several locations and average the readings. Most air-measuring instruments whose sensing element will fit in the narrow opening will provide sufficient accuracy.

Multiply the average air velocity, in feet per minute, by the net opening area, in square feet. This gives you the actual quantity of ventilation air in cubic feet per minute (cfm). For example, assume that there are four 48-in. louver sections with 15 openings of 2½ in. each. The calculation is:

$$\frac{2.5}{12} \times \frac{48}{12} \times 15 \times 4 = 50 \text{ ft}^2 \text{ of opening}$$

If the average velocity is 500 ft/min, then the actual ventilation is 50×500, or 25,000 cfm.

This type of check shows if there is enough inlet air, and if it is evenly distributed. From the readings you will know how to modify the installation, if necessary.

BAFFLE ARRANGEMENT

Figure 12-1 shows gravity louvers between the upper condensing units and the ceiling. These louvers, needed to prevent short-circuiting of the ventilation air, should not seal off the inlet air. Rooms should also have baffles at each end of the unit line-up, between the units and the outside wall, to keep the air from bypassing the units around the ends. There is normally a door in one of these end baffles. This is for service access to the louver motors and the condenser faces.

The space between air-cooled condensers and between the lower condenser and the floor should not be sealed. Sealing these spaces could cause difficulty in the winter. Heated condenser air would not be able to recirculate to maintain proper condensing temperatures.

Also, the openings in the baffle arrangement prevent undesirable backdrafts through the condensers in the summer. Such drafts can occur if the exhaust fans do not remove as much air as the total of all the condenser fans require. Backdrafts place an excessive pressure head on the condenser fans. They also cause windmilling when the condenser fans are off. This, in turn, may cause loss of oil from the fan motor bearings.

THERMOSTAT OPERATION AND LOCATION

Both exhaust fans and motorized dampers should be thermostatically controlled. It is best to operate alternate exhaust fans on one thermostat and the remaining fans on another. The motorized dampers should be of the modulating type. They are best controlled by a single thermostat. Non-modulating damper motors are not satisfactory. They can cause rapid inlet air temperature changes. This, in turn, causes rapid head pressure fluctuations and flash gas in the receivers and liquid lines.

All thermostat bulbs for the exhaust fans and the louvers should be grouped together. The best location is on the inside wall near the center of the line-up, near eye level. This seems to be the most stable location for "all-seasonal" operation. It allows all controls to sense the same temperature. It ensures that all controls will work together under all seasonal conditions.

Select the damper motor and thermostat to have a range of 6°F from fully closed to fully open positions. Set the thermostat to begin opening the dampers when the temperature rises to 70°F. They will then be fully open at 76°F. Set the exhaust fan thermostats to start one group of fans at 80°F and the other at 85°F. This system keeps the condensing unit room as near the ideal of 80°F as possible year-round without excessive short cycling of the fans and dampers.

Maintain a minimum unit room temperature of about 65°F in the winter. Lower temperatures will cause such low condensing pressures that erratic expansion valve operation and loss of refrigeration effect will occur.

LESSON 12

A simple yet reliable control system is shown in Figure 12-3 on the next page. To understand it, follow the sequence of operation as the room temperature rises. When the room temperature reaches 70°F, the damper thermostat starts the first damper motor. This motor begins to open the section of damper connected to the end switch. It also actuates the end switch. The end switch starts the second and third motors. For all practical purposes, the damper sections operate in unison. (The damper motor control circuit would remain the same if service were single-phase.)

The exhaust fans operate in stages. If the room temperature continues to rise, the first exhaust fan thermostat starts one fan at 80°F. The second thermostat will start the other fans if the temperature reaches 85°F.

VARIATIONS IN ROOM LAYOUT

The system shown in Figure 12-1 is an ideal layout for intake air and exhaust air handling. Obviously, it is not always possible to achieve this. As with all types of equipment installation, planning for optimum efficiency is often hampered by near-impossible conditions.

Figure 12-4 on page 221 shows another possible location of the exhaust fan. If possible, try to avoid the disadvantage of allowing recirculation of exhaust air. This can be particularly serious if a tractor trailer truck parks outside the room!

In areas with winters below 25°F, dampers are needed on all fans to keep the heat in the room. In milder climates, dampers are needed only on the second-stage exhaust fans. This prevents recirculation of exhaust air when first-stage fans are operating and second-stage fans are not.

In a good balcony installation, the inlet air louvers are large in area. They will completely blanket all condensers with air. A simple, inexpensive, but effective method of baffling the air is to prevent it from passing over the top of the upper units or around the end of the condensing unit line-up.

SUMMARY

There is no one right way to design an air-cooled condenser unit room. Available space and physical characteristics pose problems. Summer and winter temperatures make the most economical installation variable, depending on the location. Good room design includes the following guidelines:

- Use large intake louvers. Large intake louvers allow air to flow evenly to all units.

RAC

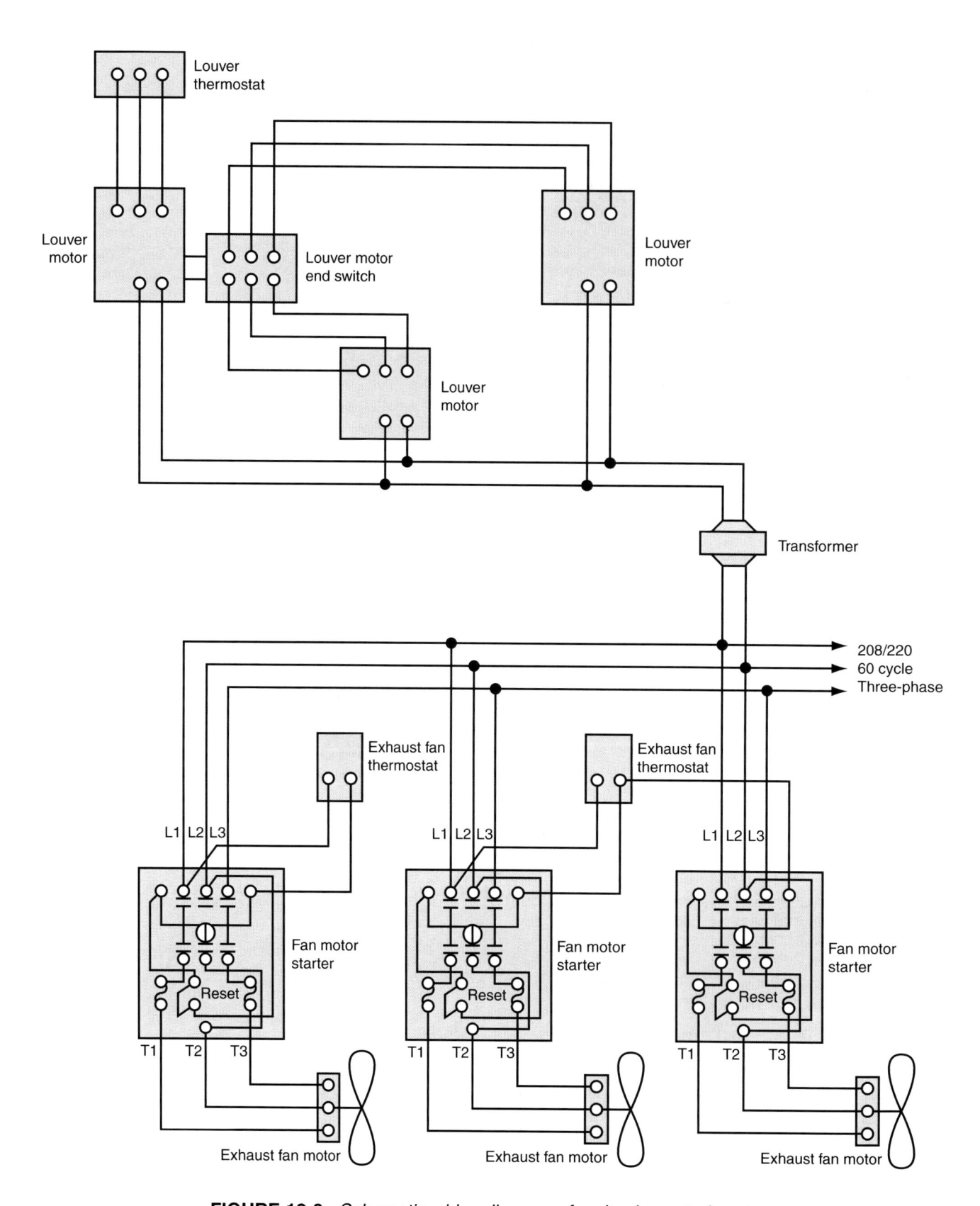

FIGURE 12-3. *Schematic wiring diagram of a simple control system*

220

- Baffle the air only enough so that it will not pass over the top of the upper units and around the ends of the unit line-up.

- Use tight-closing modulating motorized dampers if outdoor air temperatures are lower than 25°F.

- Make sure that damper and exhaust fan controls are properly located and properly set. Use separate controls for exhaust fan and air inlet dampers.

- Do not skimp on exhaust fan capacity. Base it on actual air volume.

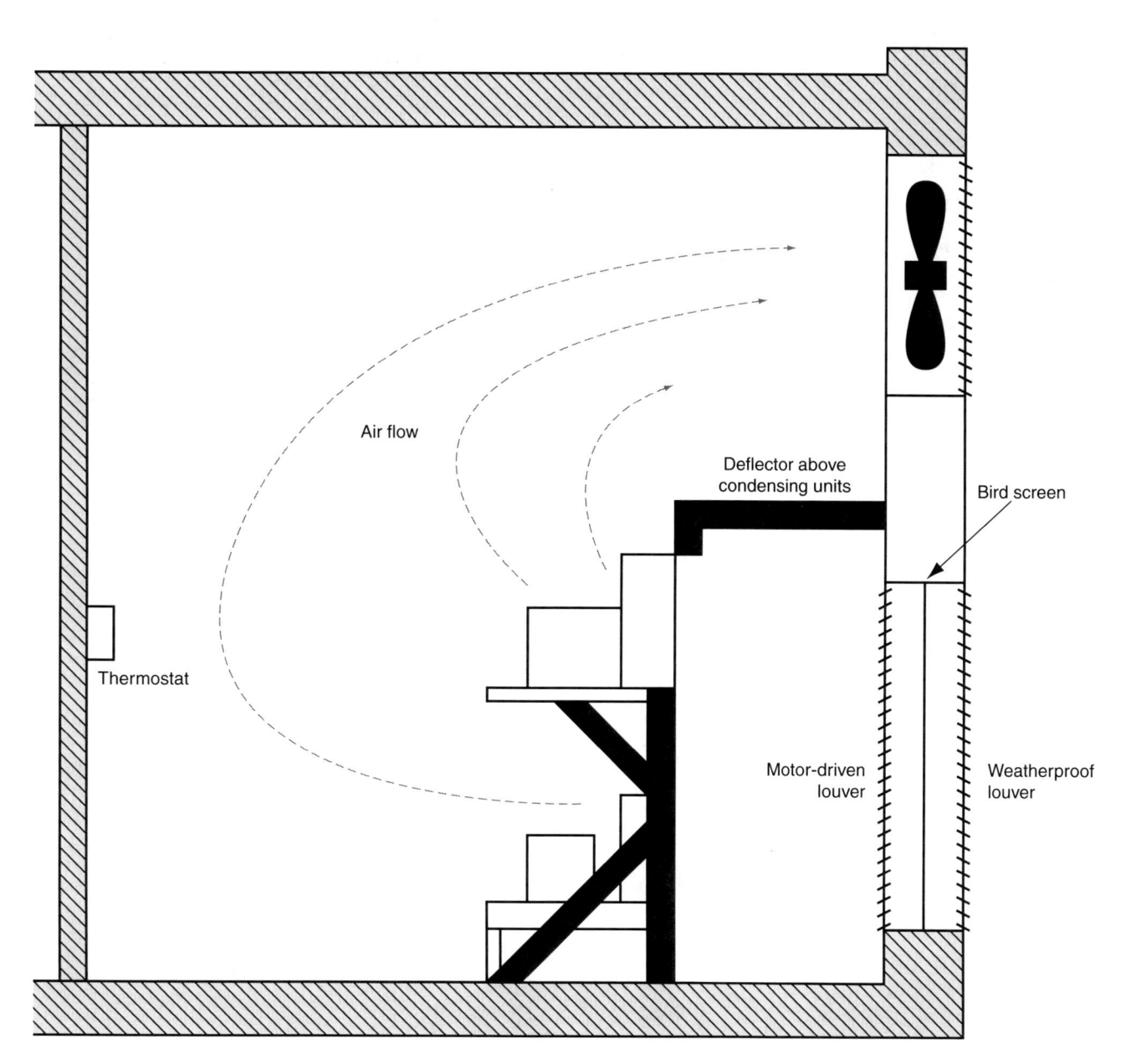

FIGURE 12-4. *Cross section of air-cooled condensing unit room design, with wall intake and wall exhaust*

REVIEW QUESTIONS

1. Name two reasons why the majority of supermarkets employ air-cooled condensing units.

2. Why are balcony installations in wide use?

3. In a room for an air-cooled condensing unit, how far horizontally should the air opening on the inlet wall extend?

4. On what basis is the total wall opening area calculated for air-cooled condensing unit room intake air?

5. How far away from the inlet air wall should the air openings for condensers be when condensing units are placed in position? Why?

6. For optimum exhaust conditions in an air-cooled condensing unit room, what is the preferred distance exhaust fans should be spaced apart on centers?

7. Which exhaust fans are noisier and less efficient, belt-driven or direct-drive?

8. If an air-cooled condensing unit room has an exhaust capability of 1,000 cfm per unit horsepower and 2½ ft² of inlet louver per unit horsepower, what will the average inlet air velocity be in feet per minute?

9. What is the primary function of the exterior intake air louver?

10. What should be the minimum percentage of net opening expected of a well-designed louver?

REVIEW QUESTIONS

11. What type of inner intake louver should be installed if winter temperatures in the area of installation may be below 25°F?

12. If an air-cooled condensing unit room has four 48-in. louver sections with 15 openings of 2½ in. each, how many square feet of opening will there be?

13. Why is a deflector or baffle required between upper-tiered condensing units and the ceiling?

14. How should exhaust fans and motorized dampers be controlled?

15. What is the minimum temperature that must be maintained during the winter in a room housing an air-cooled condensing unit?

16. Why must the minimum temperature referred to in the previous question be maintained?

17. If the damper thermostat in Figure 12-3 were set to close its contacts when the room temperature rose to 70°F, what would happen when the temperature reached that level?

18. When the room for an air-cooled condensing unit is located in an area where winter temperatures are below 25°F, how many of its exhaust fans require dampers? Why?

LESSON 13

Heat Transfer Coils

HEATING AND COOLING COILS

There are many uses for heating coils. The most common are tempering cold outside air, and preheating and reheating air in air conditioning and heating systems. There are also hundreds of varied industrial applications. Coils for heating are often installed in systems that may provide for air cleaning as well as humidification. Hot water and steam are the most common heating media. However, the use of heat from the hot gas discharge in a refrigerating system is increasing.

Cooling coils may be used to cool air with or without dehumidification. Many air conditioning systems use water to reduce the load on the compressor. Cooling coils are also used with chemical moisture absorption systems to remove sensible heat. However, most cooling coils are used for both sensible and latent cooling. They are sometimes sprayed with water to aid in air cleaning and odor absorption. Cold water and Group 1 refrigerants (ASA classification) are the normal cooling media in surface coils. Brines of various types are also used when low-temperature refrigerants are required.

Coils are normally of two types:

- bare tube coils

- coils with extended surfaces.

Bare tube coils are used in some low-temperature refrigeration applications and for various evaporative condenser coils.

The transmission of heat from air passing over a tube is impeded by three resistances:

- air-film resistances

- the resistance through the wall of the metal tube itself

- the film resistance between the fluid in the tube and the inside surface of the tube.

For the typical cooling and heating coil, the resistances of the metal wall and the inside film are low compared to the external air side resistance.

Air-film resistance can be decreased by adding to the external surface area. This is done with fins externally applied to the tubes. A water spray is used on some equipment. It increases capacity and serves other purposes as well.

COIL CONSTRUCTION

Tube surface is known as the *primary* surface. If fins are attached to the tubes, the fin surface is the *secondary* surface. The primary surface generally consists of round tubes staggered in relation to air flow. In some cases they are in line.

The most common fin is the plate type. It may be corrugated or otherwise die-shaped to increase air turbulence. Spiral fin coils are also used for these applications. Individual round or square fins applied to each tube are also common. The staggered tube arrangement with corrugated fins normally gives somewhat higher heat transfer than other types.

The bond of the fin surface to the tube is of the utmost importance for proper performance. This bond must be permanently secured to ensure continued performance after coils have been in service for some time. For spiral fin-type coils, the fins are wound on the tubes under pressure. Then they are coated with solder to maintain fin-to-tube contact. Some spiral fin coils have fins formed out of the tube material itself. With the plate-type or individual fin coils, the bond is normally achieved by mechanical or hydraulic expansion.

Heating and cooling coils are usually copper tubes with aluminum fins. Coils of all aluminum are also used. Copper tubes with copper fins are used in certain cases. Steel fins and tubes are used for certain ammonia or brine applications.

Tube sizes normally are ⅜ in., ½ in., ⅝ in., ¾ in., and 1 in. outside diameter (OD). There are 3 to 14 fins per inch. The tube spacing generally varies from

LESSON 13

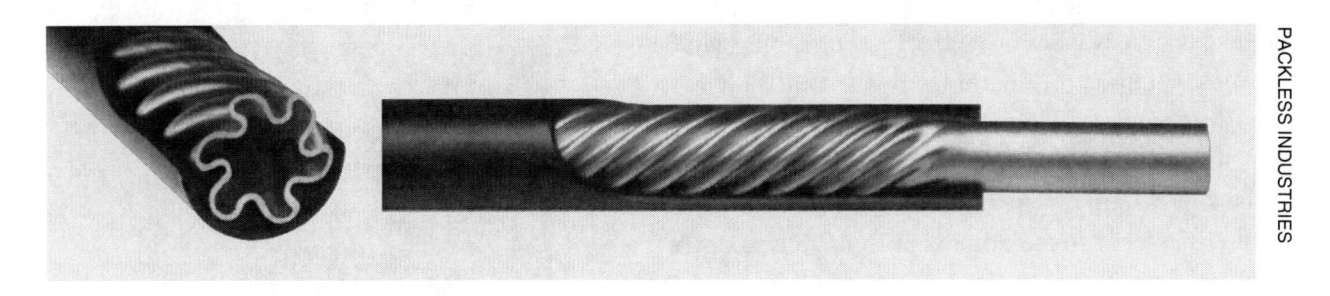

FIGURE 13-1. *Fluted bore with extended surface area*

about 1 in. to 2½ in. on center. This depends on the particular coil design and space considerations. Choose fin spacing for the duty required, bearing in mind that frost accumulation is possible on low-temperature coils. Coil casings are normally made of galvanized steel or aluminum.

Heat transfer is increased by a series of indentations on the tube surface. This amounts to an extended surface area, and provides additional turbulence for the medium traveling within the tubes. This is called a *fluted bore*, shown in Figure 13-1 in a coaxial tube-in-tube design. It also is used to a great extent in shell-and-tube condensers and evaporators.

WATER COILS

For proper water coil performance, air must be eliminated from the system and the water properly distributed. Air is eliminated in the system piping. (Water coil piping details are shown in Figure 13-9 on page 238.) Water coils are circuited with different tube arrangements for uniform water distribution. A typical coil can be arranged for a varying number of parallel water circuits, as required by specific job conditions.

Coils may use well water that contains sand and other foreign matter. If so, there should be a way to clean the individual tubes in the coil. This is done by using coils with removable plugs for each tube, or with removable headers. Water coils are normally arranged so that they can be completely drained. Drain connections are provided in the coils or in the piping at the coils.

DIRECT EXPANSION COILS

Figure 13-2 on the next page shows a typical refrigerant direct expansion coil used for air conditioning. Distributing volatile refrigerants in coils is more complex than distributing water or brine. In direct expansion coils, the coil surface should be uniformly cool. Circuiting should protect the compressor from unevaporated refrigerant.

RAC

A dry expansion evaporator with a TXV or capillary tube is the most common method of feeding a coil. With a thermal valve on a coil, there are two important design factors to consider. First, pressure drop across the coil must be kept within practical limits. This can be done with multiple feeds to the evaporator through headers or distributors. The second factor involves suction superheat, which is normally obtained within the coil itself. The feeds in these coils are designed so that they handle the same load and are generally exposed to the same temperatures. The distributor must be effective for both liquid and vapor, since entering refrigerant is a mixture of the two. Distributing tubes are normally small-diameter tubes—½ in. or 5/16 in. OD. They can be smaller or larger, depending on the load.

Coils are usually constructed to use one metering device per coil. In air heating and cooling coils, air usually blows at right angles to tubes. In coils with more than one row in direction of air flow, the media in the tubes may be circuited in various ways. Most coils have a counterflow arrangement, but parallel flow is also used. Counterflow gives the highest refrigerant mean temperature difference, which results in increased capacity.

FIGURE 13-2. *A direct expansion evaporator coil*

Flooded coils are used for some refrigeration applications. Flooded evaporators are fed by a high-side or low-side float, as shown in Figure 13-3.

APPLICATIONS

Water coils are generally installed with horizontal tubes. Coils subject to air below 32°F must be protected from freezing. All cooling coils must be provided with drip pans, because they catch condensate formed during the normal cooling cycle.

Face-and-bypass dampers, shown in Figure 13-4, are satisfactory control means with water cooling or heating coils. When they are used on direct expansion coils, other problems arise. With reduced air volume on the bypass cycle, there is a danger of freezing the coil due to lower suction temperature. On many direct expansion coil installations, the coil, or coil bank, is divided into several sections. Each is connected to an individual compressor to secure good control.

The use of capacity modulation devices on compressors has also required in many cases that the coil itself be divided. This allows a certain segment of coil to be used when the compressor operates at partial capacity. The entire coil is used when the full capacity of the compressor is used.

Under certain conditions, there may be a problem of water blowing off cooling coil fins. On some coils, water blows off at velocities below 400 ft/min. Other coils have no problem at velocities over 600 ft/min. This problem depends on the particular design of the coil relative to the type of fin, fin spacing, etc. One solution is to install eliminator plates on the leaving air side of the coil. They catch the water and run it into the drain pan.

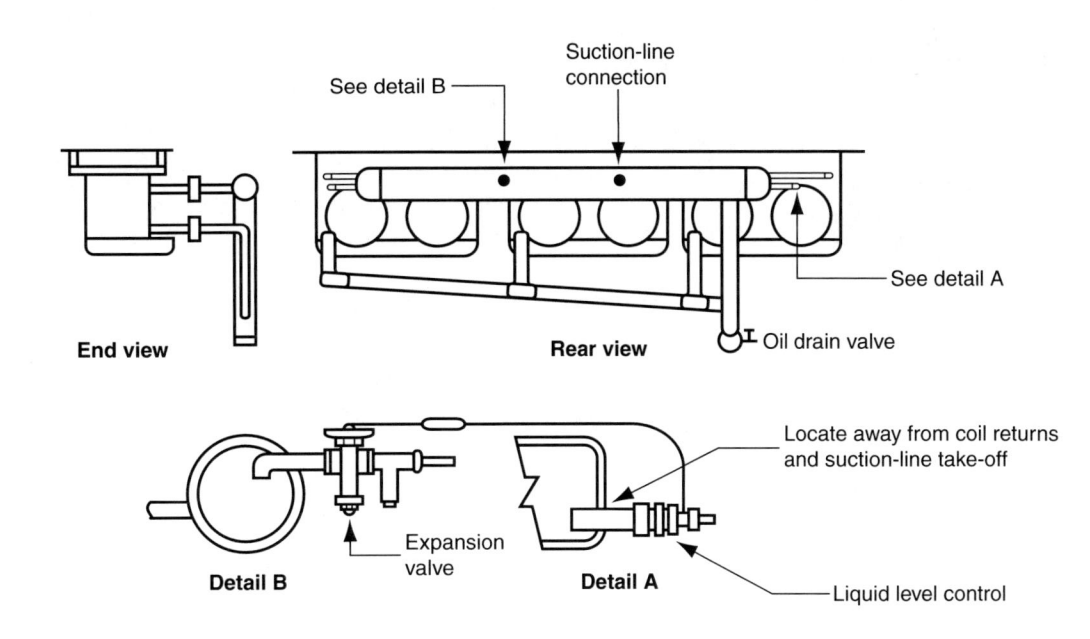

FIGURE 13-3. *How liquid level control is achieved in a typical installation for flooded blower coils with a horizontal accumulator*

Cooling coils may be stacked one above the other. If so, there should be drip troughs below each coil. They prevent condensate from the upper coils running down over the lower coils, as shown in Figure 13-5 on the next page. Sometimes, cooling coils are sprayed with water to increase heat transfer and more closely approach saturation for leaving air. When a bypass is used on a cooling coil, it may be difficult to hold the humidity if part of the air does not go through the coil.

Heating and cooling coils are normally strong enough to withstand any expansion and contraction within the coil. Be careful to avoid transferring strain from piping to the coils.

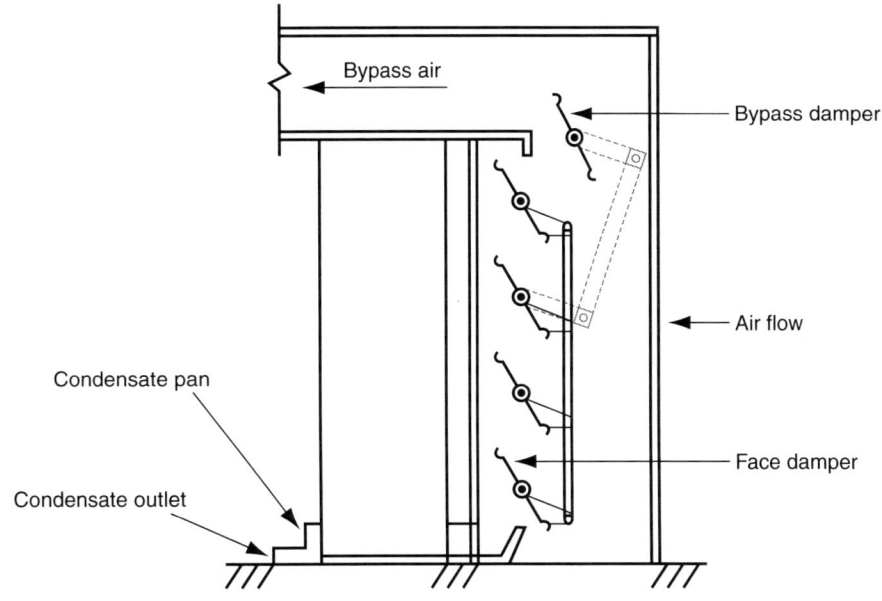

FIGURE 13-4. *Section showing face-and-bypass damper arrangement*

COIL SELECTION

There are several design factors to consider when selecting coils:

- specific duty (heating, cooling, dehumidifying, and capacity required to maintain a certain balance)

- temperature of entering air (dry-bulb and wet-bulb for dehumidification, dry-bulb only for dry cooling)

- available heating or cooling media with temperatures, pressures, etc.

- dimensional requirements

- air volume and allowable resistances

- allowable refrigerant-side resistance

- any individual installation requirements, such as the type of control to be used, etc.

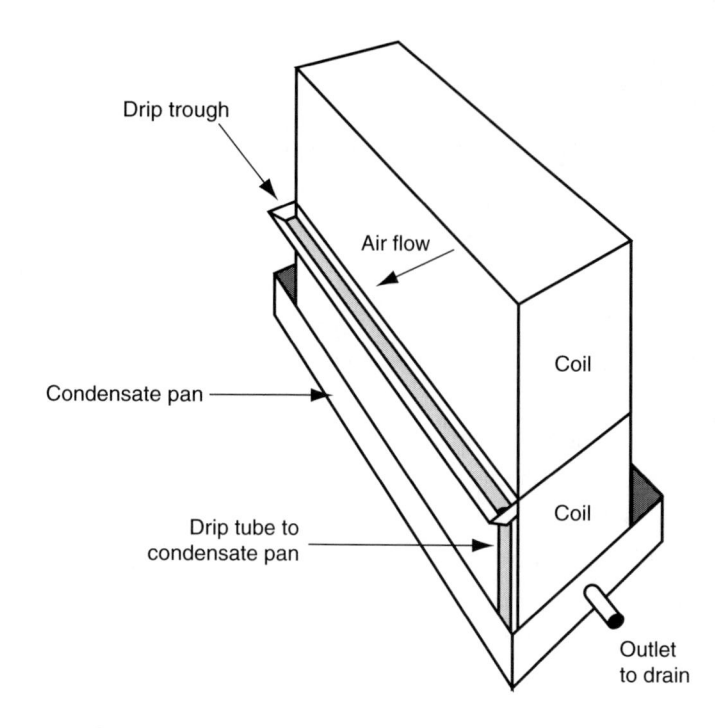

FIGURE 13-5. *Coils arranged with drip trough and condensate pan*

Figures 13-6 and 13-7 show examples of typical coils, and Figure 13-8 shows some details of their construction.

The cooling or heating medium often depends on what is available, and whether it is a new or existing installation. The problem of available space is influenced in the same way. Air quantity should be based on good design practice, but existing system conditions may dictate this factor. Air-side resistance will influence the required fan size, as well as speed and motor horsepower. The pump and pump motor available control the allowable pressure drop through a water coil. Proper performance of coils depends on the proper selection, application, and maintenance of all the equipment in the system.

FIGURE 13-6. *Typical booster-type water coils*

Rating of a coil is based on uniform velocity over the face of the coil. If velocity is not uniform, it will affect coil performance. Bringing air into a coil at odd angles or blocking off part of a coil will generally cause trouble. The most common cause of reduced air volume is a filter filled with dirt. Decreased air volume affects coil performance. Proper design and servicing eliminates these difficulties.

A dirty coil may be cleaned in several ways. It can be brushed and cleaned with a vacuum cleaner. If the deposit has hardened, wash the coils with steam or hot water and compressed air. Coils may become so dirty that they must be removed in order to be cleaned properly.

FIGURE 13-7. Header-type water coil

There are many chemical coil cleaners that do an excellent job. All instructions must be followed carefully when you are using one of them. Note whether it should be used full strength or diluted. Check for effects on materials such as copper, aluminum, steel, and plastic drain pans with PVC piping.

There are also high-pressure cleaning devices for coil cleaning. Some mix the proper proportions of chemical cleaner with water. They can apply the solution to the coil surface under pressure. Upon completion of the cleaning process, the coil surface must be rinsed with clear water. This prevents chemical reactions with the coil surface.

Observe all safety precautions, such as wearing rubber gloves, aprons, a face shield, etc., when cleaning coils. *CAUTION: Do not attempt to clean coils with fans operating!*

HEATING COILS

In normal practice, hot water heating coils are usually rated within the following limits:

- air face velocity—200 ft/min, up to 1,600 to 1,800 ft/min

- hot water temperature—150 to 280°F (higher temperatures are sometimes used in high-temperature, high-pressure hot water systems)

- water velocity—2 to 6 ft/sec

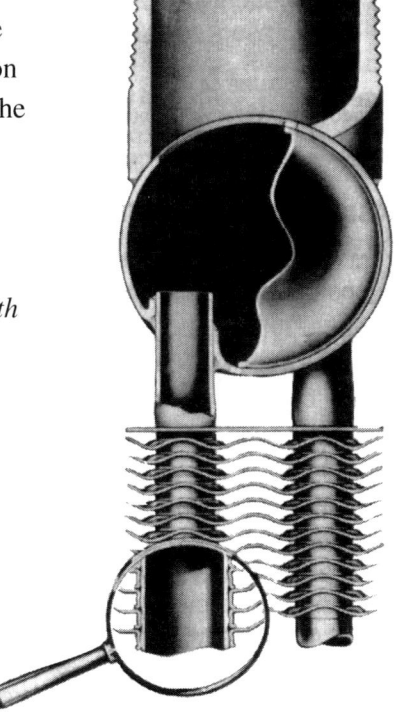

FIGURE 13-8. Section through a coil, showing the joint between tube and header and contact of the fin collar with the tube

- water quantity—based on about a 20°F temperature drop through the hot water coil

- air resistance—a variable usually within the limits of ⅛ in. to ¾ in. of water column.

The selection of water heating coils is relatively simple. It involves only dry-bulb temperatures and sensible heat. For a given duty, it is possible to select several arrangements. This will depend on the relative importance of such items as space, air resistance, cfm, water temperature drop, etc.

COOLING COILS

Cooling and dehumidifying coils are usually selected within the limits listed below:

- entering air dry-bulb temperature—60 to 100°F

- entering air wet-bulb temperature—50 to 80°F

- air face velocities—300 to 800 ft/min

- refrigerant temperatures—25 to 55°F at coil suction

- water entering temperatures—40 to 65°F

- water volume—2 to 6 gpm per ton, or the equivalent of a water temperature rise of from 4 to 12°F

- water velocity—2 to 6 ft/sec.

In designing an air conditioning system using water cooling coils, keep the following in mind:

- Always use counterflow of air to water through coils for maximum capacity from the coil. For counterflow, the cooling medium enters the coil on the leaving air side, and water leaves the coil on the entering air side. In contrast to counterflow, there is parallel flow, in which entering air and entering water enter the coil on the same side.

- The most economical minimum difference between the leaving air dry-bulb temperature and the entering water temperature is in the 6 to 8°F range. By using a counterflow design, the dry-bulb temperature of the air can be brought to within a few degrees of the entering water temperature. However, this usually requires an excessive amount of coil surface.

- The most economical face velocities of air through a cooling coil range from 400 to 600 ft/min. The lower the air velocity, the lower the air friction.

- From a cost standpoint, it is best to select as long and narrow a coil for a given face area as the job requirements permit. A long narrow coil is generally less expensive than a short wide coil. For example, assume that a coil with 8 square feet of face area is required. A coil 18 in. by 64 in. will be less expensive than a coil 36 in. by 32 in. Yet both areas are the same. Job conditions often dictate coil dimensions, but the long coil should always be considered.

- Maintain water velocity in the coil as high as possible without exceeding the maximum allowable pressure drop. Where small water volumes are available, special water circuiting can increase water velocity. Internal tube spirals are also used for this purpose. In some applications, a large volume of water must circulate, but with low water friction loss through the coil. In such applications, coils are circuited so that a maximum number of tubes are fed with water. This keeps each water pass to a minimum. There is, consequently, lower water pressure drop.

DIRECT EXPANSION COIL SELECTION

In selecting direct expansion coils, consider the following points:

- A direct expansion coil is normally selected for a given refrigeration load. Remember that the load is often determined by the capacity of the condensing unit. This could affect the coil selection and the type of circuiting used on the coil.

- When direct expansion coils are selected to operate at suction temperatures of 32 to 35°F, you must take care to prevent freeze-ups. If the entering air temperature is reduced, suction temperature could drop below freezing. This results in the formation of frost on the coil surface. There are two ways to prevent this problem. Select the coil at a higher suction temperature under maximum entering air conditions. Or, use a back pressure-regulating valve in the suction line. Doing so can prevent suction temperature in the coil from falling below a pre-set temperature.

- Install the coil for counterflow operation, with the suction connection on the entering air side of the coil. This maintains a temperature difference between the coil surface temperature and the leaving refrigerant temperature. It provides one of the control means for the thermostatic expansion valve. As this temperature difference becomes small, suction header location becomes more important. If you neglect the minor effect of pressure drop in an evaporator, the temperature of the refrigerant is constant. The importance of counterflow operation from a capacity standpoint in a direct expansion coil is far less than in a water coil. In a water coil, there is a major change in the temperature of the water passing through the coil.

The ratio of total heat to sensible heat removed varies in normal air conditioning applications from 1.0 to about 1.65. Sensible heat is then from 60 to 100% of total, depending on the application. In most comfort air conditioning installations, coil face velocities are between 400 and 600 ft/min. A velocity of 500 ft/min is very common. Refrigerant temperatures will vary from 35 to 50°F where dehumidification is required. Where no dehumidification is required, select the coil on the basis of dry-bulb temperatures and sensible heat, as you would with a heating coil.

The performance of coils used for both sensible and latent cooling must be determined by laboratory tests. Coil capacity must balance with the capacity of related equipment, such as the compressor, and the temperature of circulating air. Current industry standards call for ratings of factory-assembled self-contained air conditioners at 33.4 cfm per 1,000 Btu of cooling capacity (approximately 400 cfm per ton of refrigeration). Conditions of 80°F db and 67°F wb for entering air are considered standard. The selection of cooling coils for field-fabricated installations requires the use of coil manufacturers' rating tables. Consult such tables on the basis of load division as calculated for a particular job.

When critical industrial systems are being designed, good engineering practices must be used to determine such things as the air volume to be circulated, refrigerant temperature, etc. The air volume to be circulated is technically based on the internal sensible heat load of the room. Deviation from this value is normally for reasons of circulation or outlet air temperature.

Re-heat is required for many industrial applications and many good comfort air conditioning installations. With re-heat, design condition can be maintained regardless of outdoor air conditions. Most problems with air conditioning systems occur when the cooling requirement is considerably below design conditions. This is more of a problem when outside air dewpoints are high, with a light load condition. In hot, dry climates, the light load is not such a problem.

HEAT TRANSFER AND AIR FLOW RESISTANCE

Several variables affect the transfer of heat between the air stream and the heating or cooling medium:

- the temperature difference

- the velocity and character of the medium in the tubes

- the design and arrangement of the coil

- the velocity and character of the air stream.

The driving force is usually taken as the logarithmic mean temperature difference for heating or cooling, without dehumidification.

The design and surface arrangement of a coil is based on many factors, including:

- material type and thickness

- spacing of fins

- ratio of primary to secondary surfaces

- staggered tube or in-line tube arrangement

- corrugated fins or flat fins.

Staggered tubes and corrugated fins increase total heat transfer over in-line tubes and flat fins. Air volume is usually based on standard air at 70°F and a barometric pressure of 29.92 inches of mercury. The velocity of air is considered coil face velocity. Uniform air velocity is very important for obtaining reliable test ratings and getting rated performance in installations. With fin coils, heat transfer from the heating or cooling medium to the air stream depends on many factors. Performance of the coil must be based on actual tests on the specific surface used. Comparing coils on the basis of square feet of surface and face area can be misleading. Select coils from curves or tables of coil performance prepared by manufacturers from reliable test data.

HEATING, COOLING, AND DEHUMIDIFYING COIL PERFORMANCE

Performance of heating and cooling coils depends on three factors:

- the overall coefficient of heat transfer from the medium within the coil to the air it heats or cools

- the physical area of the coil

- the mean temperature difference between the fluid in the coil and the air over the coil.

For cooling and dehumidifying coils, this is expressed mathematically by the following equation:

$$q_t = K_t S(\Delta t_m)$$

where q_t = total cooling capacity in Btu per hour

K_t = overall total heat transfer coefficient in Btu per hour per square foot of external surface per °F

S = total external coil surface in square feet

Δt_m = logarithmic mean temperature difference between entering and leaving air dry-bulb and water temperature for water coils.

In order to calculate Δt_m, you can use the following simplified three-step formula:

1. Entering air temperature
   − Leaving air temperature
   ─────────────────
   Air temperature difference

2. Leaving water temperature
   − Entering water temperature
   ─────────────────
   Water temperature difference

3. Air temperature difference
   − Water temperature difference
   ─────────────────
   Mean temperature difference

If the cooling medium is refrigerant, refrigerant temperatures are used instead of water temperatures.

For sensible cooling and heating coils, the equation is written as follows:

$$q_s = K_s S(\Delta t_m)$$

where K_s = overall sensible heat transfer coefficient in Btu per hour per square foot of external surface per °F.

LESSON 13

For finned coils, the equation for the overall coefficient of heat transfer can be conveniently written:

$$U = \frac{1}{\dfrac{R}{f_i} + \dfrac{1}{n f_o}}$$

In this equation, the term n, fin efficiency, allows for resistance to heat flow in fins. The term R in this case is the ratio of total external surface to internal surface. For typical designs of heating or cooling coils, this ratio may vary from 7 to 30. The R term places the internal surface coefficient of heat transfer on a basis of external surface. The performance of all heating and dry cooling coils is influenced by these same factors. When cooling coils operate wet or with latent cooling, performance cannot be predicted on the basis of overall coefficients.

PERFORMANCE OF DEHUMIDIFYING COILS

When the dewpoint of air entering a coil is higher than that leaving a coil, there has been some moisture removal. A coil that removes both sensible heat and moisture is normally called a *dehumidifying* coil. In most air conditioning processes, air is considered a mixture of water vapor and dry components. When air enters the cooling coil, dry components and water vapor enter at the same dry-bulb temperature. They both lose sensible heat in contact with the first part of the coil. Moisture removal starts when the dry-bulb temperature of the mixture approaches the dewpoint of the water vapor components. The first part of a cooling coil in the direction of air flow may function as a dry cooling coil.

When moisture removal starts, cooling surfaces also continue the removal of sensible heat. They are carrying load due to both sensible and latent heat. Sensible heat removal from dry air remains approximately constant per degree of change. But latent heat removal per degree of dewpoint change varies considerably, because moisture content is different at different temperatures. For example, moisture removal of cool air from 60 to 59°F dewpoint is about 37% more than cooling air from 50 to 49°F dewpoint.

A direct expansion cooling coil should be tested with its normal refrigerant control equipment. It should be tested at both higher and lower ranges of its capacity. Most coil manufacturers prepare their own performance rating tables or curves from a suitable number of coil performance tests. There is a standard entitled *Standard Methods of Testing and Rating Forced Circulation Air Cooling and Air Heating Coils*. It is published by the Heating and Cooling Coil Manufacturers Association and the Air Conditioning and Refrigeration Institute. This standard is the accepted method in the industry for testing and rating coils.

RAC

Its general use should result in manufacturers rating their equipment on a standard basis.

PIPING

This section illustrates piping arrangements, both proper and improper, for a number of different applications. Figure 13-9 shows the recommended piping installation for a typical water cooling or heating coil. Note that water is brought into the bottom part of the inlet header and out the top of the return header. Vents and drain connections are normally provided on coils constructed for use with water. It is also common practice to vent the return line above the highest point of the coil.

The automatic control valve pictured in Figure 13-9 is a three-way mixing valve. By allowing continuous flow, it avoids "dead-heading" the pump and possibly interrupting the flow through a chiller. When the valve opens fully, port A to AB is open. All water flows through the coil. Then the valve moves into the closed position. All or part of the water flows through the bypass from port B to port AB. When two or more water coils are controlled by one automatic control valve, install balancing valves with metering gauge ports into the supply piping to each coil.

FIGURE 13-9. *Piping details of water coil*

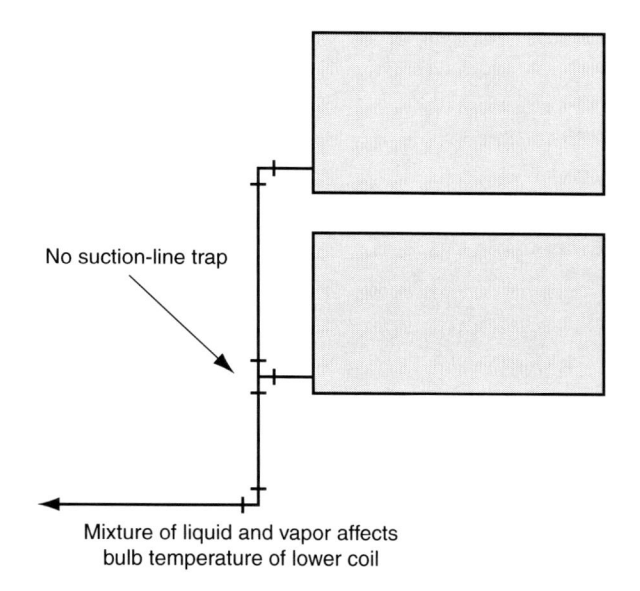

FIGURE 13-10. *Improper suction line*

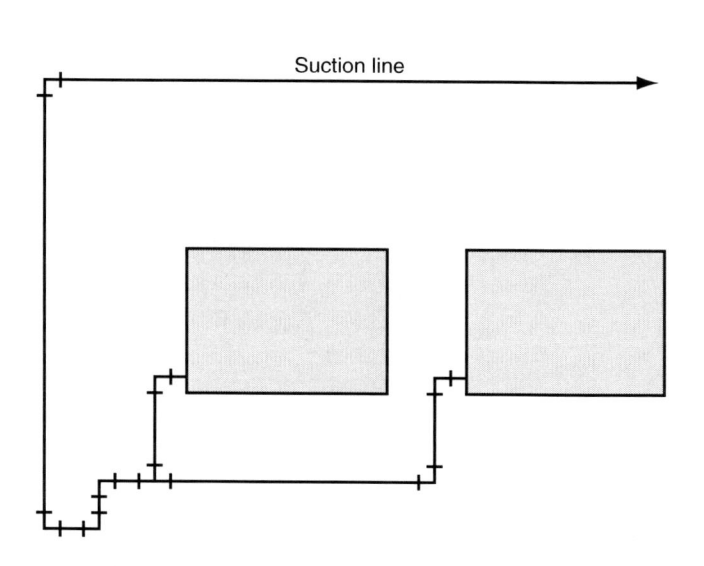

FIGURE 13-11. *Proper trapping with suction line above evaporators*

Figure 13-10 shows improper piping of a suction line from two evaporators, located one above the other. With this piping arrangement, a mixture of liquid and refrigerant vapor can flow from the upper coil down to the lower coil. Some of the refrigerant would flow into the branch "T" of the lower coil, causing loss of operating superheat at the expansion valve bulb. This would affect the proper operation of the expansion valve and could cause slugging at the compressor.

Figure 13-11 shows how the branch suction line from the coils is properly trapped. This is necessary when the suction line is run above the evaporators, especially when the condensing unit is at a higher elevation.

Figure 13-12 shows the suggested piping of coils with a trap using a double riser suction line. The traps are made with fittings as short as possible. A double suction riser system is very desirable when capacity devices are used on the compressor. Both suction risers must be run up high enough to enter the main suction on the top. This will prevent draining of refrigerant from one riser to the other. The two suction risers are sized to maintain over 1,200 ft/min velocity. Both risers will be in operation for full capacity of the system.

When the system enters a reduced-capacity stage, oil will collect at the bottom of riser B. This blocks it off and allows flow through riser A at velocities exceeding 1,200 ft/min. This will occur only if riser A has been sized smaller to match the flow rate of refrigerant at the system's reduced operating capacity. As the system returns to full capacity, an increased pressure drop in riser A will form a pressure differential across riser B. This will force the oil out of the trap gradually.

Figure 13-13 shows a properly trapped arrangement. No vapor or liquid will be susceptible to thermal bulb

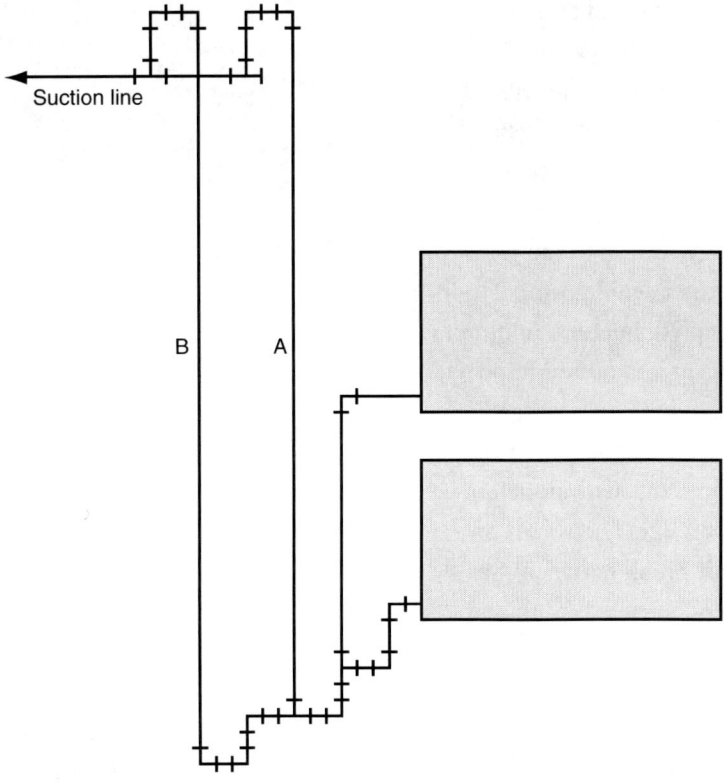

FIGURE 13-12. *Double suction riser with trap maintains proper vapor velocity at reduced compressor capacities*

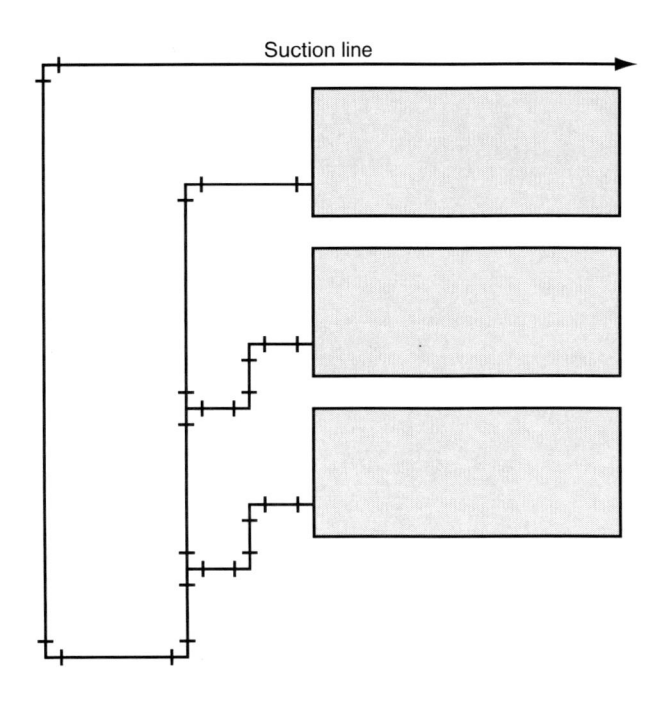

FIGURE 13-13. *Properly trapped system*

operation in coils below or alongside. Figure 13-14 shows how condensate from an air handler evaporator pan must be piped to a suitable drain. In addition to the 3-in. water seal, a 3-in. (1½-in. pipe diameters, minimum) drop is required to provide the head needed to overcome negative pressure within the air handler. The use of an air break between the condensate piping and the building drain will eliminate the possibility of sewer gases being drawn into the air supply. To prevent condensate from accumulating in the evaporator pan, run piping full size to the water seal.

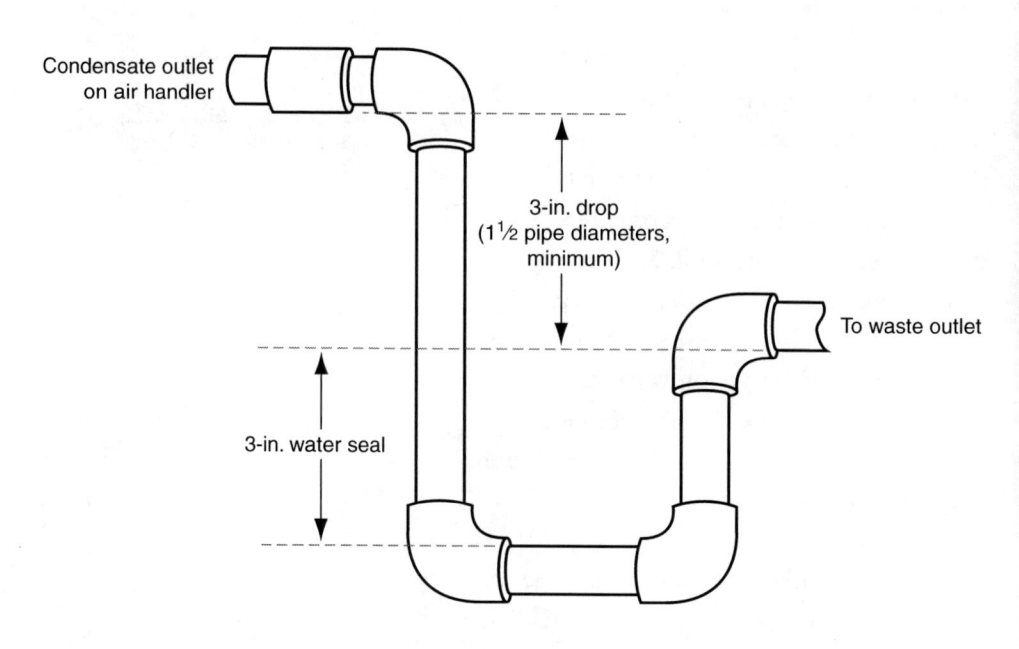

FIGURE 13-14. *Condensate drain piping*

REVIEW QUESTIONS

1. What are the two types of heat transfer coils normally used?

2. What is meant by the "primary" and "secondary" surfaces of a coil?

3. Water coils are circuited to provide _____ water distribution.

4. What provisions are made in water coils that use water containing foreign matter?

5. What flow arrangement of cooling coils is generally accepted as standard?

6. What precautions must always be taken with water coils when below-freezing air is being handled?

7. What effect do face-and-bypass dampers have on water coils and refrigeration coils?

8. What condensate provisions should be made when cooling coils are stacked one above the other?

9. When piping coils, what consideration must you give to expansion and contraction?

10. List several means for cleaning dirty coils, depending on the severity of restriction.

11. What safety precautions must you take when cleaning coils?

REVIEW QUESTIONS

12. What is the primary safety rule that you must observe when cleaning coils?

13. What are the acceptable ranges of water velocity and water volume per ton in chilled water cooling coils?

14. What is the most economical minimum difference between the leaving air dry-bulb temperature and the entering water temperature?

15. What precaution must be taken when direct expansion coils are selected to operate at suction temperatures of 32 to 35°F?

16. What is the range of refrigerant temperatures in direct expansion coils where dehumidification is required?

17. Why are three-way valves applied to control the water flow through water coils?

18. What provision must you make when piping the suction-line riser of a system that can operate at reduced capacities?

LESSON 14

Multiple Rack Systems

INTRODUCTION

The purpose of this Lesson is to familiarize you with the operation principles of multiple rack refrigeration systems. Although there are several companies that manufacture quality rack systems, this Lesson concentrates on one particular rack and walks the reader through its various components. All rack systems deal with the same problems, and while some methods of dealing with them are unique, others require maintenance practices that are used industry-wide.

THE SUPERPLUS REFRIGERATION PROCESS

The Hussmann SUPERPLUS® Refrigeration System (shown on page 258 at the end of this Lesson) consists of a rack containing:

- Two to seven Copeland compressors or two to six Carlyle compressors, all of which are semi-hermetic, with:
    1. high- and low-pressure controls
    2. oil pressure safety controls
    3. primary overload protection
    4. compressor cooling fans for low-temperature applications (or 0.75 to 3-hp rating).

- The rack is factory-plumbed to include:
    1. suction, discharge, and liquid headers
    2. Turba-Shed® oil separator and return system

RAC

3. dual receiver tanks
4. suction filters on each compressor
5. liquid filter-drier and sight glass
6. liquid level indicator.

- A factory-wired control panel with:
  1. pre-wired distribution power block
  2. individual component circuit breakers and contactors
  3. compressor time delays
  4. color-coded wiring system.

- Items supplied separately for field installation:
  1. liquid drier core
  2. vibration isolation pads
  3. loose-shipped items for accessories.

The SUPERPLUS is designed with twin receivers for increased receiver volume. The compact design reduces height and width requirements, yet provides convenient access to components for easy maintenance and service. Because service is of prime interest, it should be noted that the low center of gravity inherent with the twin receiver design minimizes vibration, extending system life and reducing service needs.

Typically, supermarket refrigeration falls into low- or medium-temperature ranges. An average low-temperature rack maintains a suction temperature of –25°F and has a low-end satellite operating at –33°F. A common medium-temperature rack operates at +16°F with a low-end satellite at +7°F. High-end satellites are often applied to prep room cooling.

Look at Figure 14-1 to get a general overview of the SUPERPLUS system and its components. In this Lesson, the following constants are maintained to assist the reader:

- In the diagrams, refrigerant flow direction is generally clockwise.

- Electrical solenoid valves carry the same initial abbreviations as in the electrical schematics.

- Refrigeration lines not actually in the cycle being discussed are shown closed, or are removed.

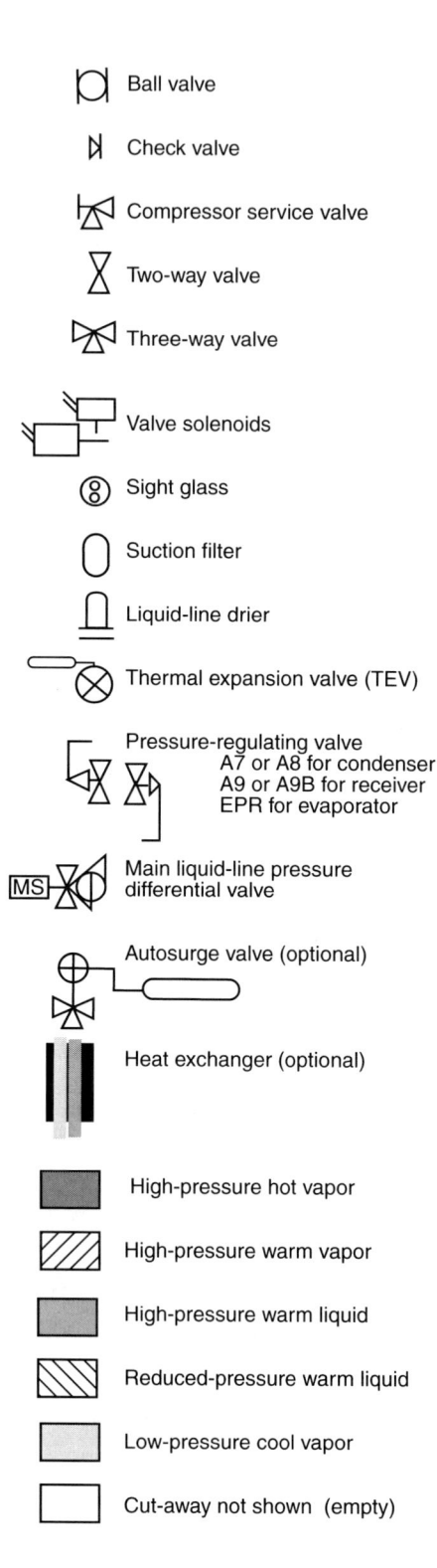

Ball valve
Check valve
Compressor service valve
Two-way valve
Three-way valve
Valve solenoids
Sight glass
Suction filter
Liquid-line drier
Thermal expansion valve (TEV)
Pressure-regulating valve
  A7 or A8 for condenser
  A9 or A9B for receiver
  EPR for evaporator
Main liquid-line pressure differential valve
Autosurge valve (optional)
Heat exchanger (optional)
High-pressure hot vapor
High-pressure warm vapor
High-pressure warm liquid
Reduced-pressure warm liquid
Low-pressure cool vapor
Cut-away not shown (empty)

LEGEND

LESSON 14

- All illustrations maintain the same fill patterns for specific refrigerant states and pressures. (See the legend on the opposite page, which applies to all of the diagrams in this Lesson.) Pressures in oil lines also retain a fixed pattern.

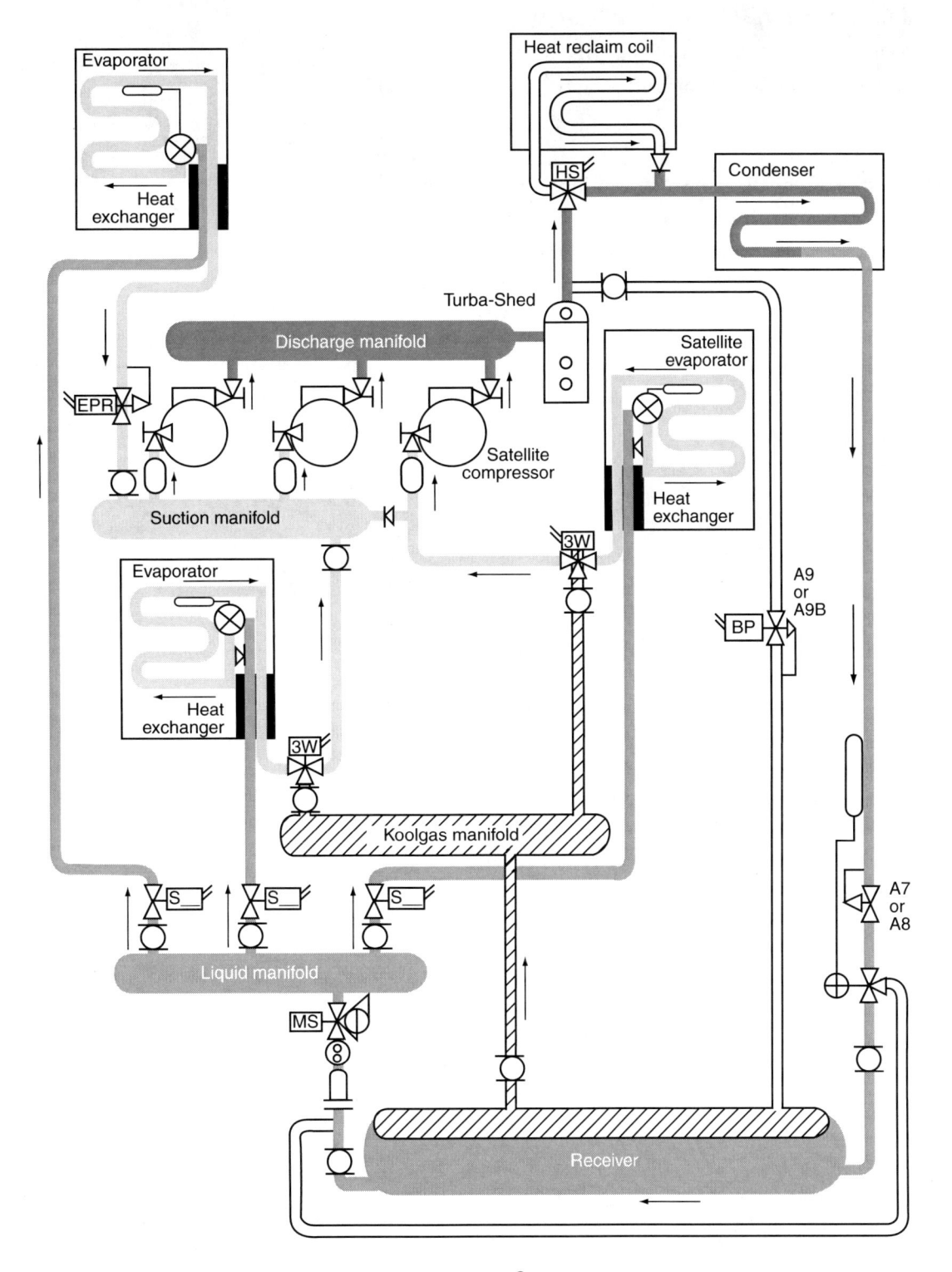

FIGURE 14-1. *SUPERPLUS® Refrigeration System*

245

RAC

THE BASIC REFRIGERATION CYCLE

You can trace the basic refrigeration cycle in Figure 14-2. Beginning with the *parallel compressors*, vapor refrigerant is compressed into the *discharge manifold* and flows to the *Turba-Shed*. The Turba-Shed separates vapor refrigerant from liquid oil by means of centrifugal force and screen baffles. The oil is stored in the bottom of the Turba-Shed and returned to the compressors.

A three-way *heat reclaim valve* (HS), shown in Figure 14-3, directs the refrigerant either to the condenser or to a heat reclaim coil. When the HS solenoid is deenergized, the three-way heat reclaim valve directs the refrigerant

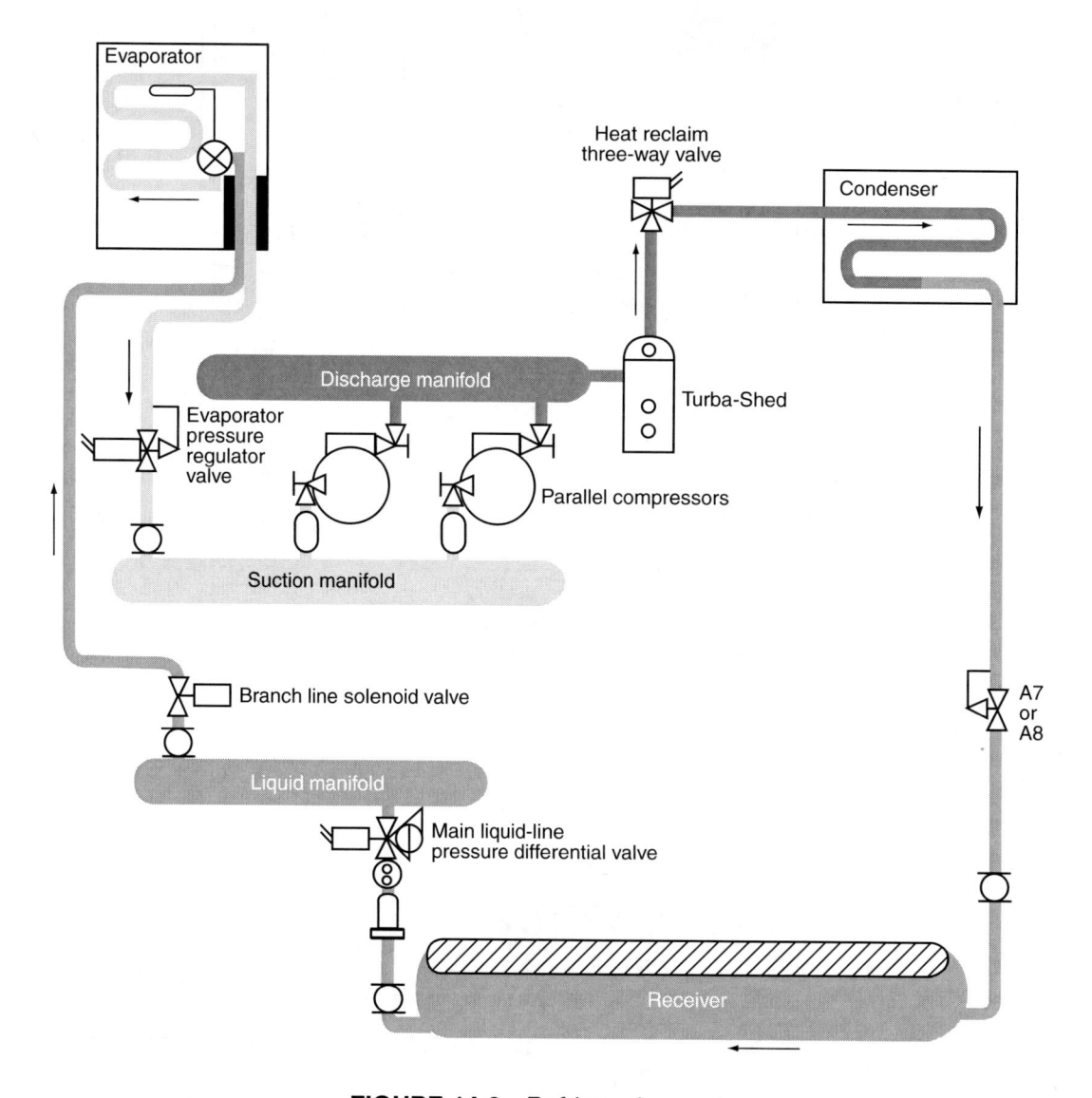

FIGURE 14-2. *Refrigeration cycle*

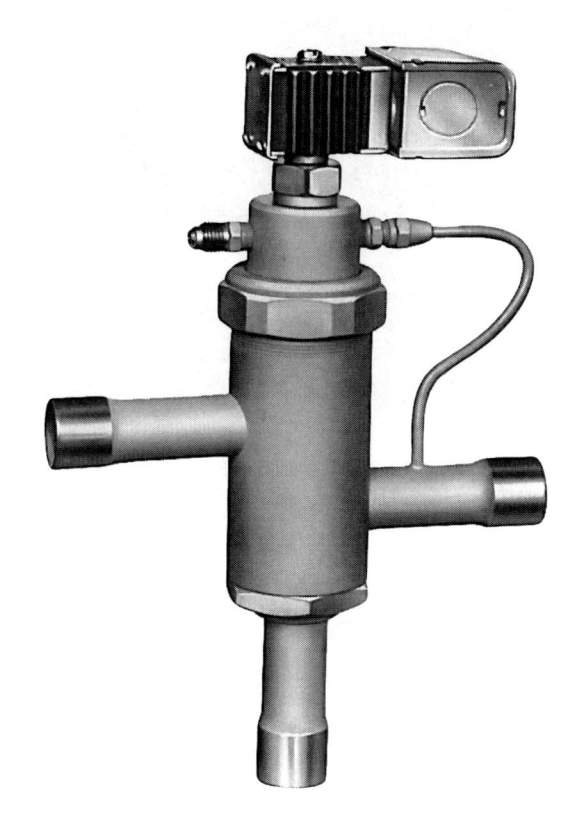

FIGURE 14-3. *Heat reclaim valve*

FIGURE 14-4. *A8 flooding valve*

to the *condenser*. The condenser then discharges the unwanted heat from the system.

The A7 or A8 *flooding valve* (the A8 is shown in Figure 14-4) maintains head pressure in low ambient conditions by reducing the available condensing area. The flooding valve restricts the flow of liquid refrigerant from the condenser. By preventing the liquid refrigerant from leaving the condenser as fast as it is forming, it causes the condenser to flood with its own condensate.

The *twin receivers* act as a vapor trap and supply the main liquid solenoid with quality liquid refrigerant. Sufficient liquid, vapor, and pressure are critical to the operation of the system. The system maintains these balances in the twin receivers for use as needed.

The *main liquid-line pressure differential valve* (MS), two models of which are shown in Figure 14-5 on the next page, functions during the Koolgas® defrost cycle to reduce pressure to the liquid manifold. This solenoid-operated valve never closes completely, but restricts the liquid line, reducing the pressure in the liquid manifold. The reduced pressure allows the reverse flow of refrigerant necessary for Koolgas defrost. The *liquid manifold* distributes liquid refrigerant to all branch liquid lines.

RAC

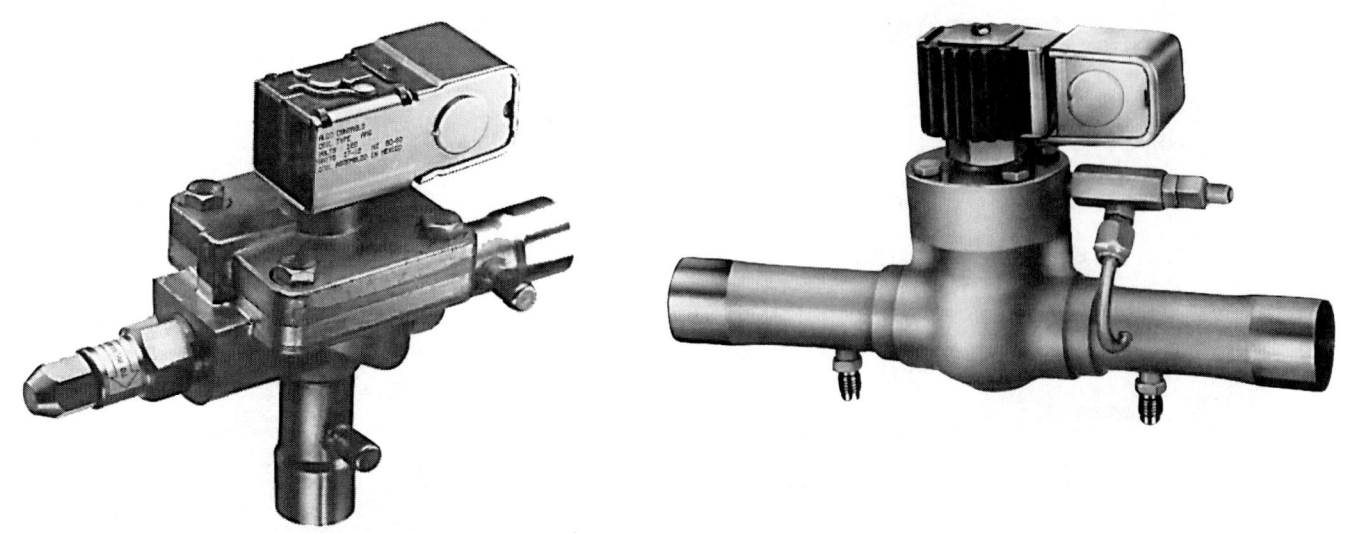

FIGURE 14-5. Main liquid-line pressure differential valves

The *branch liquid-line solenoid valve* (S_), shown in Figure 14-6, closes off refrigerant supply to the evaporator, but allows a backflow of refrigerant into the liquid manifold.

The *thermal expansion valve* (TEV), shown in Figure 14-7, is located in the merchandiser. It meters liquid refrigerant through its orifice to the low-pressure side of the system, where it evaporates absorbing heat from the coil.

An *evaporator pressure-regulating valve* (EPR), shown in Figure 14-8, may be used to control the evaporator

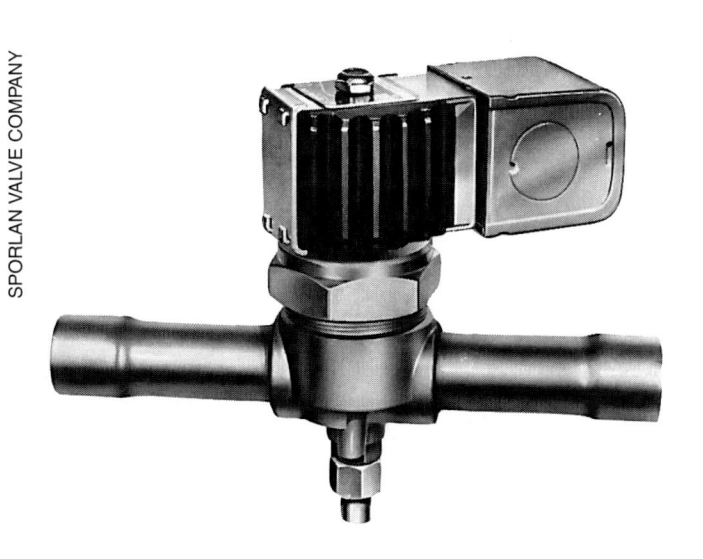

FIGURE 14-6. Branch liquid-line solenoid valve

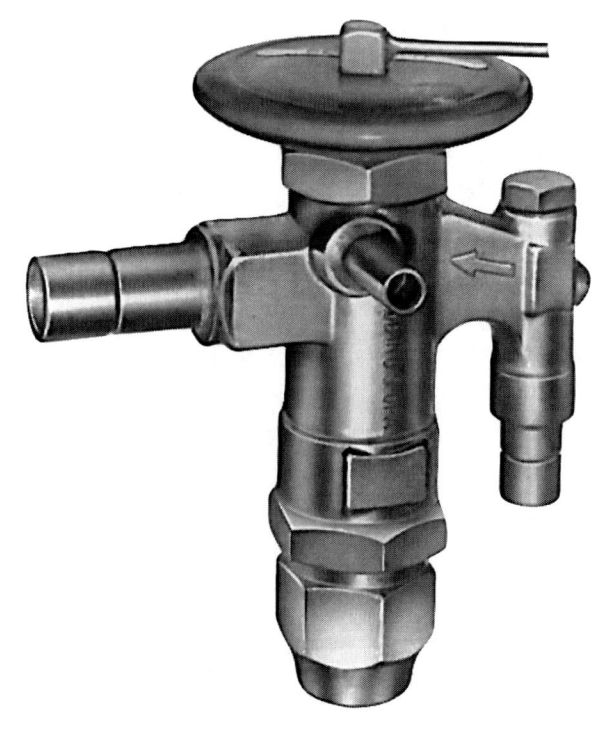

FIGURE 14-7. Thermal expansion valve (TEV)

temperature by preventing the evaporator pressure from dropping below a certain setpoint. A SORIT, BEPR, or CDA valve may be used for this purpose.

At critical locations along the refrigerant path, service valves or ball valves allow for isolation of components.

HEAT RECLAIM CYCLE

The heat reclaim cycle is diagrammed in Figure 14-9. The three-way heat reclaim valve (HS) routes the discharge heat-laden vapor to a remote-mounted coil or water heating coil. The heat energy removed from the merchandisers can be returned for a desired function. A *check valve* ensures that no backflow and flooding take place when the heat reclaim cycle is off. The heat reclaim cycle removes superheat from the refrigerant vapor, then dumps the vapor into the condenser to discharge latent heat and produce quality liquid for the refrigeration process.

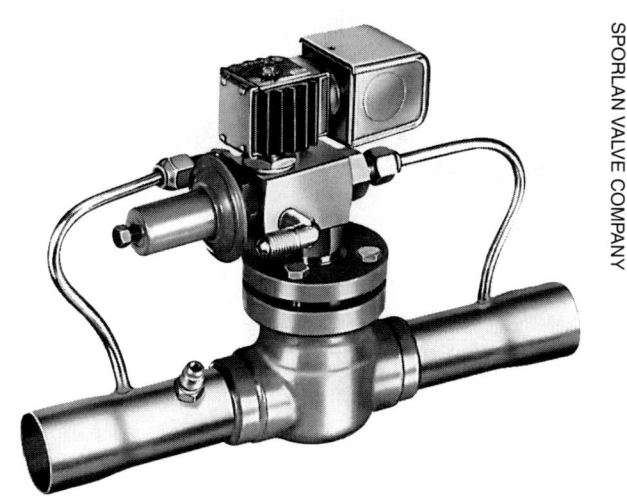

FIGURE 14-8. *Evaporator pressure-regulating valve (EPR)*

RECEIVER PRESSURE AND VAPOR TEMPERATURE REGULATION

Receiver pressure

Receiver pressure regulation is illustrated in Figure 14-10 on the next page. The A9 or A9B *pressure-regulating valve* responds to receiver pressure. (The A9 is shown in Figure 14-11 on the next page. The A9B includes a solenoid shutoff or opening option.) If the receiver pressure drops below its setpoint, the A9 valve opens, directing hot, high-pressure vapor to the receiver.

Receiver temperature

During Koolgas defrost, if the Koolgas manifold temperature drops below 85°F, the A9B solenoid opens its valve, directing hot, high-pressure vapor to the receiver. Electrically, the circuit is supplied with power *only* during Koolgas defrost. The circuit is

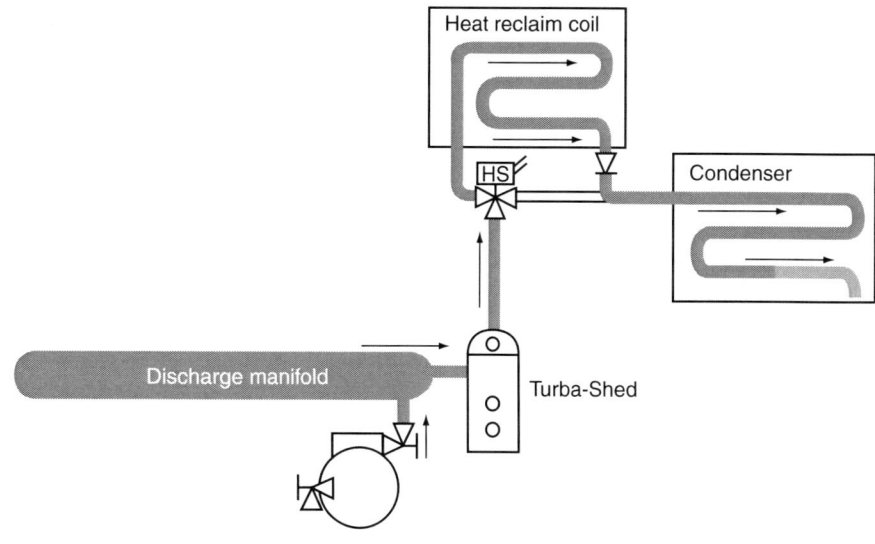

FIGURE 14-9. *Heat reclaim cycle*

closed by a thermostat that responds to the Koolgas manifold temperature.

KOOLGAS DEFROST CYCLE

Figure 14-12 shows the Koolgas defrost cycle. Beginning with the receiver, the Koolgas cycle splits in two directions—receiver vapor and receiver liquid. The high-pressure liquid flowing from the receiver is throttled by the main liquid-line solenoid valve (MS), causing a pressure reduction in the liquid manifold.

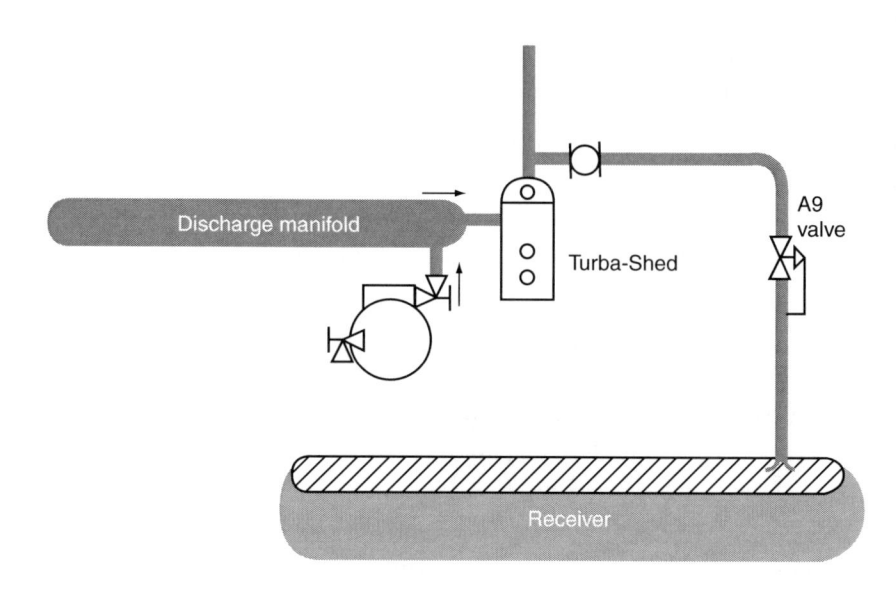

FIGURE 14-10. *Receiver pressure regulation*

The branch liquid-line solenoid valve (S_) is designed to allow backflow into the reduced-pressure liquid manifold. When a branch of refrigeration cases enters the defrost cycle, its branch valve allows refrigerant to flow into the liquid manifold. The valve solenoid is energized both for refrigeration and for defrost.

The receiver vapor flows directly into the *Koolgas manifold*. This Koolgas vapor maintains the same high pressure as the receiver. A three-way valve closes the suction line to the *suction manifold* and opens the Koolgas line to the *evaporator*. Koolgas vapor flows backward through the evaporator, giving up heat to the evaporator for defrost.

The Koolgas vapor condenses and flows into the reduced-pressure liquid line through a *bypass check valve* around the TEV. From there it is returned to the liquid manifold.

If a SORIT, BEPR, or CDA valve is used to control evaporator temperature, as shown in Figure 14-13, the three-way valve is not used. When defrost is called for, the suction line control valve closes and a two-way Koolgas valve (KS) opens the line from the Koolgas manifold to the evaporator.

OIL CYCLE

Figure 14-14 on page 252 shows the satellite oil system used by the SUPERPLUS system. Discharge refrigerant carries droplets

FIGURE 14-11. *A9 bypass valve*

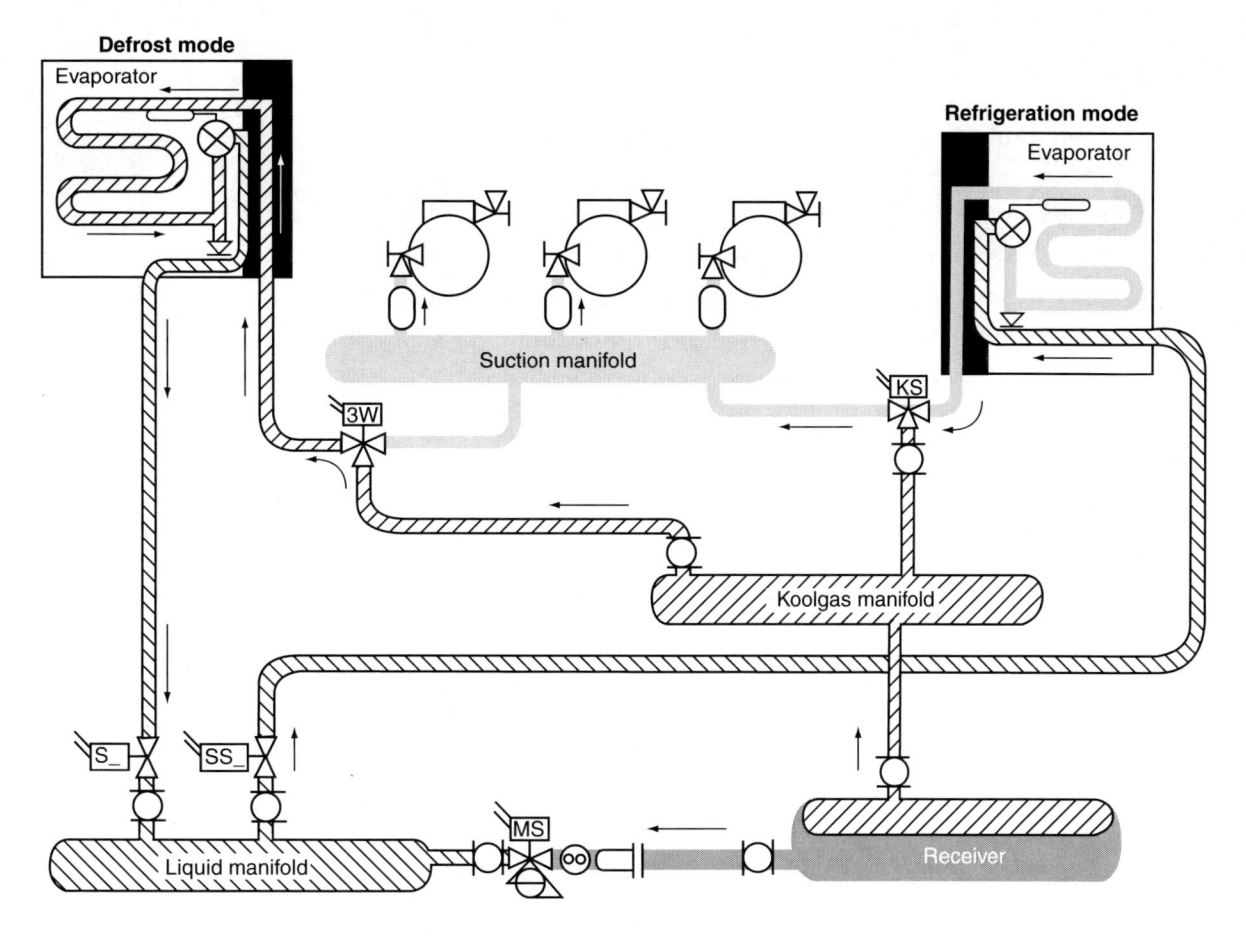

FIGURE 14-12. *Koolgas defrost cycle*

of oil from the compressors' lubrication system. The Turba-Shed returns the oil from its reservoir along the high-pressure line to the *oil pressure differential regulator valve*. This valve reduces the oil pressure to between 10 and 15 psig above the crankcase pressure, providing an even flow of oil to the *oil level regulators*.

To balance oil level among the compressors, an *equalizing line* returns any excess oil in one oil level regulator to the rest of the system. A check valve is placed in the equalizing line between the low-end satellite and the rest of the system. The check valve is necessary to keep the low-end satellite from filling up with oil. With a high-end satellite, note that there is no equalizing line.

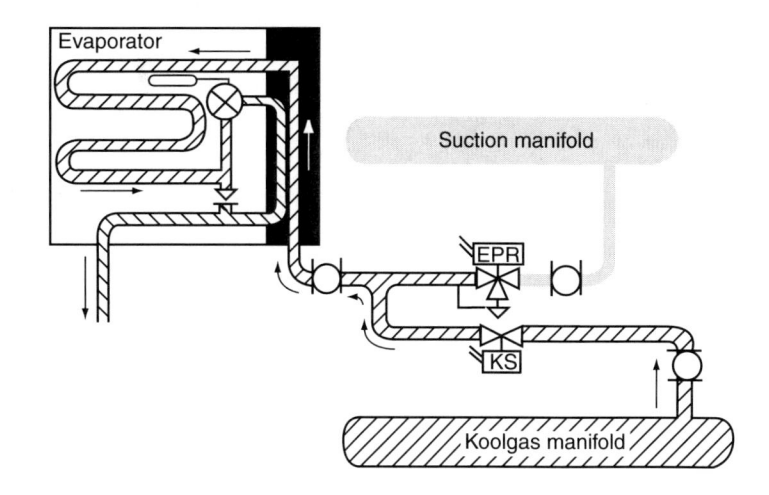

FIGURE 14-13. *Koolgas defrost with BEPR, SORIT, or CDA valve*

RAC

SUBCOOLING

Autosurge for ambient subcooling

Figure 14-15 shows how the *autosurge valve* works to provide ambient subcooling. The A9B valve needs to be working properly in order for the autosurge valve to function during Koolgas defrost. The autosurge valve directs the flow of refrigerant either *through* the receiver (flow-through), or *around* the receiver (surge) in response to the ambient subcooling obtained in the condenser.

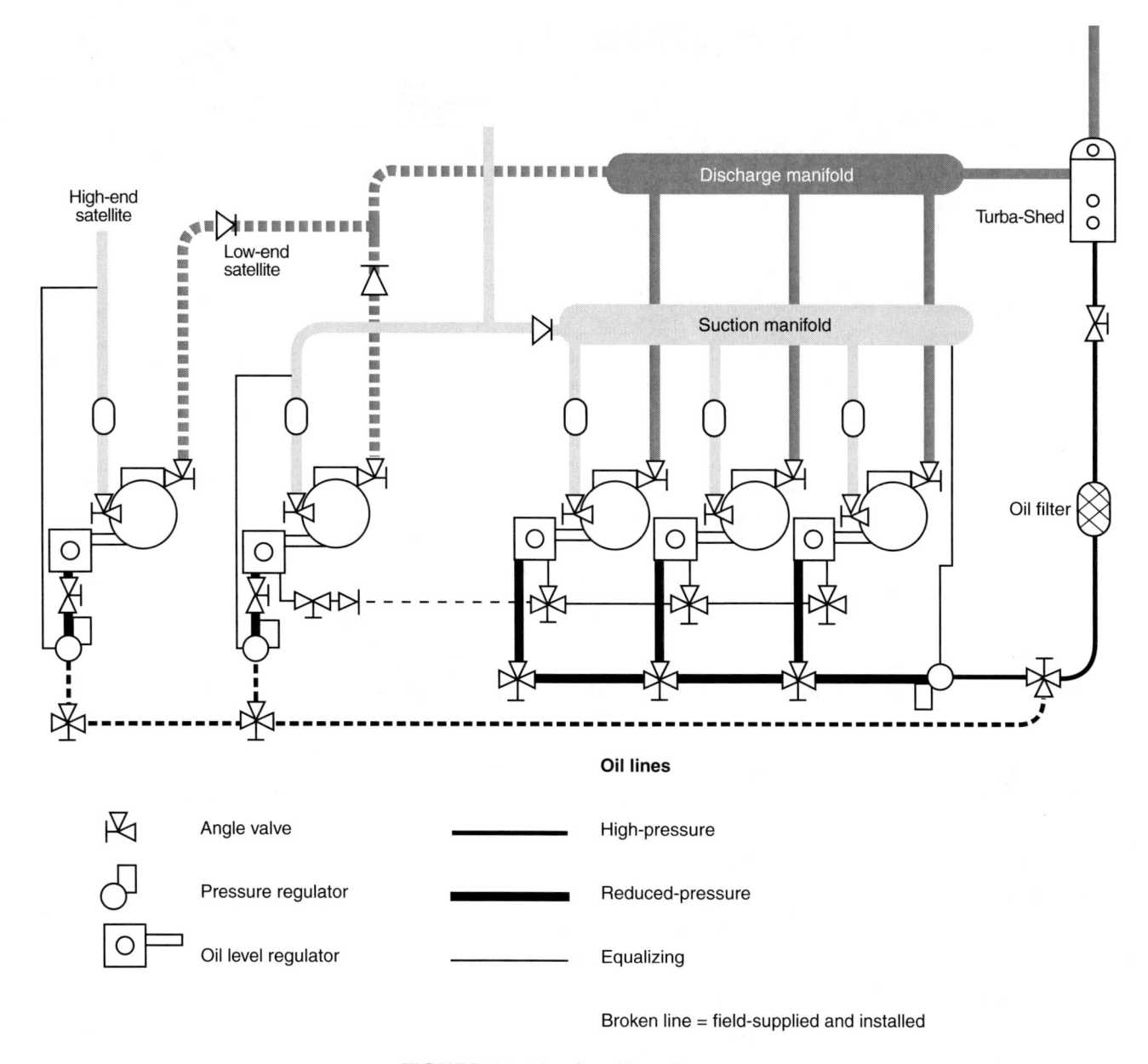

FIGURE 14-14. *Satellite oil system*

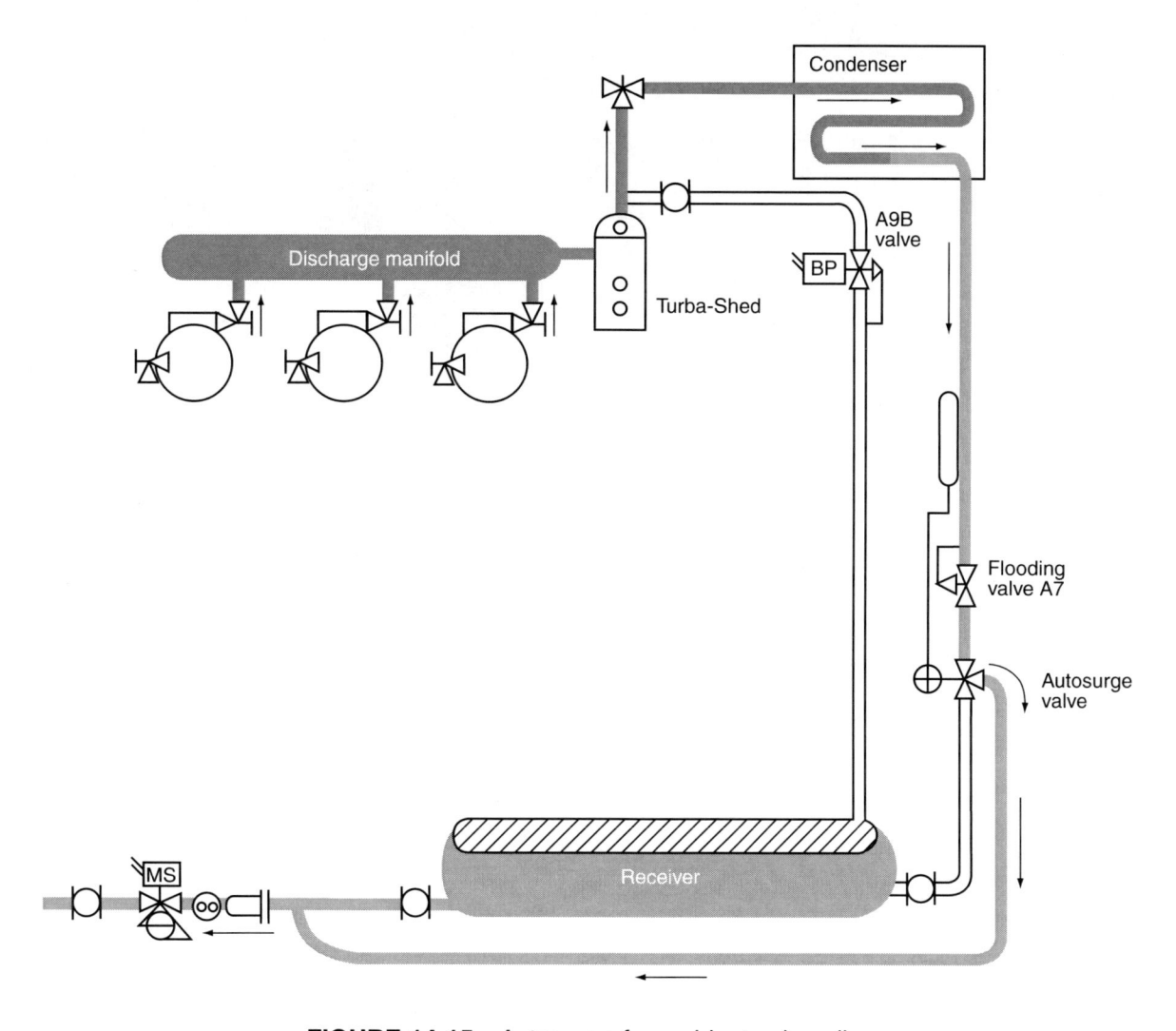

FIGURE 14-15. *Autosurge for ambient subcooling*

The autosurge valve reacts to the condensing pressure through its equalizer line, and to the temperature of the liquid refrigerant returning from the condenser through a bulb mounted on the liquid return line upstream from the flooding valve. When the temperature of the refrigerant returning from the condenser drops below its condensing temperature, the system has achieved ambient subcooling. The valve is factory-set at 10°F of subcooling and is *not* field-adjustable.

Mechanical subcooling

By lowering the temperature of the liquid supplied to the TEV, the efficiency of the evaporator can be increased. The lower-temperature liquid refrigerant means that less flash gas exits the TEV. Since mechanical subcooling uses a direct expansion device, it is not limited by ambient temperature. Figure 14-16 on the next page shows two different methods of mechanical subcooling.

A. Shell-and-tube type

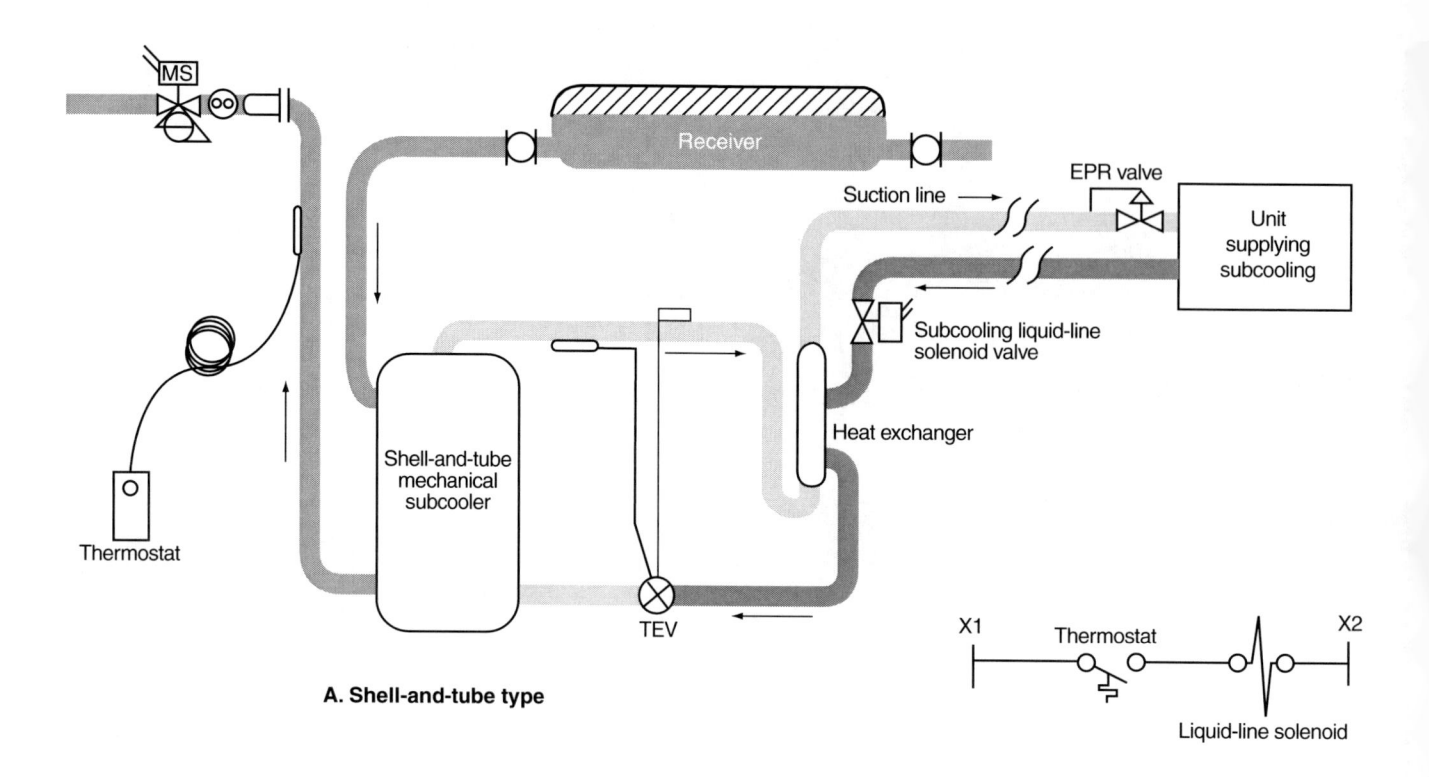

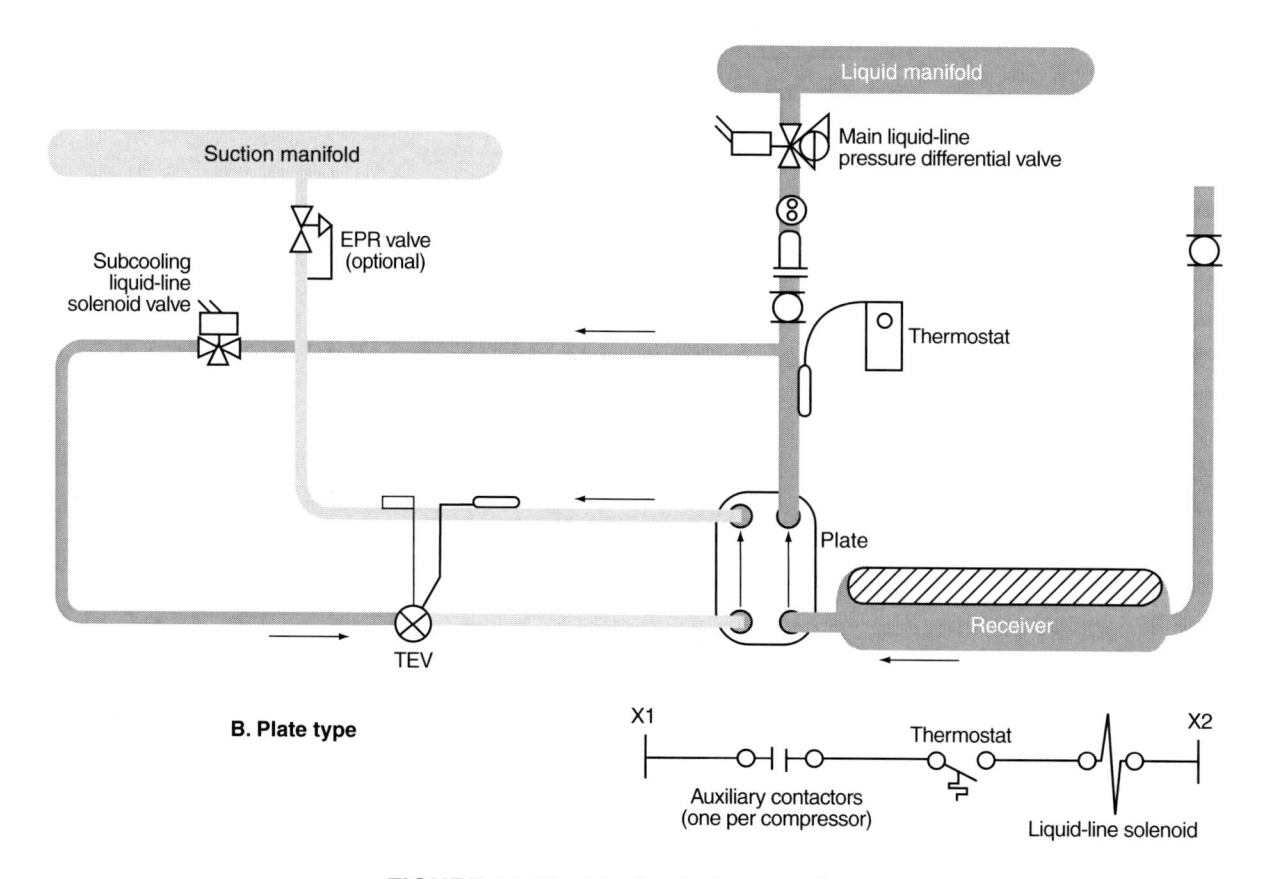

B. Plate type

FIGURE 14-16. *Mechanical subcooling*

LESSON 14

A liquid-line solenoid valve and a TEV control refrigerant to the subcooler. An EPR prevents the subcooler temperature from dropping below the desired liquid temperature. Electrically, a thermostat responding to the main liquid-line temperature controls a solenoid valve on the liquid supply line.

COMPOUND RACK

Liquid injection provides for proper superheat levels entering the second-stage compressors of a compound system. This prevents excessive discharge temperatures at the second stage.

As shown in Figure 14-17, a TEV in the liquid refrigerant line regulates the refrigerant flow into the first-stage discharge manifold in response to its superheat temperature. Electrically, a thermostat responding to the first-stage discharge temperature controls a solenoid valve on the liquid supply line. Power is supplied to this circuit through any one of the parallel auxiliary contactors on each first-stage

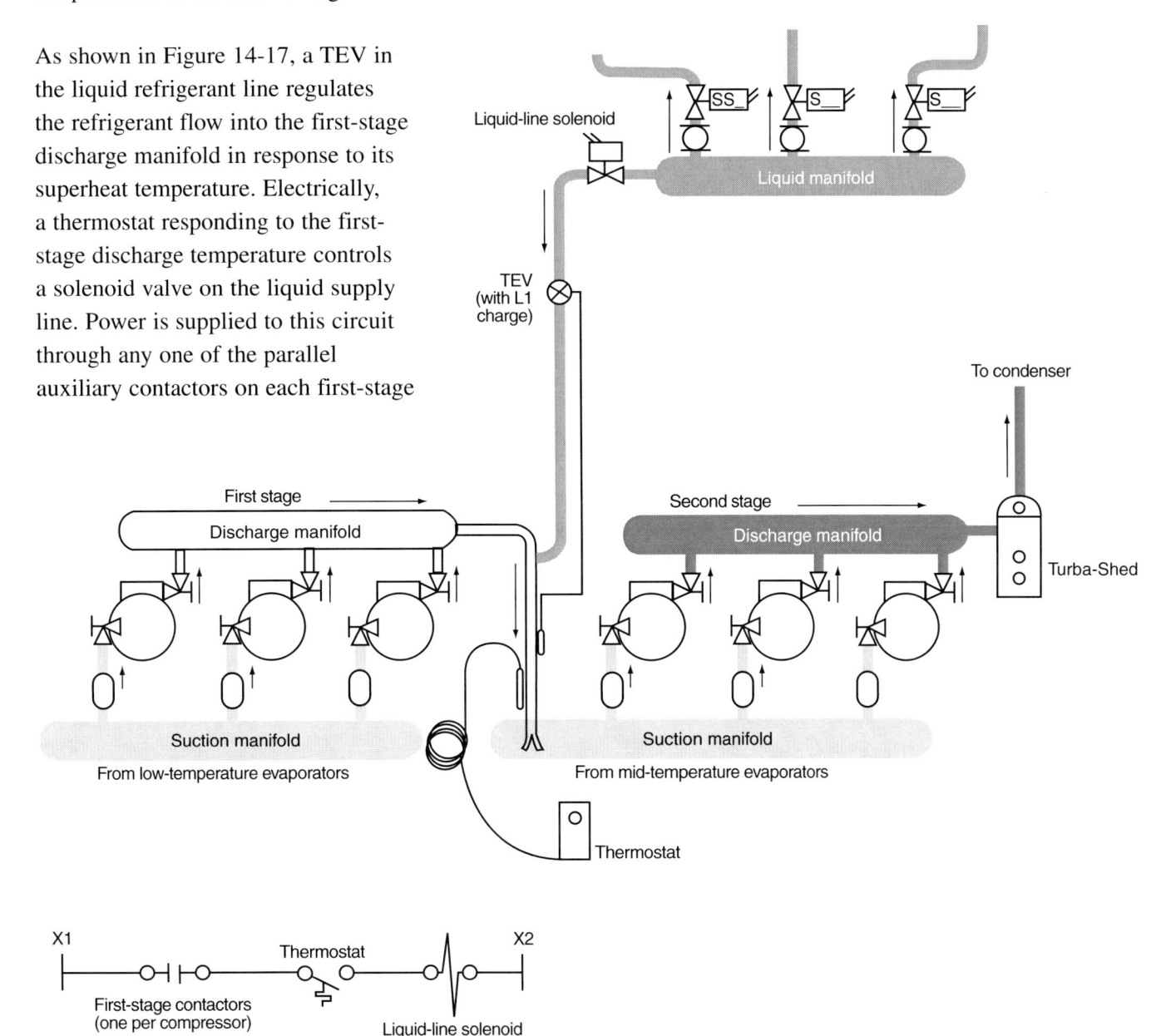

FIGURE 14-17. *Compound rack*

255

compressor contactor, so at least one first-stage compressor must be running in order for the liquid injection to work.

DEMAND COOLING

The demand cooling system shown in Figure 14-18 is designed to inject saturated refrigerant into the suction cavity when the compressor internal head temperature exceeds 292°F. Injection continues until the temperature is reduced to 282°F. If the temperature remains above 310°F for one minute, the control shuts down the compressor.

The *temperature sensor* employees a negative temperature coefficient (NTC) thermistor to provide signals to the *control module*. The NTC resistance drops on temperature rise. The control module responds to the temperature sensor's input by energizing the injection valve solenoid when 292°F is exceeded. Too high or too low a resistance from the thermistor circuit will cause the module to shut down the compressor after one minute.
The *injection valve* meters saturated refrigerant into the suction cavity of the compressor.

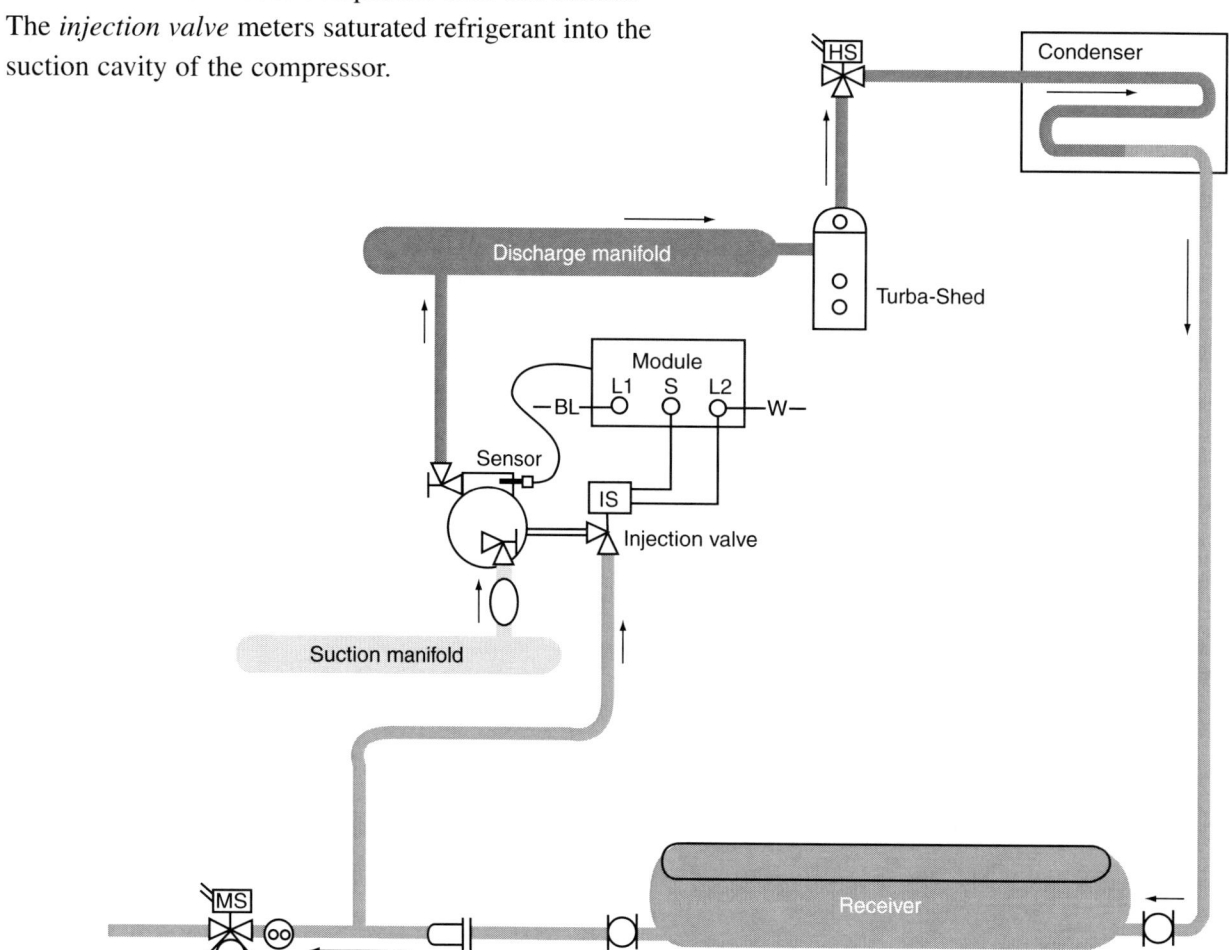

FIGURE 14-18. *Demand cooling*

LESSON 14

SAFETY TIPS

The following safety tips come with the reminder: being safe is *your* responsibility!

- Always wear proper eye protection when you are working.

- Wear proper hearing protection whenever you work in a machine room.

- Stand to one side—never work directly in front of:
  1. any valve that you are opening or closing (manual refrigeration valves, for example, or regulator valves on brazing tanks and nitrogen tanks)
  2. electrical circuit breakers
  3. refrigeration lines that you are cutting or opening.

- Always use a pressure regulator with a nitrogen tank. Observe the following guidelines:
  1. Do not exceed 2 lb of pressure, and vent lines when brazing.
  2. Do not exceed 350 lb of pressure for leak-testing the high side.
  3. Do not exceed 150 lb of pressure for leak-testing the low side.

- Use only a striker to light a torch.

- Determine whether a circuit is open at the power supply or not. Remove all power before opening control panels. *Remember*—some types of equipment have more than one power supply.

- Always supply proper ventilation.
  1. Refrigerants and nitrogen can displace oxygen, causing suffocation.
  2. Refrigerants exposed to flame can produce phosgene, a poisonous gas.

- Be sure that refrigerant lines are free of pressure before cutting. Check:
  1. both sides of a two-way valve
  2. all lines to a three-way or four-way valve.

- Dangerous hydraulic explosions may result if you:
  1. isolate liquid lines or a compressor when they can absorb heat over an extended time period
  2. overfill pumpdown refrigerant containers.

- *Never* vent refrigerants into the atmosphere.

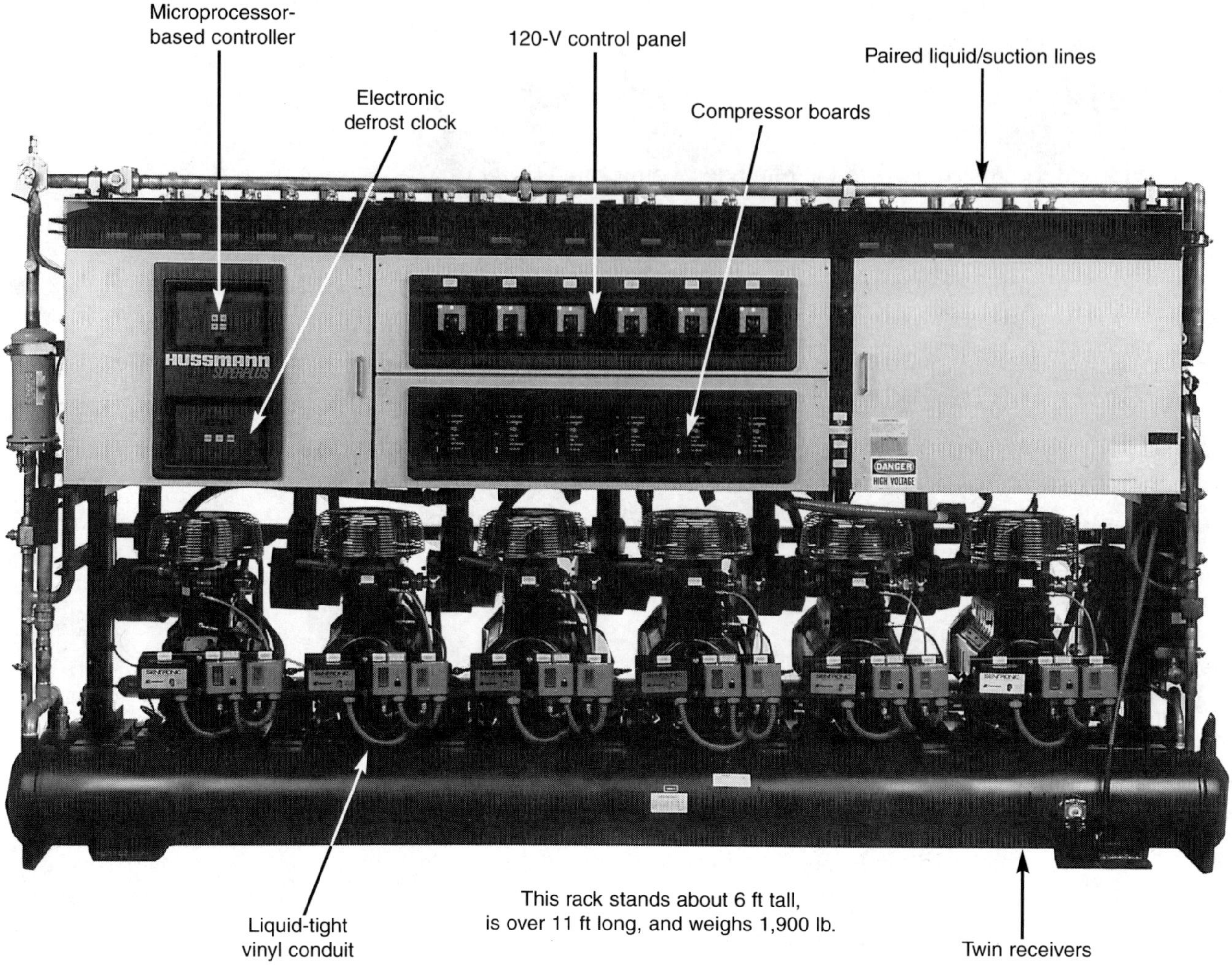

HUSSMANN CORPORATION

REVIEW QUESTIONS

1. The SUPERPLUS design features twin receivers, which lowers the overall system height, and therefore its center of gravity. This in turn reduces system _____.

2. A typical low-temperature rack maintains a suction temperature of _____.

3. In the basic refrigeration cycle, vapor refrigerant is compressed by the compressors and sent to the _____.

4. The three-way heat reclaim valve directs the refrigerant either to the _____ or to a(n) _____.

5. What is the function of the flooding valve?

6. The branch liquid-line solenoid valve shuts off refrigerant flow to the _____, but allows a backflow into the _____.

7. The thermal expansion valve meters liquid refrigerant to the _____ side of the system.

8. A SORIT, BEPR, or CDA valve may be used as a(n) _____ valve.

9. Superheat is removed from the refrigerant vapor during the _____ cycle.

10. What is the minimum temperature to which the Koolgas manifold can drop before the solenoid-operated pressure-regulating valve opens?

11. Why is an equalizing line necessary in a satellite oil system?

REVIEW QUESTIONS

12. The autosurge valve works to provide _____.

13. Methods of mechanical subcooling are not limited by ambient temperature. Why not?

14. If you must open a refrigerant line, where should you stand?

15. When testing a nitrogen tank for leaks, you should not exceed _____ lb of pressure for the high side, or _____ lb of pressure for the low side.

16. Why is it important to supply proper ventilation when you are working with refrigerants?

17. When is it permissible to vent refrigerants to the atmosphere?

Refrigeration and Air Conditioning

RSES

Compressors, Condensers, and Cooling Towers
Student Supplement

RSES
The HVACR Training Authority